SPIRITUAL GIFTS

A Fresh Look

DAVID LIM

Gospel Publishing House
Springfield, Missouri
02–0636

To May,
whose constant encouragement, suggestions, and prayers inspired the completion of this book.

Library of Congress Cataloging-in-Publication Data

Lim, David, 1946–
    Spiritual gifts : a fresh look : commentary and exhortation from a Pentecostal perspective / David Lim.
        p. cm.
    Includes bibliographical references and indexes.
    ISBN 0–88243–636–8
    1. Gifts, Spiritual. 2. Fruit of the Spirit. 3. Gifts, Spiritual—Biblical teaching. 4. Fruit of the Spirit—Biblical teaching. 5. Bible. N.T. Epistles of Paul—Criticism, interpretation, etc. 6. Pentecostal churches—Doctrines.
    I. Title.
    BT767.3.L545   1991   90–23950
    234'.13—dc20

Printed in the United States of America

Table of Contents

Foreword

In many parts of the world today the cutting edge of evangelism and church growth is the burgeoning Pentecostal movement. From humble beginnings at the turn of the century, the revival has produced large and growing denominations in virtually every country in the world. The larger church world has entered into the Pentecostal blessing as well. Charismatic fellowships are found today in many of the older denominations. Crucial to the contribution of the Pentecostal revival to the contemporary church world is the Pentecostal understanding of the person and work of the Holy Spirit. It is quite surprising, in view of this, how few books on that subject have been generated by the presses of the great Pentecostal denominations in the last generation. Most of the recent titles dealing with pneumatology, as a matter of fact, have been produced by non-Pentecostals. For Pentecostals many of them are useful. Some, however, reflect perspectives that challenge important elements in Pentecostal belief. That a need exists for a fresh look at the biblical teaching about the Holy Spirit by a "card-carrying" Pentecostal is clearly manifest.

In recent years, the charismatic renewal has brought many people in diverse places into new depths of Christian experience. Many are discovering the power of the Holy Spirit in their lives. Much of this is very positive. A phenomenon associated with the renewal, however, is the perplexing variety of teaching bombarding new and tender converts. Besides creating considerable confusion about the Spirit's activity in the Church among the charismatics, this cross-current influences some traditional Pentecostal churches. We rejoice that the Spirit today is being poured out on all flesh, but questions raised by the recent renewal demand fresh answers.

David Lim has endeavored to fill a pressing need for a scholarly, yet practical handbook on life in the Spirit. He comes to his task with a fine combination of qualifications. His academic credentials disclose an earned doctorate from a highly respected American evangelical seminary. His special field of expertise is New Testament studies. He has been a successful pastor, missionary, Bible college instructor, seminary professor, and administrator. He is in considerable demand as a preacher: a favorite in camps, conventions, and institutes. His wide travel and broad exposure to the literature and influences on the contemporary Pentecostal world are evident in the substantial bibliography and in the wisdom with which he addresses significant issues. Dr. Lim exhibits in his own person that rare combination of piety and learning that mark the true scholar-saint, a mix not altogether common in the traditional Pentecostal movement.

Particularly appealing is the ability of the author to deal with controversial topics with clarity and conviction, but without defensiveness. The book commends itself for its warmth, its pastoral and edifying tone.

Many volumes contain helpful material but are not easy to read. This book—although it discloses that the author has read the relevant material and is conversant with the technical dimensions of biblical study—offers a fine piece of craftsmanship without evidence of the tools that made it possible. Consequently, layperson, college student, and pastor will equally delight in reading this book. It is easy to picture this book as the basis for a Bible study series in a local church, a weekend seminar, or a ministers retreat. Certainly, pastors the world over will profit from the author's practical and theological insights so clearly expressed.

I am delighted that Dr. Lim's research has furnished a helpful guide that articulates with fresh emphasis the main themes that have nourished the Pentecostal revival from its inception. He underscores old truths in new ways. He brings stability. Although this work serves as a useful apologetic for Pentecostal experience and understanding in a turbulent era, it does more than this. It conveys the spirit and passion of a missionary. As the Assemblies of God, mobilized worldwide, embarks on its Decade of Harvest, here is a resource for encouraging believers to enter with confidence and delight into ministry in the anointing and enabling of the Spirit.

WILLIAM MENZIES
PRESIDENT
ASIA PACIFIC THEOLOGICAL SEMINARY

Preface

This book was written with several perspectives in mind. First, in the area of gifts we must move from scholarship to practice. Too many works focus on either one or the other, often to the detriment of both. Paul's was a task-oriented, missions-oriented theology. He wrote to help the churches move freely in God's power to accomplish His purpose. For Paul, gifts were not optional, but essential to the church's operation.

Second, I have written, in the main, for all serious students of the Word, with or without theological background. I have sought to be concise. Some individual paragraphs represent the key points of a lecture given either at Asia Pacific Theological Seminary (APTS) or in a seminar. Bible teachers should find it easy to water the seed-thoughts to develop these areas. The footnotes reflect more of the discussion on exegetical and theological issues.

Third, I have tried to keep a wholistic perspective: including both biblical commentary and pastoral concerns. Although parts of the book may represent an apologetics point of view, my primary purpose has been to help churches begin exercising the gifts as well as to guide those churches already exercising the gifts so their healthy, ongoing ministry might be maintained. Churches do not need an occasional exercise of gifts but a development of life-styles of sensitivity to God and others.

Fourth, because students from twelve countries attend APTS, I have become aware of the fact that varying cultural and church situations require differing applications; each church must discuss how these principles affect them. The genius of the Pentecostal revival is that we are not all shaped by the same mold. The body of Christ contains diversities of temperaments, worldviews, educations, and leadership styles. The Spirit uniquely anoints that diversity to reach a greater number of people. The explosive growth of the Church in recent years is in Third World countries. And that is as it should be. After all, Pentecost must lead to missions.

Fifth, although I have not especially written to either plumb spiritual depths or scale academic heights I hope that this work is helpful in both arenas. The larger church world, until recent years, has had the truths about the Holy Spirit and spiritual gifts obscured. Christians worldwide are sensing the need to rediscover the patterns of the primitive church, to realize experientially the pattern for power that revolutionized its generation. For them, I wish to stand at the door and usher them in. Still, over the past fifteen years scholars have written prolifically in this area. Some, who were skeptical or opposed to the charismatic revival, have written with tremendous openness and insight, sounding as though they had hands-on experience in this area. I have tried to include their insights in the dialogue on key issues. I am grateful for the Bible college and seminary libraries that allowed me access to their books and periodicals collections.

A book of this nature is not written alone. In 1977, the Pentecostal Assemblies of Canada published *Charismata: A Fresh Look from a Pentecostal Perspective,* my first writing on gifts. That formed a basis for the first half of this work.

For the present work, William MacDonald offered valuable criticism. William Menzies, APTS president, friend, and brother, has given invaluable counsel. Special acknowledgment goes to Tom Sanders and Glen Ellard and his editing staff (with an assist on the Greek from Clancy Hayes) at Gospel Publishing House who worked so patiently and diligently with me in the final revision stages. I have learned much about writing from them. Thanks to Ian and Heather Henderson who lent their computer expertise. I am grateful to Wonsuk Ma, whom I consulted on key points of Old Testament perspectives. Dozens of significant people have impacted my life, thus the writing of this book. None have been more influential than Dwight MacLaughlin. As my pastor during my teen years he taught me the vital importance of laying a strong biblical foundation for all that we do. He lived Pentecost for me.

Special tribute goes to my wife, May, whose feedback and insights inspired key applications of the book. She proofread vital segments, drew the diagrams, and team-taught these materials with me in Chinese. My daughters, Faith, Lydia, and Deborah, wholeheartedly supported this project. Many of my hours that should have been theirs are their gift to the readers of this book.

Thanks to my Asian brethren who encouraged me to share these materials throughout Southeast Asia. My prayer is that these materials will be an effective tool to help you in reaching the harvest for Christ.

Acknowledgments

Acknowledgment is made to the following for permission to quote from the publications indicated:

Augsburg Fortress Publishers, *Agape and Eros* by Anders Nygren; *The Bible and the Role of Women* by K. Stendahl.

Ave Maria Press, *Healing* and *The Power to Heal* by Francis MacNutt.

Baker Book House, *Christian Calling and Vocation* by Henlee H. Barnette; *Showing the Spirit: A Theological Exposition of 1 Corinthians 12–14* by Donald A. Carson; *A Commentary on the Pastoral Epistles* by J. N. D. Kelly; *The Synoptic Problem* by Robert H. Stein.

Banner of Truth Trust, *God's Ultimate Purpose: Ephesians 1:1–23* by David Martyn Lloyd-Jones.

Bantam, Doubleday, Dell Publishing Group Inc., *Ephesians: Translation and Commentary on Chapters 4–6* by Markus Barth.

Cambridge University Press, *The Last Twelve Verses of Mark* by W. Farmer; "Cursing Jesus (1 Cor. 12:3): The Jews as Religious Persecutors" by J. Duncan M. Derrett; "Tongues, A Sign for Unbelievers?" by B. C. Johanson; "1 Cor. xiii and 1 Cor. xiv" by Nils Johansson; "Liturgical Order and Glossalalia in 1 Corinthians 14:26c–33a" by William Richardson.

Collins Publishers, *The Christian Experience of the Holy Spirit* by H. Wheeler Robinson.

Dallas Theological Seminary, "A Symposium on the Tongues Movement: The Purpose of Tongues" by Zane C. Hodges; "The Ministry of Women in the Apostolic and Postapostolic Periods" by H. Wayne House; "Tongues and the Mystery Religions of Corinth" by H. Wayne House.

Evangelical Theological Society, "Public Roles for Women in the Pauline Church: A Reappraisal of the Evidence" by James G. Sigountos and Myron Shank; "A Reconsideration of the Ending of Mark" by John Christopher Thomas.

Harcourt Brace Jovanovich, Inc., *The Four Loves* by C. S. Lewis.

Harper & Row, Publishers, Inc., *A Commentary on the First Epistle to the Corinthians* by Charles Kingsley Barrett; and *Mark* by Larry W. Hurtado.

Interpretation, "When is the End Not the End? Literary Reflections on the Ending of Mark's Narrative" by Norman R. Petersen; "The Service of Worship: An Exposition of 1 Corinthians 14" by E. Schweizer.

Journal of Biblical Literature, "A Pattern of Prophetic Speech in 1 Corinthians" by Thomas W. Gillespie; "The Bridge Between Mark and Acts" by Alfred E. Haefner; and "Luke's Description of John Mark" by B. T. Holmes.

Judson Press, *The Ministry of the Spirit* by Adoniram Judson Gordon.

Kregel Publications, *The Revival in Indonesia* by Kurt Koch; *New Testament Teaching on Tongues* by Merrill F. Unger.

Marshall Pickering, *Isaiah 40–66* by R. N. Whybray.

Moody Press, *The Pastoral Epistles* by Homer A. Kent; *The Gospel of Isaiah* by Alan A. MacRae; *Isaiah: The Glory of the Messiah* by Alfred Martin and John Martin.

Oxford University Press, "The Interpretation of Tongues: A New Suggestion in the Light of Greek Usage in Philo and Josephus" by A. C. Thistleton; *The Gospel Message of St. Mark* by Robert H. Lightfoot; *The Text of the New Testament* by Bruce M. Metzger.

The Paternoster Press Ltd., "Function or Office? A Survey of the New Testament Evidence" by Ronald Y. K. Fung.

R. Brockhaus, *The New International Dictionary of New Testament Theology* by Colin Brown.

Scholars Press, *Literary Patterns, Theological Themes and the Genre of Luke-Acts* by Charles H. Talbert; "A Pattern of Prophetic Speech in 1 Corinthians" by Thomas W. Gillespie; "The Bridge

Between Mark and Acts" by Alfred E. Haefner; "Luke's Description of John Mark" by B. T. Holmes.

T & T Clark Ltd., *Church Dogmatics* by Karl Barth.

University of Chicago Press, *A Greek-English Lexicon of the New Testament and Other Early Christian Literature* by Walter Bauer.

University Press of America, *The Gift of Prophecy in 1 Corinthians 12–14* by Wayne Grudem; *Spirit Baptism, A Pentecostal Alternative* by Harold Hunter.

Ward and Laurel Gasque, "F. F. Bruce: A Mind for What Matters."

The Westminster Press, *Isaiah 40–66* by Claus Westermann; *Spirit of the Living God* by Dale Moody; *Baptism in the Holy Spirit* by James D. G. Dunn; *The Letter to the Romans* by William Barclay; *The Letters to the Corinthians* by William Barclay; *Saint Mark* by Dennis E. Nineham.

William B. Eerdmans, *Romans* by Matthew Black; *The Epistle to the First Corinthians* by Gordon Fee; *Isaiah: Scroll of a Prophetic Heritage* by William L. Holladay; *The Gospel According to Mark* by William Lane; "Comfort" by G. Stahlin in *Theological Dictionary of the New Testament,* ed. Gerhard Kittel and Gerhard Friederich.

Zondervan Publishing House, *Pentecost and Missions* by Harry R. Boer; *How to Read the Bible for All Its Worth* by Gordon Fee and Douglas Stuart; *First Corinthians* by Harold Mare; *Mark: Evangelist and Theologian* by Ralph P. Martin; *The Holy Spirit and His Gifts* by J. Oswald Sanders.

Every effort has been made to trace copyright holders—without results in a few instances. This will be rectified in future editions if the relevant information can be obtained.

Introduction

The subject of the gifts of the Spirit admits several views. Many churches have made the gifts optional, intentionally or unintentionally. Some think the gifts were only for the first century. Others believe tongues are the least of the gifts, so they stress only what they consider the greater gifts. Pentecostals, on the other hand, have sometimes stressed the more spectacular gifts, thus not encouraging the quieter gifts. Because of the teaching that one may *possess* gifts, people of low self-esteem may infer that they do not and could not possess the gifts. By making maturity and holiness prerequisites to ministering gifts, the immature and "not so holy" have been left out.

Extremes in doctrine and practice have caused some people to shrink from a complete Spirit-led ministry. An overemphasis on emotion void of any biblical foundation has led to faith-shattering experiences for some. A lack of love and acceptance has hindered the effective exercise of the gifts. Some churches have forgotten their Spirit-inspired goals and focused on less worthy objectives. The apostle Paul said, "Do not put out the Spirit's fire" (1 Thessalonians 5:19). Spiritual gifts are God's tools to lead us to maturity and ministry. Properly understood and exercised, the gifts can cause the Church to grow.

We shall examine the biblical basis of the baptism in the Holy Spirit, the priesthood of the believer, the departure from the first-century pattern, the move toward renewal, and the incarnational nature of the gifts.

The Biblical Basis of Spiritual Gifts

Some scholars argue that one cannot use historical portions of the Bible to teach doctrine.[1] If so, Pentecostals are wrong in appealing to Old Testament records and to Luke-Acts narrative material to establish their doctrinal position on the work of the Holy Spirit.

But Old Testament historians wrote with a purpose. The Bible is not just history, but salvation history. Within the first twelve chapters of Genesis are key themes of the Bible: creation, humanity in the image of God, redemption, selection of the people of God, judgment for sin, proper worship, the glory of God versus the wiles of the devil, and God's plan and purpose in missions. Appearing in Genesis, these themes are thereafter unfolded throughout the rest of the Bible. The books of Exodus through Numbers have provided much material on which the Church has based its teaching of typology. The Book of Judges reveals the repeated cycle of prosperity, backsliding, judgment, repentance, and blessing in Israel's experience. All this is meant to teach God's faithfulness, human depravity apart from God, and the human need to repent. "All Scripture is God-breathed and is useful for teaching" (2 Timothy 3:16). Jewish Hellenistic historians did the same thing in their writing of history with a purpose.[2]

The outpouring of the Holy Spirit is not unique to the New Testament era. The Old Testament records five major visitations of the Israelites by God: during the times of (1) the Exodus, (2) the judges, (3) the kings, (4) the pre-exilic prophets, and (5) the post-exilic prophets. The giving of the Spirit was not for salvation, but for service. In each period God anointed only key leadership for special ministries. Accompanying that anointing were the outward signs of prophecy, miracles, military prowess, and divine wisdom.

---

[1]See Gordon D. Fee and Douglas Stuart, *How to Read the Bible for All Its Worth* (Grand Rapids: Zondervan Publishing House, 1982), 87ff.

[2]I. Howard Marshall, *Luke: Historian and Theologian,* New International Greek Testament (Grand Rapids: William B. Eerdmans, 1970), 55–56; and Roger Stronstad, *The Charismatic Theology of Luke,* (Peabody, Mass.: Hendricksen Publishers, Inc., 1984), 6–7.

After the post-exilic period, scriptural prophetic inspiration was not manifested for four hundred years. Pious Jews of the intertestamental period, particularly at Qumran, felt they were living in the midst of darkness, corruption, and perversity. Just like the prophets, they longed for the Messianic Age, when the Spirit would be poured out abundantly upon everyone. With the coming of the Christ, the latter days would begin, for Isaiah had prophesied that the Messiah would be uniquely Spirit-anointed for ministry (see Isaiah 11:2; 42:1).

LUKE-ACTS' APPROACH

Luke testified to the fulfillment of the outpouring of God's Spirit. He focused on the Spirit's infillings of Elizabeth, Mary, Zechariah, John the Baptist, Anna, and Simeon. He described the Spirit as physically descending on Jesus after His baptism, leading Him into the wilderness to be tempted by the devil, and empowering Him for His ministry. Jesus' inaugural sermon featured the theme of the Spirit's anointing. By emphasizing the work of the Spirit, Luke pointed to the arrival of the Messianic Age, the latter days.

Scholars, both liberal and conservative, have recognized that Luke was not simply recording history.[3] When relating Spirit enablement for service, Luke deliberately used the same terminology (e.g., "clothed," "filled," and "poured out") as the translators of the Old Testament had when they produced the Septuagint. He did this to show the continuity of the Spirit's work from the Old Testament into the Messianic era: Pointing back to Israel's experiences of the Spirit, Luke used those experiences to teach what lay ahead in Christ's ministry and the work of the Church. When the Messiah came, the Holy Spirit would once again set people apart with accompanying outward signs, as had happened in the former days.[4]

---

[3]Stronstad, *Charismatic Theology of Luke*, 9.

[4]Liberal scholar Hengel, conservative scholars Marshall, M. Barth, Turner, Pinnock, Ervin, and Stronstad see Luke-Acts as interpretative history. I am indebted to Stronstad for his research in the areas of Luke-Acts theology and the continuity of the Spirit's experience in the Old Testament and the New.

Certain Luke-Acts narratives are written to describe normative features of the mission and character of God's people. This being so, his narratives have historical-theological intent. According to I. Howard Marshall, Luke's "view of theology led him to write history."[5]

When describing Jesus' being anointed of the Spirit, Luke deliberately pointed to a physical, attestable sign: The Holy Spirit descending in a form like a dove (Luke 3:22). Jesus' filling with the Spirit parallels the infilling of the 120 on the Day of Pentecost. Note the parallels between Luke 3:21 to 4:2 and Acts 1:12 to 2:14:

1. Both were praying before the descent of the Spirit.
2. The Spirit came visibly (Luke: dove; Acts: tongues of fire).
3. Both were set apart for their ministries.
4. Both immediately began ministering. (Jesus confronted Satan in the wilderness and then began preaching in Capernaum; the 120 in the upper room witnessed to Jesus' resurrection power.)[6]

The Spirit in Acts continues to do for the Church what He began to do in the Book of Luke in the ministry of Christ. The primary intent of the Spirit's infilling in Luke-Acts was not to bring salvation, but to equip for service.[7]

In contrast to the Old Testament era of the Spirit being poured out upon selected persons, the New Testament era features the Holy

---

[5]Marshall, *Luke*, 52.

[6]Charles H. Talbert, *Literary Patterns, Theological Themes, and the Genre of Luke-Acts*, Society of Biblical Literature Monograph Series, no. 20 (Missoula, Mont.: Scholars Press, 1974), 16.

[7]Much discussion has taken place over the last several years on the purpose of the infilling of the Spirit in Acts, particularly since the publication of James D. G. Dunn's *Baptism in the Holy Spirit* (Philadelphia: Westminster Press, 1970). Dunn's thesis is that none were fully saved until they were filled with the Spirit and that the infilling of the Spirit was for incorporation into the body of Christ (i.e., salvation). Although F. F. Bruce shows how much he has been swayed by such arguments in his recent work, *Epistles to the Colossians, to Philemon, and to the Ephesians*, The New International Commentary on the New Testament (Grand Rapids: William B. Eerdmans, 1984), many other scholars have written persuasively to counter Dunn. Barth and Turner in evangelical circles and Ervin, Horton, and Stronstad in Pentecostal circles are among them.

Spirit promised to all believers. Christ commanded his disciples to wait to be "clothed with power from on high" (Luke 24:49). And afterwards, anointed, Peter preached, "The promise [of the Spirit] is . . . for all whom the Lord our God will call" (Acts 2:39). The baptism in the Holy Spirit is a promise, a gift, and a command. This gift the Early Church assumed all believers would appropriate (see Acts 2:4,17–18,38–39; 10:44–46; 11:8; 19:1–2).

On the Day of Pentecost after Jesus' ascension, Peter quoted from Joel to explain the disciples' powerful experience as the outpouring of the Holy Spirit upon all flesh (Joel 2:28–29; Acts 2:17–18). Today some insist that no one was fully saved before Pentecost: because the Spirit is needed in regeneration and the Spirit had not been poured out until then—the beginning of the Church Age. However, the disciples present were already saved because they had encountered and believed in the resurrected Jesus (e.g., John 20:22). Furthermore, the disciples were commanded to wait in Jerusalem for clothing with power, not salvation. At Pentecost, Peter offered the same promise of the gift of the Holy Spirit to all those who would repent and believe in Christ (Acts 2:38–39).

In Acts 2, the 120 spoke in identifiable languages. Acts 2:6,8 use the word *dialektos,* from which we get the word "dialect." Acts 2:11, in reference to the same event, uses the word *glossais,* from which we get the word "glossal." Such description indicates a speaking to God in a language unlearned by the speaker.

Acts 8 reports the case of the Samaritan believers being baptized in the Holy Spirit. They had been baptized in water. They had seen many miracles. James Dunn argues that this was a "defective salvation" because Acts 8:12 says they "believed Philip . . ."[8] But one has only to read the rest of the verse: ". . . as he preached the good news of the kingdom of God and the name of Jesus Christ, they were baptized, both men and women." The Samaritans had "accepted the word of God" (Acts 8:14); the terminology indicates salvation. Dunn himself indicates that Philip's baptism was not repeated: "Their baptism was fully Christian."[9] It seems strange

---

[8]Dunn, *Baptism in the Holy Spirit,* 63–65.
[9]Ibid., 61, 63.

that Philip would baptize those whose response and commitment were "defective" and not be called to answer for such a rash action among the despised Samaritans, as Peter later had to do in Jerusalem after he baptized Cornelius and his household (Acts 11:1,18).

Simon perceived the Holy Spirit was given (Acts 8:18). A total perception is indicated by the Greek word *idon,* which could include seeing and hearing. Although his heart was wrong, he could clearly see and hear that something unique was occurring. Although tongues is not mentioned in Acts 8, most commentators readily admit that what Simon perceived was speaking in tongues. As a matter of fact, some call this the Samaritan Pentecost.[10]

Acts 9 records Paul's salvation experience on the road to Damascus. When Ananias came to Paul, he called him "brother" (v. 17), for Paul was already part of the family of God. Ananias expressed two reasons for his coming: that Paul would " 'see again and be filled with the Holy Spirit' " (Acts 9:17). Clearly, Ananias' statement has nothing to do with winning Paul to the Lord. Paul needed an empowering from the Lord. He was not saved just to get to heaven; he was saved to serve. That is why the emphasis of Luke-Acts is the infilling of the Holy Spirit. Thus Paul later stated that he spoke in tongues more than the Corinthians (1 Corinthians 14:18). He coveted God's equipping to do God's work.

Acts 10:44 to 11:18 relates the outpouring of the Spirit upon the Gentiles of Cornelius's household. The Gentiles had the same experience of speaking in tongues as the disciples at Pentecost (Acts 10:47; 11:15,17; 15:8). Because of this, Peter was able to determine that they, too, had received the baptism in the Holy Spirit.

He was not amazed that Gentiles could become believers; the Old Testament had foretold that. But just as Jews expected Gentiles to become proselytes, so most Jewish Christians before the Jerusalem Council of Acts 15 would naturally have felt that Gentile Christians needed to embrace Jewish practices. Peter and the Jerusalem church shared that bias (see Acts 10:28; 11:2–3; 15:1).

---

[10]See F. F. Bruce, *The Book of Acts,* The New International Commentary on the New Testament (Grand Rapids: William B. Eerdmans, 1977), 183. Also, many other non-Pentecostal scholars readily agree that the experience at Samaria included tongues.

Consequently, Peter was amazed that Gentiles (they likely became believers during Peter's preaching) could receive the Holy Spirit "just as we [Jews] have" (Acts 10:47). They had experienced the Holy Spirit—apart from any other qualification—at the same time they were saved. Before Pentecost the disciples had believed; at Pentecost they were filled: The Baptism in the Holy Spirit was an additional experience. Cornelius's household was saved and filled at the same time. Peter implies that the experience of this gift, as at Pentecost, was separate from salvation (Acts 11:17). He began to understand that faith alone qualifies both Jewish and Gentile believers to experience all spiritual blessings.

Over twenty years after Pentecost, on his third missionary journey, Paul went to "some disciples" at Ephesus to ask the crucial question about receiving the Holy Spirit (Acts 19:1–2).[11] Apollos had taught about Jesus accurately enough, but he had known only of John's baptism (Acts 18:24–28). Paul came to teach the Ephesian believers more and to baptize them with Christian baptism.

Some argue that the Ephesians were not Christians when Paul came. But the word "disciple" is not used of followers of John the Baptist after his death, for they became disciples of Jesus (see also the usage of the word "disciple" in Acts 6:1; 9:10; 16:1). The disciples in Achaia (Acts 18:27) were clearly believers, for they "by grace had believed." Why would not the disciples in Ephesus (Acts 19:1) be in the same category of believers? Evangelism of the lost does not include the question of receiving the Holy Spirit.

---

[11]The issue is on a point of Greek grammar in Acts 19:2. Dunn argues that it should be translated "Did you receive the Holy Spirit when you believed?" Horton, Ervin, Stronstad, and Barth argue most convincingly that it should read, "Having believed, did you receive?" In other words, in this case the action of the aorist participle in Greek should be taken as preceding the main verb: They had already believed. Have they now received? The context indicates that this is a possible usage of the aorist participle. Turner takes a mediating position by agreeing with Dunn on the grammar but disagreeing on the theology: "The aorist participle, *pisteuantes,* should probably be taken as coincident with *elabete;* though against Dunn it must be said that one does not ask Paul's question unless a separation between belief and Spirit-reception is conceivable" (transliteration inserted for the Greek; Max M. B. Turner, "The Significance of Receiving the Spirit in Luke-Acts: A Summary of Modern Scholarship," *Trinity Journal* 2 [Fall 1981]: 131).

Even if one insists that the Ephesians were not full believers when Paul first arrived, they clearly would be after he had them baptized in water. That act preceded his laying hands upon them and their speaking in tongues and prophesying. The Early Church expected a separate, distinct, and vital experience of an enablement of power in the Holy Spirit. Spirit reception for the Ephesians was similar to the Samaritans: an experience separate from salvation.

Dispensationalists often say the Book of Acts represents only a transition period between Jewish and Gentile eras. They believe that tongues served as a sign to unbelieving Jews of Gentile acceptance in the Church.

But tongues did not serve that purpose at Cornelius's household, and they did not serve that purpose in Ephesus. The issue at the time of Paul's third missionary journey could not have been that of the acceptance of Gentiles within the Church. That issue would have been essentially resolved through the Jerusalem Council of A.D. 49 and the vast numbers of Gentiles already in the churches.

Thus the biblical evidence to show the universality of the outpouring of the Holy Spirit in the New Testament era is more than sufficient. Throughout Acts every new group was filled with the Spirit. More than a growing organization, the Early Church was a throbbing, vital organism energized by the Spirit himself.[12]

MARK'S APPROACH

The Book of Mark reveals Jesus as the powerful, Spirit-anointed servant-Messiah who comes against the forces of Satan.[13] In the

---

[12]Harry R. Boer, *Pentecost and Missions* (Grand Rapids: Zondervan Publishing House, 1961), documents that the Early Church did not go forth primarily on the motivation of following the Great Commission, but under the impetus of the Pentecostal experience. This is significant because it comes from one whose reformed theology background emphasizes the work of the Holy Spirit as incorporation into the body of Christ, not as empowering for service.

[13]Ernest F. Scott, *The Spirit in the New Testament* (London: Hodder and Stoughton, 1923), 67, and Morna D. Hooker, *The Message of Mark* (London: Epworth Press, 1983), 16, see a strong emphasis on the Spirit in Mark. M. Robert Mansfield *"Spirit and Gospel" in Mark* (Peabody, Mass.: Hendricksen, 1987), 17–19, suggests the primary purpose of Mark was to show how Jesus is the Spirit-filled one, permanently endowed to fulfill his task. This emphasis takes precedent over any other designation for Christ in Mark, including Son of Man references.

prologue of this Gospel, the Holy Spirit is mentioned three times: John the Baptist prophesies that Jesus will baptize with the Holy Spirit (1:8), Jesus himself is baptized with the Spirit (1:10), and the Spirit leads Jesus into the wilderness to face Satan (1:12). The four detailed cases in the Gospels showing Jesus casting out demons are all recorded by Mark, showing how the Spirit-filled Jesus came against the evil spirits (see Mark 3:20–30). Mark writes these things to encourage Gentile Christians facing intense persecution in Rome.

Mark's Gospel follows the order and detail of Peter's sermon in Acts 10. Even the abruptness of the ending of Mark corresponds to the sudden ending of Peter's sermon at Cornelius's house by the sovereign intervention of the Holy Spirit.[14]

Many have been willing to accept the simplistic approach that Mark was Peter's secretary, taking dictation.[15] Though much influenced by Peter, clearly Mark wrote independently and originally,

---

[14]Note the following comparison of Peter's sermon with Mark's outline:

Acts		Mark
10:36	Introduction	1:1
10:37–8	Spirit Anoints Jesus	1:10
	Ministry Begins	1:14
10:38	Describes Powerful Ministry	1:16–10:52
10:39	Focus on Jerusalem	11 to 14
10:39b	Crucifixion	15
10:40–41	Resurrection	16
10:44	Sudden interruption/Sudden ending of Holy Spirit	16:8

Mark 16 concludes with a promise of a personal meeting with Peter in Galilee. No fulfillment is recorded in Mark. In Acts 10 Jesus encounters Peter, this time in a vision and through the outpouring of the Spirit upon Cornelius's household. The many parallels seem deliberate.

[15]Papias discusses this influence, cited by Eusebius, *Hist. Eccl. III.*, xxxix.15.

revealing great intellect and persuasive abilities yielded to the Holy Spirit's inspiration.[16]

Then why should Mark use the Acts 10 sermon? And if so, why the sermon outline in Acts 10 and not those of Acts 2, 3, or 4? The obvious reason for Acts 10 was the centrality of the Cornelius event for the Early Church. Peter, after struggling with God over His commands about unclean animals, went to Cornelius's house. He preached a straightforward gospel. But as a Christian Jew at this stage of Church history, his natural inclination may have been to add something in the way of Jewish legalisms or observances for Cornelius's household.

Before Peter had any chance to do this, the Holy Spirit intervened. And the Gentiles saw that on themselves, too, the Holy Spirit had been poured out. They could not be treated as second-class citizens in the kingdom of God; they too had received power to fulfill their mission to the world. The Gentile church must have rehearsed the Cornelius event line by line and detail by detail with excitement and great frequency.[17]

Peter himself repeated the story. He "explained everything to them [i.e., the Jerusalem brethren] precisely as it had happened" (Acts 11:4). He climaxed his explanation with an account of his

---

[16]Many present-day scholars call Mark a historian and theologian in his own right. For example, see Ralph P. Martin, *Mark: Evangelist and Theologian* (Grand Rapids: Zondervan Publishing House, 1972); William Lane, *The Gospel According to Mark*, New International Commentary on the New Testament (Grand Rapids: William B. Eerdmans, 1974); Robert Mansfield, *"Spirit and Gospel"*; Hugh Anderson, *The Gospel of Mark*, The New Century Bible Commentary Series (Grand Rapids: William B. Eerdmans, 1976); Larry W. Hurtado, *Mark*, The Good News Commentary (San Francisco: Harper and Row, 1983); Dennis E. Nineham, *Saint Mark* (Philadelphia: The Westminster Press, 1963).

[17]Many identify a strong relationship between Mark and Acts. Peter was Mark's mentor. Alfred E. Haefner, "The Bridge Between Mark and Acts," *Journal of Biblical Literature* 77 (1958): 67–71, sees Acts 1:13–14 and Acts 3–4 as the natural continuation of Mark 16:8. B. T. Holmes, "Luke's Description of John Mark," *Journal of Biblical Literature* 54 (June 1935): 64, says that Luke's allusions to John Mark in Acts "implied to his first reader that Mark handled a written memorandum about Jesus in the course of the first Gentile mission to Cyprus." It is suggested Mark sought to write a continuation of his Gospel, and Luke makes similar use of this sequel in his second volume. In fact, the longer ending of Mark may be a précis, a summary of charismatic elements of Acts serving as its preface.

preaching to, and the Holy Spirit's coming upon, Cornelius's household (vv. 15–16). Years later, Peter reported the same event at the Jerusalem Council (Acts 15:7–11). And James referred to Simon Peter's story as pivotal to the whole discussion (Acts 15:13–14). For many Gentiles, the Acts 10 event at Cornelius's house was more significant than the Acts 2 event of Pentecost.

As Mark unfolded his Gospel, its background for Christians of the first century was the Cornelius event. The excitement built as the story progressed. The great interruption of Peter's message and the outpouring of the Spirit were anticipated. The life and ministry of Jesus was not only historical fact but present reality for the Early Church. The inbreaking of the Spirit of God through the ministry of Jesus was carried on even to the Gentile world.

The issue of several possible endings for the Gospel of Mark does not invalidate this thesis, but rather confirms it.[18] The main proposals put forward about the conclusion of Mark are the shorter ending that concludes with Mark 16:8[19] and the longer ending that includes Mark 16:9–20.[20]

Most recent scholars insist the shorter ending was Mark's original intent.[21] Mark closed his Gospel by repeating the theme that char-

---

[18]The issue of the various endings of Mark's gospel cannot be dealt with fully in this book. Most scholars concur that the shorter ending was the original one. I have summarized the three basic options concerning the ending at 16:8:

1. Mark was somehow prevented from finishing his gospel. It should have at least one account of a resurrection appearance as a fulfillment of the passion predictions. Mark 16:8 ends with a weak preposition, "for." It could be translated, "They were afraid, you see . . ." It seems incomplete and awkward.

2. The conclusion was lost or destroyed by accident. This option is not likely. Mark could have rewritten it, or the ending could have been copied from the many early copies of the Gospel.

3. Increasingly, present-day scholars propose the abrupt ending was intentional.

[19]Manuscripts Aleph and B and most modern translations end Mark at 16:8, leaving Mark with an utterly abrupt ending, as if the author suddenly stopped.

[20]Some minor manuscripts give other abrupt endings, and Codex Washingtonius expands the longer ending of Mark 16. The discussions of the two major possible endings serves the purpose of confirming my thesis.

[21]Difficulties with the shorter ending focus on the following three arguments: First, although the word *gar* (for) is used to end sentences, paragraphs, and topics, it is not used to end a book. Second, five times the phrase "to be afraid" is found

acterized all of Jesus' activity throughout this gospel (4:41; 5:15,33,36; 6:50; 9:6,32):

> Astonishment and fear qualify the events of the life of Jesus. . . . "[T]he gospel of Jesus the Messiah" (Ch. 1:1) is an event beyond human comprehension and therefore awesome and frightening. . . . [C]ontrary to general opinion, "for they were afraid" is the phrase most appropriate to the conclusion of the gospel.[22]

Hugh Anderson summarizes and agrees with the arguments for the shorter ending:

> Again the *silent* dread with which the record closes can be taken as a sign of the awe and reverence of those for whom the old world has run its course and the new day of God is actualized. . . .
>
> . . .
>
> If Mark's ending was at 16:8, abrupt though it is, he could hardly have declared more effectively that God's Word is mightier than man's words. . . .[23]

It is Anderson's opinion that the empty tomb and the angel are sufficient to point to a new meeting with the risen Christ in Galilee. The Book of Mark exhibits a restraint in manifesting power for the whole world to see. Jesus' word in itself is pure and trustworthy and can be understood by his followers.

Robert Lightfoot says that the abrupt ending emphasizes "human inadequacy, lack of understanding, and weakness in the presence of supreme, divine action and its meaning."[24]

Larry Hurtado suggests Mark may have wanted to confront readers with a story of Jesus' resurrection that was somewhat "open-ended and unconcluded."[25]

---

in Mark, but never absolutely except in 16:8 (the purported ending of the Gospel). Third, Mark 14:28 and 16:7 refer to a meeting in Galilee, but no such meeting is recorded.

[22]Lane, *Mark*, 592.

[23]Anderson, *Mark*, 354, 358.

[24]Robert H. Lightfoot, *The Gospel Message of St. Mark* (Oxford: Clarendon Press, 1950), 92.

[25]Hurtado, *Mark*, 271.

Norman Petersen says the abrupt ending of 16:8 forces the reader to understand what Mark is saying about the time in which the reader lives: It is a matter of eschatological urgency. Verse 8 "interrupts the continuity of expectations about the Kingdom."[26] It has arrived, but the end is not truly yet. This period between the beginning of the end and conclusion of the end is the age of the Spirit's activity through the new people of God.

Note the words these scholars have used: "astonishment and fear," "silent dread . . . awe and reverence," "God's Word . . . mightier than man's words," an "open-ended and unconcluded" story that "interrupts the continuity of expectations." The Resurrection event—typical of all of Jesus' teaching ministry, miracles, and life—left all with feelings of amazement and inadequacy.

Now note the phrases Acts uses to describe those who evaluated the Cornelius event. The same awe produced by Jesus' ministry was produced by the Gentile reception of the Holy Spirit:

"The circumcised believers who had come with Peter were astonished that the gift of the Holy Spirit had been poured out even on the Gentiles" (Acts 10:45).

"Who was I to think that I could oppose God? . . . They had no further objections [lit., they kept quiet] and praised God" (Acts 11:17–18).

"The whole assembly became silent as they listened to Barnabas and Paul telling about the miraculous signs and wonders God had done among the Gentiles through them" (Acts 15:12).

Mark may have intentionally closed his gospel in an open-ended way for his readers to contemplate the amazing power and might of God. Jesus was the uniquely Spirit-filled one. The Resurrection, accomplished by the Holy Spirit, overwhelmed his followers. That same Spirit came upon the 120 at Pentecost and upon the Gentiles at Cornelius's house. All were amazed.

---

[26]Norman R. Petersen, "When Is the End Not the End? Literary Reflections on the Ending of Mark's Narrative," *Interpretation* 34 (April 1980): 157.

Dennis Nineham, however, counters the arguments for a deliberately abrupt ending:

> If St. Mark did intentionally end his Gospel with this paragraph, he was certainly behaving with considerable literary sophistication and making great demands on the understanding of his readers.[27]

But what seems so difficult for some scholars in the twentieth century to realize was more than obvious to the first generation of Mark's Gentile readers: The sudden coming of the Holy Spirit at Cornelius's household, showing how God both accepted the Gentiles and blessed them with every blessing. The importance of that event cannot be overestimated, especially as segments of Judaism and Jewish Christianity continued to resist Paul's teaching of grace to the Gentiles (e.g., Acts 21:17ff. and Galatians). Mark's theme was that God can break into any situation, at any time, no matter how difficult, just as the Holy Spirit broke in at Cornelius's household. The synoptic Gospels were likely written in the A.D. 60s. The Gospel writers and the church of the 60s were responding with a great amen to confirm that God indeed was doing these very things.

Of course, many Bible students accept the longer ending of Mark (vv. 9–20) as the inspired ending.[28] There is no reason to reject this portion of Scripture. This ending includes three emphases: physical Resurrection, the Great Commission, and the miracles that follow the preaching of the gospel. Coincidentally, or intentionally, these three teachings also reflect what happened at Cornelius's house-

---

[27]Nineham, *Saint Mark*, 442.

[28]Good textual evidence supports the longer ending as well. Manuscripts A, C, D, and K, the Vulgate, and numerically the vast majority of manuscripts record the longer ending. Good family representation also exists: Byzantine (A, E, H, K), Caesarean (W), Western (D and Diatessaron A. D. 170), Alexandrian (C), and Coptic manuscripts. Bruce M. Metzger, *The Text of the New Testament* (Oxford: Clarendon Press, 1968), 229, thinks that the longer ending was added so early that undoubtedly the church accepted it as canonical. W. Farmer champions the longer ending as the more difficult reading, and therefore necessarily the original one (W. Farmer, *The Last Twelve Verses of Mark* [London: Cambridge University Press, 1974], 57). See also John Christopher Thomas, "A Reconsideration of the Ending of Mark," *Journal of the Evangelical Theological Society* 26 (December 1983): 407–419, on manuscript evidence. See also Stanley M. Horton, "Is Mark 16:9–20 Inspired?" *Paraclete* (Winter 1970): 7–12.

hold.[29] Peter preached on the life, death, and resurrection of Christ. He obeyed the Great Commission to reach even to the Gentiles. Then Cornelius's household received the miraculous outpouring of the Holy Spirit. All of these teachings are confirmed by the rest of the New Testament.

PAUL'S APPROACH

Paul himself taught the Corinthians about speaking in tongues, though some of them misused this gift.

Some critics say the tongues at Corinth was simply gibberish, coming from the Corinthians heathen background of idolatry. If so, why didn't Paul simply tell them to stop? Instead, he wished that all would speak in tongues. He spoke in tongues more than all of them. He perceived no basic difference between the tongues he spoke and the tongues they spoke. He thought of tongues at Corinth as God-given, meaningful prayer and worship, capable of interpretation and edification of the believer.

The Corinthians' experience and the disciples' experience on the Day of Pentecost have many similarities.[30] It is as if Paul deliberately parallels the two, implying the nature of these experiences are indeed the same. Note the following:

1. All were gathered in one place (Acts 2:1; cf. 1 Corinthians 14:16,23).
2. The gifts are incarnational in nature (Acts 2:4; cf. 1 Corinthians 14:32).
3. Both occasions consider negative responses (Acts 2:6,13—drunkeness; cf. 1 Corinthians 14:23—insanity).
4. A positive response is expected of open hearts (Acts 2:11; cf. 1 Corinthians 14:16,24–25).

---

[29]The longer ending seems to combine some elements from Matthew and Luke. If it was not part of the original Mark, it was added very early in the second century. This passage contains nothing extra-biblical. It is not written in the apocryphal style of much of the church fathers between A.D. 100 and A.D. 150.

[30]O. Palmer Robertson, "Tongues: Sign of Covenantal Curse and Blessing," *Westminster Theological Journal* 38 (Fall 1975): 43–53, and Stanley Horton, *What the Bible Says About the Holy Spirit* (Springfield, Mo.: Gospel Publishing House, 1976), 230–31, make most of these observations.

5. Tongues serve as a sign to unbelievers (Acts 2:12,15,38–39; cf. 1 Corinthians 14:22–25).
6. Salvation comes through ministry in an understood language (Acts 2:37,41; cf. 1 Corinthians 14:25).
7. A variety of gifts are manifested (Acts 2:43; cf. 1 Corinthians 14:26).
8. A focus on teaching, fellowship, worship, gifts as signs, ministry to one another, and the evangelism of the lost results (Acts 2:41–47; cf. 1 Corinthians 14:3,6,15,22,24,26).

Luke and Paul were coworkers. Although they wrote with different purposes, they did not contradict each other. Luke-Acts was written with deliberate patterns and purposes in mind: Paul's ministry is paralleled to Peter's ministry to attest Paul's apostleship to the Gentiles. While Luke emphasized empowering for service and dynamic experiences in the Spirit, Paul focused on the Spirit's work in church growth, Christian living, the development of ministries, and the exercise of gifts. From terminology in Acts 19:1–2, Romans 12:1–21, 1 Corinthians 12 to 14, Ephesians 4:7–13 and 5:19–20, Colossians 3:16, 1 Thessalonians 5:19–21, and other passages, it is evident that Paul taught the churches about spiritual gifts everywhere he went.

Jude uses Pauline language on tongues to exhort believers: "Build yourselves up in your most holy faith and pray in the Holy Spirit" (Jude 20; cf. 1 Corinthians 14:4,15).

Hebrews 6:4–5 speaks of those "who have shared in the Holy Spirit, who have tasted the goodness of the word of God and the powers of the coming age." This passage, along with Hebrews 2:4, is a clear reference to the gifts of the Spirit poured out in the last days. It is obvious that this church was a charismatic one.

The Priesthood of the Believer

Essential to our understanding of spiritual gifts is the doctrine of the priesthood of all believers. Every believer has both a responsibility and a privilege to come to God directly. Having this spiritual vocation of being a priest to God, each believer should fulfill it in one type of ministry or another.

But both Protestants and Catholics have often missed the point. The Protestant interpretation often leaves the individual to solve his own problems, since, after all, he is a priest to God and can get his own answers. Protestants say, "God bless you, brother, I'll pray for you" and leave him without genuinely discerning his needs and ministering to them. The reason some churches have many weak and sickly among them is that Christians fail at "discerning the Lord's body" (1 Corinthians 11:27–31, KJV).[31] Christians take Communion, worship God, and hear sermons without sensing the needs that are in the family of God and seeking to be of help. The calamity is not that one may take Communion in an unworthy manner and be punished by God. The calamity is that Christians may attend church, go through all the motions, and miss the real needs of others. This happened at Corinth. This kind of hypocrisy can only be condemned by God and the world. Roman Catholics miss the beauty of every-believer priesthood. They go through a priest for ministry, forgiveness, needs, rather than understanding their own responsibility to minister to one another.

God's original intention was that all Israel (the people of God) were to be priests. "You will be for me a kingdom of priests and a holy nation" (Exodus 19:6). But while Moses was receiving instructions from God on Mount Sinai, the disobedient Israelites made a golden calf to worship. Only the Levites rallied around Moses in faithfulness to God. From among the Levites (namely, the descendents of Aaron) would come the priests, representing the nation in performing specific tasks of worship. They were not supposed to do the work of repentance and sacrifice, but to be the representatives of the people in the ritual aspects of worship. The other tribes, however, quickly surrendered full responsibility to them to do all priestly functions. Further, in Old Testament times, only specific

---

[31]Most scholars have approached 1 Corinthians 11:27–31 from the traditional perspective of self-examination before partaking Communion: If I sin, God may punish me for taking Communion unworthily. Gordon Fee is one scholar who does not. See *The Epistle to the First Corinthians*, The New International Commentary on the New Testament (Grand Rapids: William B. Eerdmans, 1987), 563–64. The context of the passage implies consideration of others in the body of Christ as the primary issue, not personal holiness.

individuals were anointed by the Spirit: judges, prophets, priests, and kings.

Isaiah 61:1–2 was prophetic of the anointing and ministry of the Messiah: He would bring good news, heal the brokenhearted, announce release for the captive, and proclaim the year of the Lord's favor.

Then, concluding this passage, 61:6 says, "You will be called priests of the Lord, you will be named ministers of our God." All Israel had a priestly, mediatory role to the nations. Jesus chose this Isaiah passage for His inaugural sermon, revealing the purposes and empowering of His ministry.

The prophet Joel said that the Spirit would descend on all flesh (Joel 2:28–29). Peter said that that fulfillment began at Pentecost (Acts 2:16ff.). He later said, "You are a chosen generation, a royal priesthood, a holy nation" (1 Peter 2:9, NKJV; see also v. 5). The descent of the Spirit had to do with all the people of God fulfilling their function as priests.[32]

The last book of the Bible describes the consummation of God's plan with several references to the royal priesthood of all believers: Jesus having "made us to be a kingdom and priests" (Revelation 1:6; see also 5:10). From the beginning to the end of the Bible, God's plan is that all of His people should be priests to Him and their fellow human beings. And Jesus, our elder brother, is our great High Priest.

Rather than supporting the dichotomy of professional and lay ministries, the Bible features two basic types of gifts: enabling gifts and ministry gifts. Ephesians 4:11 lists four enabling gifts (or five, if one identifies pastor and teacher as two separate gifts). They are to equip the saints for the work of the ministry.

---

[32]The concept of all the people of God becoming a prophetic people has been put forward by Stronstad, *Charismatic Theology of Luke*, 25–26, 80–81. He points to Joel's prophecy as the unique verse in the Old Testament that referred to the prophethood of all believers and thus deliberately used by Peter in his sermon at Pentecost. If this is a valid conclusion, its implications are rich. The ministry of Jesus our High Priest realizes the ministry foreshadowed by Elijah, Jeremiah, and Isaiah. Jesus is both Prophet and Priest. The people of God are not only priests, to minister to one another, reconciling and interceding; we also have a prophetic

In the King James Version a comma is inserted after the word "saints" in Ephesians 4:12, giving the enablers three jobs: perfect the saints, do the work of the ministry, and edify the body of Christ. By this interpretation the professional clergy are supposed to do all the work. This is clearly wrong. By making laypeople passive beneficiaries and developing a pseudo clergy-laity gap, many heresies of doctrine and authority have developed throughout church history.

The original Greek manuscripts contained no punctuation. Punctuation was added later for the clarity of future readers. Without the comma, the passage clearly shows that the work of the ministry belongs to all saints. The verb *katartidzo* signifies a right ordering and arrangement, a bringing to maturity and completeness. The NIV translates it "prepare"; the RSV, "equip." When a body is healthy it can fulfill its mission. When enablers help the body of Christ function in unity, the Church will do the work of ministry.

The priestly ministry of the believer is twofold. Foremost is ministry to God. Our lives are to be a spiritual act of worship (Romans 12:1). Worship reflects who we are, our motives and life-style. The church, when it gathers, worships most effectively when its members live godly lives. In turn, by worshipping together, we learn better how to order our lives. True worship comes from the realization of who God is and the acknowledgment of His sovereign control. We worship with heart, mind, soul, and strength. We see the world from God's perspective, beyond personal problems, cultural or racial barriers, and relational difficulties. We worship because God alone is worthy of our worship.

A part of true worship is sacrifice. Jesus became our sacrifice, indicating that we too should pour out our lives for others. We may need to die to carnal desires and personal ambitions. The well-being of the body of Christ must take preference over selfishness. The cause of Christ is our reason for existence. Paul considered the Christian life a sacrifice to God (Romans 12:1; 15:16; Philippians 1:6).[33]

---

role, to proclaim the good news until the final judgment day. Our lives, actions, and words must speak to a sinful world incisively and prophetically.

[33]"Began" and "carry on to completion" in Philippians 1:6 are two Greek words signaling the beginning and ending of a sacrifice.

Ministry to God includes intercessory prayer. Spiritual work depends upon prayer: We must win the battle in the spiritual realm before we win it in the material realm. We are to intercede for everyone (1 Timothy 2:1). We are to approach God boldly. Jesus grants the keys of the Kingdom and tells His followers about fulfilling God's plans by binding and loosing things on earth (Matthew 16:19). The power of the gospel applied properly can open doors of access, bind fears, and set people free to be who they truly are in God's plan.

A priest must set himself apart for the sacred task. Prayer, diligent study of the Bible, rest, and waiting in God's presence all demand a life-style that makes time to hear from God. Too many noises in today's world drown out the voice of God to us.

Second, practice of a true priestly ministry to God will lead us to our fellowman. After we begin to see the world from God's perspective we draw strength to face the challenge of winning the world. We find renewed joy and power in our dynamic relationship with God. We build each other up. We eagerly seek to fulfill God's will.

Our worship bears missionary implications: Jesus died to reconcile a world to himself; God gives us a ministry of reconciliation. We must seek to build bridges to others so they can be brought to Christ, so their healing can take place. "Therefore confess your sins to each other and pray for each other so that you may be healed" (James 5:16). We are to restore the straying brother or sister (Galatians 6:1). Our whole life should reflect an awareness of our tasks as royal priests to our families, our church, and the non-Christian world. The ministry of the Church consists of "its worship, its self-giving love, and its testimony concerning the reconciling power of Jesus Christ."[34]

This, then, is the pattern of the New Testament: All have opportunity to be anointed of the Holy Spirit and be used of God. The Holy Spirit is given freely that all, not just a select few, may exercise their differing ministries.

Every first-century Christian was aware he had a ministry that

---

[34]Murray, J. S. Ford, *Church Vocations: A New Look* (Valley Forge: Judson Press, 1970), 70.

the Holy Spirit would bless. Apostles, prophets, evangelists, and pastor-teachers were to equip the believer for his tasks. Real fellowship and in-depth interaction with fellow believers caused Christianity to develop the strength to reach out to a pagan world and win it for Christ. All were coworkers in the greatest enterprise the world has ever known. Because of the doctrine of the priesthood of all believers, the gifts of the Spirit were widely exercised.

Departure from the First-century Pattern

The Church, however, soon departed from the ministry pattern of every believer a priest. With this departure, the manifestation of the Spirit's gifts also declined. As heresies threatened the Church from within and persecution from without, forcing or drawing believers away from congregations, ministerial responsibility and authority soon became centralized in the clergy. Thus Ignatius, bishop of the strong church at Antioch at the beginning of the second century, could say that the bishop is "as the Lord." Apart from the bishop's authority, no Eucharist or marriage could be performed. So by the middle of the third century, Cyprian was asserting, "He has not God for his Father who has not the Church for his Mother."[35]

In other words, church membership became tantamount to eternal life. The bishop as head could declare who had his sins forgiven: Heretics were not allowed to hold church membership. This position no doubt combated some heresies, but it also gave rise to a major problem that has pervaded the Church to this day.

Since it was assumed that other believers did not know as much as the bishop or have the same authority, they were given less responsibility. Thus a clergy-laity distinction developed (much like it had in the Old Testament) and the bishop gradually became the authority of the church. He could determine his successor and bestow spiritual gifts through the laying on of hands, doctrines neither borne out by biblical exegesis nor practiced in the first-century church. The error was in assuming a person, rather than God, had the

---

[35]*Dec unit* 6, quoted in "The Cyprianic Doctrine of the Ministry," a chapter by John Henry Bernard in Henry B. Swete, ed. *Essays on the Early History of the Church and the Ministry* (London: MacMillan and Co., 1918), 239.

authority to bestow gifts and grant forgiveness. An error that became known as sacerdotalism, it implied that few possessed spiritual virtue and that only those few could impart it. In this way, the majority of believers lost the awareness that they could receive and exercise spiritual gifts.

This naturally led to the development of the Roman Catholic Church and the strength of the papacy. During the Middle Ages, education and Bible study were available only to the privileged few. The vast majority of people were uneducated. Even among the clergy few had access to the Bible, to say nothing of their knowledge of biblical languages. Supposedly, only some were able to interpret the Bible. The common person could not. The organized church became the custodian of Scripture. With that, the authority of Scripture became the authority of a few people in high religious positions. Their instruction was not to be questioned.

The situation would not have been so bad if those in authority had continued to faithfully teach the Bible and develop the individual priesthood of the believer. Unfortunately, humanism, greed, and politics were among the forces dominating the Roman Church's thinking. Disgusted with the corruption evident at Rome and Friar Johann Tetzel's promising of release from purgatory for offerings to beautify the Vatican, Martin Luther posted a detailed protest.

The Move toward Renewal

The Protestant Reformation renewed emphasis on reading the Bible and stirred many scholars to translate the Word of God into the language of the people. Three great cries of the Reformation were *sola fide, sola scriptura, sola gratia:* "only faith, only Scripture, only grace." Reformers refused to accept any authority other than Scripture.

Reformers revived the doctrine that every believer was a priest unto God. The Reformation not only sought to correct some abuses but actually changed the course of Western civilization, both sacred and secular. However, as with other spiritual movements, the Reformation succumbed to the tendency toward rigid orthodoxy, replacing fervent spirituality with another set of rituals. Some believers became lax, emphasizing orthodoxy in doctrine over power in life.

Then came the age of pietism, which emphasized personal experience and devotion. Pietists did not believe correctness in doctrine alone was sufficient. They recognized the need for the illumination of the Bible by the Holy Spirit. Emphasis was given to the scientific study of languages and the historical-grammatical interpretation of Scripture to discover the latter's application to daily life. Many saw the need of a missionary vision.

John Wesley was greatly influenced by the pietistic movement. English evangelicalism, in turn, produced William Carey, who helped initiate the modern missions movement. In England and America great revivals were led by men such as the Wesley brothers, George Whitefield, Jonathan Edwards, Charles Finney, and D. L. Moody. Both the missions movement and the great revivals emphasized the need for personal salvation, commitment, and holiness. The Holy Spirit was at work preparing God's people for His work.

At the turn of the twentieth century, a mighty Pentecostal outpouring began. Once again Christians realized they could have divine enablement through the gifts of the Spirit for accomplishing the work of God. Throughout church history specific groups of people had known and practiced manifestations of the Spirit. The revival of the twentieth century, however, transcended specific groups and affected every denomination, touching the Christian church in every country.

But the church faced the challenge of a worldwide population explosion. By the 1950s, the earth's population was greater than the total of all who had lived between Adam and the beginning of the twentieth century. By 1987 over five billion people inhabited the earth. How is the church to fulfill Christ's commission to proclaim the gospel to all peoples? Well-organized churches, a few charismatic leaders, and greater use of media are not the total solution. Only in freeing every believer for ministry can the church fulfill this challenge.

Today, the doctrine of the priesthood of every believer is more widely understood and practiced. Among those proclaiming this doctrine, four basic positions on the gifts of the Spirit predominate.

The first, held by ultra-conservative believers, is, We have a completed Bible; we do not need the gifts as the first-century church did.

A second view is that the gifts are optional, some gifts being more important than others. A fresh breeze began to blow upon believers of all denominations, many Catholics, Presbyterians, Baptists, Methodists, and Episcopalians being filled with the Holy Spirit. Consequently, nearly every denomination has had to evaluate this Pentecostal experience and what it might mean for them. Some regard tongues as "of the devil." Others feel tongues are the "least of the gifts" and therefore can be neglected or overlooked; one needs the "better gifts." Some believe the baptism in the Holy Spirit is optional.

A third basic position considers the baptism in the Holy Spirit a badge of holiness. A spiritual elitism develops. Some believe they are more spiritual than others. In its extreme form, this position teaches that some possess gifts and have the ability to impart them at will.

Essentially, this position poses the same problem faced by the second-century church, the problem that led to a church hierarchy. Whereas that was an organizational sacerdotalism, this position represents a spiritualized sacerdotalism: Pressing into service the allegorical method of Scripture interpretation, proponents actually make experience an authority as valid as Scripture itself. Those who are perceived as more spiritual supposedly possess great abilities to discern demons in fellow believers, to have visions and dreams on behalf of others, and to utter prophecies directing others' lives. The less spiritual stand in awe at the overwhelming demonstrations of gifts manifested by them.

A fourth position appears to be the biblical one. It allows each believer to be led of the Spirit of God. Decision making is based on a humble examination of biblical truths and on listening to the whole membership of the body of Christ rather than to any one person. The Lordship of Christ causes believers to seek growth in His image. Growth into maturity is a result of that decision making. Basically this position says that all believers are priests, the Spirit is poured out on all people, all members of the body of Christ are important and mutually reliant, every member needs to learn how to submit to the other members, and every believer should exercise spiritual gifts for the work of the ministry today. God's church has always been healthiest when all the members could share freely and openly. When ordinary people are entrusted with the liberating truth of Jesus Christ, they undergo the same life-changing experiences as any other saint of God.

The Incarnational Nature of the Gifts

Two very different views reveal basic misunderstandings of the nature of the gifts of the Spirit. Some define the gifts as primarily natural abilities, while others define the gifts as totally supernatural. The first view equates the gifts with natural talents dedicated to the Lord. Artists, doctors, and musicians who so dedicate their talents are considered to be exercising spiritual gifts. Miracles were prevalent in the first century only because the Bible was not yet complete. Proponents of this view think the developments of modern science, particularly in medicine, do away with the need for a gift such as healing. Others use a checklist for people to determine their gifts according to a self-evaluation form. This is a sort of spiritualized vocational preference test designed to help people find their gifts. Although this view helps people find their ministries in the church, it sometimes minimizes the supernatural aspect of spiritual gifts.

A second view characterizes the gifts as totally supernatural, denying human faculties. Those having this view argue that anything pertaining to the physical, or fleshly, part of a person is evil. Therefore, when God speaks through people, He bypasses their minds and simply uses their tongues. The more spectacular gifts of healing, miracles, prophecy, tongues, and interpretation are highly esteemed.

If the gifts were totally supernatural, then they would be infallible. But God's Word tells us to evaluate each gift in the light of edification, exhortation, comfort, and the Bible itself. Donald Gee states:

> A view of the gifts of the Spirit contained in a slogan that they are "a hundred percent miraculous" has obtained considerable acceptance in some quarters. We are told that "there is no element of

the natural in them at all.'' This is the pardonable language of enthusiasm for enforcing the truth that a supernatural element in spiritual gifts does exist, and we can respect the statement as such. But it will not do as a statement covering all the facts. We need a more balanced view. If we do not achieve it, we shall perpetuate the extremes that have marred the Pentecostal testimony from its beginning. Indeed, in that way lies considerable danger.[36]

As Gee implies, it is not truly biblical to accept either of the extreme positions. Spiritual warfare demands supernatural equipment. However, God does speak through people; He does not negate or bypass who they are. From the Garden of Eden until now, God's desire has been to fellowship with His human creation, to communicate with them, to develop their total beings to serve Him. If God wanted to work without using human beings, he could use angels.

Crucial to understanding gifts is the knowledge that the opposite of *spiritual* is not *physical*, but *sinful, carnal*. Often we have sought to deny all that is within us because we are sinful. We fail to realize that God has redeemed us and He seeks to perfect the image of Christ in us. God uses us! Because some have thought of the gifts as totally supernatural, they have emphasized the more spectacular gifts to the detriment of the less spectacular gifts. Just as *physical* is not to be equated with *carnal*, so also *spiritual* is not to be equated with *spectacular*.

But if the gifts are neither all natural nor all supernatural, what is their nature? At the point where the supernatural (all of God) meets the natural (all of man), the gifts begin. *The gifts are incarnational.*

For example, Christ was incarnated. He was fully God, yet fully human. He was God in the flesh, yet one person. He was not schizophrenic—a part-time God and a part-time human.

Another illustration of incarnation, the coming together of God and man, is the Bible: both a divine book and a human book. Men wrote it with their vocabularies, cultural backgrounds, idioms of

---

[36]Donald Gee, *Spiritual Gifts in the Work of the Ministry Today* (Springfield, Mo.: Gospel Publishing House, 1963), 10.

speech, and historical situations. But the Bible is God's book, verbally inspired to the human authors. It is accurate and authoritative. It is an objective revelation of God's truth.

Although the church and the individual are by no means on the same level as Jesus Christ and the Bible, the church was divinely instituted, established by Christ. Yet all who work with the church know how human it is! So, also, the mystery hid from all the ages is "Christ in you, the hope of glory" (Colossians 1:27). As we yield ourselves to all God has for us, we can share gifts. He helps us do for His kingdom what we cannot do by ourselves. J. Rodman Williams says the presence of the *charismata* "enhances natural capacities and functions."[37]

Thus, God touches all our abilities and potential with supernatural power. All Spirit-imparted abilities to minister and meet the needs of the church are derived from the enabling of the gifts of the Spirit.

Although W. J. Conybeare would classify gifts as "the extraordinary and the ordinary," why make the division? It is clearly arbitrary.[38]

It may well be said that some gifts are more spectacular to the observer than others, some are more spontaneous, some rely more on instantaneous inspiration, or power, and still others seem to be crowning blessings on natural abilities. Generally speaking, the gifts of 1 Corinthians 12:8–10 appear to be more spectacular and spon-

---

[37]J. Rodman Williams, *The Era of the Spirit* (Plainfield, N.J.: Logos International, 1971), 58. See also, R. E. McAlister, *The Manifestations of the Spirit* (Toronto: Gospel Publishing House, n.d.), 20, 34; Samuel Chadwick, *The Way to Pentecost* (Berne, Indiana: Light and Hope Publications, 1937), 108; J. Oswald Sanders, *The Holy Spirit and His Gifts* (Grand Rapids: Zondervan Publishing House, 1940), 111–112; Melvin L. Hodges, *Spiritual Gifts* (Springfield, Mo.: Gospel Publishing House, 1964), 26.

[38]"These miraculous powers are not even mentioned by the Apostolic writers as a class apart . . . but are joined in the same classification with other gifts, which we are wont to term natural endowments or 'talents.'. . . It is desirable that we should make a division between the two classes of gifts, the extraordinary and the ordinary; *although this division was not made by the Apostles at the time when both kinds of gifts were in ordinary exercise* [my emphasis]." W. J. Conybeare and J. S. Howson, *The Life and Epistles of St. Paul* (Grand Rapids: William B. Eerdmans, 1949), 334–335.

taneous than those mentioned in Romans 12:6–9. Yet both Romans 12 and 1 Corinthians 12 use the same basic word for gifts, *charismata,* indicating they are of the same nature. And although Ralph Riggs called the list of 1 Corinthians 12 "the official list" and the list of gifts in Romans 12 "supplementary," he too looked upon the latter as "likewise gifts of the Spirit."[39]

Rather than saying some gifts are natural and some are supernatural, it is perhaps better to focus on the *exercise* of the gifts, placing such exercise on a continuum from "natural" to "supernatural" (see figure 1). As exercised more effectively, the gift moves toward the supernatural: Less human ability is observed and God's working becomes more evident.

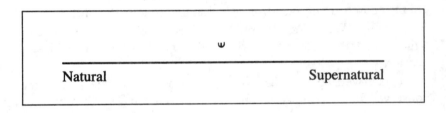

Figure 1. The Incarnational Exercise of the Gifts

Some of the gifts would immediately be placed toward the supernatural side of the continuum. However, other gifts, for example, a word of wisdom and a word of knowledge, may not appear quite so supernatural. Yet they may produce as powerful a change as a gift of miracles.

More gifts are not manifested today because we fail to recognize the nature of spiritual gifts and their importance in the church. Gifts have been considered optional to ministry. They have been relegated to super-spiritual Christians and, as in the Old Testament, charismatically-endowed leaders. The genius of the New Testament church

---

[39]Ralph M. Riggs, *The Spirit Himself* (Springfield, Mo.: Gospel Publishing House, 1962), 115–16.

was not in its leadership but in the vitality and ministry gifts of every believer. Melvin Hodges says:

> The exercise of spiritual gifts should not be considered as something apart from the normal exercise of the Body of Christ but part of the normal spiritual development of each member in the life of the Spirit.[40]

Gordon Atter adds, "We have the manifestation of the Spirit . . . to do the job as effectively as we ought to do it."[41] Williams says:

> There is the realization of a new immediacy between God and man. The "strange" signs—such as prophecy, healing, miracles, exorcism, speaking in tongues, discernment of spirits—are only strange so long as there has not yet been an interpenetration of the divine and the human, the supernatural and the natural. When this occurs . . . then what is alien to ordinary existence becomes (without losing its wonder) a part of the regular ongoing life and activity of the community.[42]

Ministering a gift is not to be equated with holiness, maturity, or accuracy. These factors help in the effective sharing of gifts, but are not its prerequisites. Since all believers are to minister gifts, manifesting gifts is no sign of spiritual attainment. Spiritual manifestations are to be judged against the clear biblical revelation. God gives the gift: He is to be glorified. As each member exercises a gift, he himself matures, interaction among believers takes place, and the body of Christ is edified.

We have put gifts on such a high, spectacular, and perfect plane that most believers are afraid that they may be "in the flesh" or unworthy to share. Ironically, at the same time, because few in the church seem to be able to exercise gifts, those who do may develop a sense of spiritual pride. And others may seek a particular gift because of how people may look up to them.

---

[40]Hodges, *Spiritual Gifts*, 26.

[41]Gordon F. Atter, *Rivers of Blessing* (Toronto: Full Gospel Publishing House, 1960), 86–87.

[42]Williams, *Era of the Spirit*, 57.

When God touches us, however, we should realize we are simply sinners saved by grace. J. Oswald Sanders says it is the fruit of the Spirit that is the evidence of spirituality. For in examining the nature of the Spirit's gifts, he finds

> they are for the most part gifts of service. Not one of them directly concerns character. They are God's equipment and enabling for effective service.[43]

Howard Courtney, writing from the Foursquare point of view, says:

> [T]o expect absolute perfection at all times in any gift that operates through fallible man or through human instruments is laying oneself open to the possibility of severe shock.[44]

Actually, the Corinthian church should have long ago disabused us of the notion that perfection was a criterion for operating the gifts: Paul said they were still babes and carnal. At the same time, he did not tell them to stop the use of the gifts; he taught them, rather, their correct use. A healthy body must exercise in order to grow. A church must minister spiritual gifts to mature and develop the holiness and fruit Christ expects.

However, having said that gifts are not a sign of spiritual attainment, an incarnational approach to gifts proposes that human agency plays an important part in the communication of the gift. The gifts are shared when God touches us. We are a part of the message. Our character, life, faith, vocabulary, sincerity, problems, and successes in life immediately become part of what others see and hear when the gift is shared.[45] Concerning the human part in exercising a word of knowledge, Maynard James says,

---

[43]Sanders, *Holy Spirit and His Gifts,* 110.

[44]Howard P. Courtney, *The Vocal Gifts of the Spirit* (Los Angeles: B. N. Robertson Co., 1956), 28. See also, R. B. Chapman, "The Purpose and Value of Spiritual Gifts," *Paraclete* 2 (Fall 1968): 24–28.

[45]Melvin L. Hodges, "Operations, Ministries and Gifts," *Paraclete* 7 (Spring 1973): 21: "There is also an area of human responsibility. Our consecration to God, the way we use what He gives us, our faith and dedication to His cause, play a part in opening the way for the gifts to be manifested."

> This gift is given by the Holy Ghost alone and can never be obtained by man's natural powers. This does not mean that the Lord ignores diligent and prayerful Bible study when He bestows the word of knowledge. Indeed, it will be found that the saint this supernatural knowledge comes from is usually both devout and disciplined.[46]

But are not the more spectacular gifts of healing and miracles totally supernatural? In what way are they incarnational? First, the credibility of the miracle and the message accompanying the miracle is dependent upon the messenger himself. A preacher whose financial practices, family life, or morality is questioned will be ineffective and may do more harm to God's kingdom than good. In a local congregation the person who does not relate well to his own family or holds hostility toward others will limit his ministry, primarily because of the response of others. If one's life is consistent with the message, that message is more readily received.

Besides the issue of credibility, a significant aspect of the gifts has been overlooked: The church is often the instrument through which the Holy Spirit effects healing.

What could happen if congregations truly learned to "rejoice with those who rejoice" and "mourn with those who mourn" (Romans 12:15)? Christians would see the needs and hurts of others as their own needs and hurts. They would be motivated to pray fervently and earnestly. They would reach out in love and support. There is a whole category of healing that can occur only in the context of the loving, supportive Christian family.

This stress-filled world has witnessed more emotional difficulties, marital breakdowns, drug and alcohol abuse, child abuse, and torn families than ever before. Life often catches people with their defenses down and without genuine structured support. The only solution is the loving, caring family of God.

Healing can flow through the church. During the worship service, alert Christians can pray for those around them, becoming sensitive to what God is saying, becoming a channel for God's blessings. In

---

[46]Maynard James, *I Believe in the Holy Spirit* (Minneapolis: Bethany Fellowship, 1965), 108.

a church like this, many miracles can take place, even before the altar call. During the week we can do the same. We can become His hands extended to needy people.

God has ordained that gifts be ministered through human vessels. The deepest sharing comes when the church knows and responds to the one who shares, in strength or in weakness. Perfection in the person who operates the gift is not the issue—genuineness and sincerity are. Outsiders may minister gifts to a local congregation, but deep fellowship and interaction help us to appreciate one another more and also to become more responsive to the gifts. Our task is to learn how to minister so that others will receive our ministry with gratefulness and maximum benefit.

In summary, there are four views on the nature of the gifts.

First, the gifts are natural abilities dedicated to the Lord. Second, God totally negates the human faculties. The person is only a secretary, or empty vessel, giving a message word for word, as if it had been dictated. Third, some believe holiness and spirituality determine God's bestowal of gifts. More holiness means more gifts. Weak and immature Christians need not apply. Fourth is the incarnational view. God makes full use of the vessel—his mind, thoughts, background, and current situation. The vessel himself is *part* of that message, thus his life and way of sharing the gift are vital parts of what builds up others. The keys are sensitivity to the Spirit, to one another, and to sharing the gift at the proper time. Gifts are tools of ministry. Through the fruit of the Spirit we manifest these tools effectively. W. I. Evans exhorts:

> The need of the Pentecostal people is not primarily to pray for the gifts. Gifts are here. Our need is to seek God and press into God in living faith so that the gifts lying around dormant, enough to set the world on fire, may come into exercise.[47]

The church will be as relevant as the people who compose it and will change even as the people grow with the times and mature in Christ. Rather than ministry being accomplished primarily by a professional clergy, the whole body of Christ will be engaged.

---

[47]W. I. Evans, *This River Must Flow* (Springfield, Mo.: Gospel Publishing House, 1954), 70.

PART ONE

Commentary

Introduction

To have a proper theology of the Church we must understand the role of the gifts of the Spirit in building, empowering, directing, shaping, and vivifying the Church. The biblical perspective comprises a loving, interacting congregation that is mutually dependent, caring for one another. Some have greater roles of authority and responsibility than others, but everyone is equally important. Everyone has a ministry.

1

1 Corinthians 12:1–11

1 Corinthians 12:1–3
Past and Present in the Spiritual Realm

[1]Now about spiritual gifts, brothers, I do not want you to be ignorant. [2]You know that when you were pagans, somehow or other you were influenced and led astray to mute idols. [3]Therefore I tell you that no one who is speaking by the Spirit of God says, "Jesus be cursed," and no one can say, "Jesus is Lord," except by the Holy Spirit.

First Corinthians was written in response to several questions and problems that arose in the Corinthian church. Several scholars today identify the essential problem as one of an overrealized eschatology. That is, some Corinthians believed that the blessings of the Kingdom had already arrived and that they had personally been initiated into the secrets of that Kingdom. Their teaching may have been influenced by some form of Hellenistic dualism that despised bodily existence and exalted spiritual revelation. They claimed to "speak in the tongues . . . of angels" (13:1) and denied the need of a physical resurrection (15:12–34) because they had already arrived spiritually. They discouraged sexual relationships in marriage (7:1–7) and despised Paul's suffering and ministry (4:8–13).[1] This sense of spiritual superiority caused divisiveness among them as well as between some of them and Paul.

---

[1]Fee, Martin, and Carson infer overrealized eschatology at Corinth. Gordon Fee believes the Corinthians were more divided against Paul than among themselves. Carson counters that this view (1) would divorce chapters 7 to 16 from 1 to 4, (2) would make the questions asked seem more theoretical than real (unless there was division, why ask these questions at all?), and (3) 1 Corinthians 13 emphasizes

53

Paul answered each issue they inquired about as thoroughly as possible, but indicated that other questions had to await his personal arrival in Corinth before being settled (11:34). For now, Paul felt it more of a priority to answer their questions about spiritual gifts. Some felt that exercising gifts indicated deeper spirituality. Others may have been wondering about the carnal attitudes and behavior of some who were ministering gifts. Paul wanted to clear up any misunderstanding on the subject of gifts. Knowledge is preferable to ignorance. Avoidance of sensitive issues would not help.

Frederic Godet says, "the term *Charisma* indicates rather their [i.e., the gifts'] origin, the word *Pneumatika* (14:1) their essence."[2] In other words, the gifts originate with God, and their essential nature is from the Holy Spirit. *Charisma* was not found in the Septuagint or in Greek writings before the Christian era. It occurs almost exclusively in Paul's writings (one usage being in 1 Peter). Paul considers the Church and the gifts integral to each other: If this is the Church, these are the gifts. If these are the gifts, they picture the Church.[3]

Some scholars state that because the Corinthians overvalued certain types of spiritual manifestations, they used the word *pneumatika* ("spirituals") and Paul sought to correct that with his word *charismata* ("gifts").[4] They note that when Paul focuses on the problem

---

love for one another so strongly that Paul must be trying to unify the factions. Donald A. Carson, *Showing the Spirit: A Theological Exposition of 1 Corinthians 12–14* (Grand Rapids: Baker Book House, 1987), 18–19. Whatever the case, one can readily see that the factions among them also produced friction with Paul.

[2]Frederic L. Godet, *Commentary on First Corinthians*, vol. 2 (Edinburgh: T. and T. Clark, 1886), 173. I transliterate throughout this book for the sake of the reader who is unfamiliar with the Greek alphabet. Godet and others, of course, use the characters of the Greek alphabet in their works.

[3]Ronald Y. K. Fung, "Ministry, Community and Spiritual Gifts," *Evangelical Quarterly* 56 (January 20, 1984): 15. He further says, "In Paul, ecclesiology is closely dependent upon Christology; it is also a reflection of pneumatology. Thus ecclesiology, 'charismatology' and 'diakoniology' are closely integrated in the thinking of Paul, unified as they are by the twin focus of Christ and the Spirit" (p. 20). In other words, the church reflects who Christ is through the work of the Spirit.

[4]For Paul, *charismata* refers to regeneration (Romans 5:15–16), eternal life (Romans 6:23), the call of Israel (Romans 11:29), gifts (Romans 12:6–7;

in chapter 14, he switches to *pneumatika* (14:1). Also, Paul says, "Since you are eager to have spiritual gifts . . . build up the church" *(pneumaton* 1 Corinthians 14:12).[5]

Those scholars who take this view, however, also take a problem-centered approach to gifts at Corinth.[6] Although Paul does confront problems at Corinth, his correction is positive so that there may be a greater exercise of the gifts. Thus, Ralph Martin does not consider the two terms negative. Rather, he considers *charismata* the broader term, referring to God's concrete actions, and *pneumatika* the narrower term, relating to the exercise of gifts in public worship.[7] Paul has, in fact, already used the word "spirituals" positively (e.g., 1 Corinthians 2:15; 3:1; 9:11) and will do so again (14:1,12). Even though the Corinthians did think of themselves as more spiritual, it is difficult to attribute the word "spirituals" to their personal terminology alone.

Paul contrasts their former condition with their present condition (12:2; cf. Ephesians 2). As Gentiles, they had worshipped mute idols and were given to ecstatic frenzies. They had felt that the more the divine spirit moved upon a person, the less became his self-control; the less his self-control, the more he possessed of the divine spirit. Godet explains:

> Their rule was: the more *pneuma* (spirit) the less *nous* (intelligence). The judgment accorded with Greek and even Jewish prejudices. Plato said in *Phaedrus:*
>
>> "It is by madness (the exaltation due to inspiration) that the greatest of blessings comes to us" and in the *Timaeus* he says:

---

1 Corinthians 12:4, 8–10), marriage and celibacy (1 Corinthians 7:7), and Timothy's gift (1 Timothy 4:4 and 2 Timothy 1:6). In 1 Peter 4:10 the word refers to spiritual gifts. In any case, it is clear that *charisma* is grounded in *charis* (grace). Grace places us in the body of Christ. *Charisma* enables the believer to fulfill his function of service.

[5]See, for example, Ralph Martin, *The Spirit and the Congregation: Studies in 1 Corinthians 12–15* (Grand Rapids: William B. Eerdmans, 1984), 65–66.

[6]Scholars have "overspecified what can be learned from a few individual words." Carson, *Showing the Spirit*, 24.

[7]Martin, *Spirit and Congregation*, 8.

"No one in possession of his understanding has reached Divine and true exaltation."[8]

The Jews often felt that way about their prophets whose utterances seemed more emotional or ecstatic.[9] Apparently one of the Corinthian factions felt the same way. As a result, some may have believed the teacher was less than the prophet and the prophet less than the one who spoke in tongues of angels. Paul's problem was how to answer those who defended their actions by saying, "The Spirit told me" or "God made me do it." Paul emphasizes that we are now more in control as new creations in Christ than when we were pagans without Christ.

A contrast is made between speechless idols and the God who speaks to and through us. God does not violate, attack, or destroy one's personality, but brings a person to his potential. Just as the prophets of Baal worked up an ecstatic frenzy on Mt. Carmel, these Gentiles were also beside themselves, trying to work up their own answer. They had zeal coupled with ignorance.

The imperfect passive verb and passive participle in 12:2 emphasize how much they had lost control *(egesthe apagomenoi*—lit. "you were led, being led away"). The use of the imperfect tense may indicate a habitual pre-Christian life-style, perhaps even some type of demon possession, as though they were carried away by an overwhelming current of force. "The pagans were led by no intelligent, conscious guidance, but by an occult power behind the idol (10:19ff)."[10]

By using the phrase, "Therefore, I tell you [make known to you]" (12:3), Paul speaks officially and authoritatively, like the Seleucid rulers of the interbiblical period who customarily gave their official decrees in this form. Paul had examined the issues and shows the

---

[8]Godet, *First Corinthians,* 174.

[9]Numbers 24:4,16; Hosea 9:7. Also, Philo the Alexandrian Jew of the early second century.

[10]George G. Findlay, "St. Paul's First Epistle to the Corinthians," in *The Expositor's Greek Testament,* ed. W. Robertson Nicoll (London: Hodder and Stoughton, Ltd., n.d.), 886. Carson, on the other hand, thinks the first two verses refer simply to their ignorance as pagans and verse three to what Paul wants to make known to them. Carson, *Showing the Spirit,* 26.

basic differences between the gifts of the Spirit and pagan worship. The Corinthians had asked him. Now he was answering with authority.

Pagan frenzy caused people to speak anything.[11] If someone claiming an angelic vision teaches a different gospel, Paul says, "Let him be eternally condemned (Galatians 1:8). Any spirit denying the fully-God, fully-human, incarnational nature of Jesus is of the Antichrist (1 John 4:2–3). On the other hand, no one speaking by the Spirit of God calls Jesus accursed. The Holy Spirit will lead us to love Christ more and build upon proper scriptural foundations. The test of genuineness is the lordship of Christ in ethics and practice, not the possession of a gift or giving an utterance purportedly "by the Spirit." For the Christian, the lifeless pagan deities could never be Lord. Every knee shall bow and every tongue confess that Jesus Christ is Lord (Philippians 2:10–11).

All religions in the Roman Empire were considered legal as long as they included worship of Caesar. Only the Jews were allowed to serve God without worshipping Caesar. Increasingly, the legality of the Christian faith was tested. Paul tried to establish the right of Christians to worship God only and yet be loyal subjects of the government. He sought to have government on the side of Christianity (in the Philippian jail, before Festus, before Agrippa).

Although the New Testament church experienced little persecution at first, to confess Jesus is Lord would eventually invite harassment from the government. While everyone else was saying Lord Caesar because of the Roman government decree, the Christian was called upon to boldly proclaim his faith in Christ by saying Lord Jesus. The first political persecution took place in Rome about A.D. 49 when some Jews were rioting "at the instigation of Chrestus."[12] The second persecution came with Nero's changing mental

---

[11]H. Wayne House, "Tongues and the Mystery Religions of Corinth," *Bibliotheca Sacra* 140 (April-June 1983): 134–150, suggests Paul is saying they should be sure their tongues are not the same as in their pagan past of Apollo and Dionysius worship—the mysticism, ecstasy, individualistic experiences that did not necessarily value harmony.

[12]Suetonius, *Life of Claudius*, xxv.4. "Chrestus" was a common name; it also sounded much like "Christos," Christ. It may be this persecution that caused Aquilla and Priscilla to leave Rome for Corinth.

condition between A.D. 62 and 65. First Corinthians was written between the two persecutions, around A.D. 55.

The key question of this passage is, Who at Corinth would call Jesus accursed? The Greeks did not often use the term *anathema*. Would it be antagonistic Jews? Pharisaic Jews could speak about Messiah, the Christ. Doctrines concerning resurrection from the dead, angels, casting out demons, prophetic utterances, salvation, redemption, and the kingdom of God would not be difficult to accept in the synagogues throughout the Roman empire. But for many Jews, the Messiah could not be put to a cross. Because of the cross, Jesus was accursed to them. They were still looking for Christ.[13]

A second possible source of such a curse would be the influence of an incipient Gnosticism, similar to the views of Cerinthus and the Ophites of perhaps eighty years later.[14] This early form of Gnosticism stated that flesh was evil and spirit was good. Therefore, Jesus, being physical, was accursed. Christ, according to their view, was pure spirit and therefore blessed. These Gnostics could claim to be spiritual and at the same time say Jesus was accursed.

Others say Paul is merely being hypothetical, that calling Jesus accursed was not a real problem in the church at Corinth. If it were a real problem, Paul would answer it more directly. Perhaps Paul is stressing the incarnational aspect of gifts by implying that doctrine, conduct, and confession must line up with one another. One cannot make strange, radical statements that have no basis in the Bible, no matter how "spiritual" they sound.[15]

---

[13]A summary of recent thinking on this position is given by J. Duncan M. Derrett, "Cursing Jesus (1 Corinthians 12:3): The Jews as Religious Persecutors," *New Testament Studies* 21 (July 1975): 544–554.

[14]Howard M. Ervin, *These Are Not Drunken As Ye Suppose* (Plainfield: Logos Books, 1968), 187–93.

[15]Other explanations of who said *Anathema Jesus* follow: Christians resisting a Spirit-given revelation by using blasphemous utterances, Christians fearing that tongues-speaking actually cursed Jesus without their knowing it, a textual problem for *anathema* which may read *ana athe emar maran Iesous* (" 'I am coming,' said our Lord Jesus"), and a simple contrast between those pagans who oppose Jesus and the Christian confession. Those discussed in the text seem to me to be the main ones. See Gordon D. Fee, *The First Epistle to the Corinthians*, New International Commentary on the New Testament (Grand Rapids: William B. Eerdmans, 1987), 578–81 for further discussion of the options.

Whether the problem was Jewish persecution, incipient Gnosticism, or unfounded, radical utterances, Paul deliberately states that the Christian confession in life and word is Jesus is Lord. Origen said the Ophites were required to equate Jesus with the serpent. But to say Jesus is anything less than Lord and fully God amounted to heresy.

1 Corinthians 12:4–6
Gifts, Service, Working

⁴There are different kinds of gifts, but the same Spirit. ⁵There are different kinds of service, but the same Lord. ⁶There are different kinds of working, but the same God works all of them in all men.

Paul begins his discussion of "spirituals" (12:1) by focusing on three words: "gifts," "service," "working." "Gifts" are the tools. "Kinds of service" relates to the varying functions of persons in the body of Christ,[16] the ways tools can be used to get the job done. These two words ("gifts" and "ministries," KJV) are often used interchangeably in churches today but a distinction should be made: "Service" ("ministries," KJV) is from the Greek *diakonia,* which refers to a type of service. The Early Church chose seven men to administer the allocations of charity while the apostles gave themselves to a ministry of preaching and teaching (Acts 6:1–4). Each person has a different ministry and thus may be said to possess that ministry. Gifts, however, are spontaneously granted tools through which we fulfill our ministries.

In the current discussion on gifts and ministries there are two views. Do gifts determine ministries, or are ministries enhanced by whatever gifts God may grant? If the former, then we need to determine our gifts, put them together, then find where we with our ministries fit best. The focus is vocational. By answering enough questions on what is typical of each gift, a person may determine the gifts he possesses. In favor of this view are passages like Ephe-

---

[16]Siegfried Schatzmann, *A Pauline Theology of Charismata* (Peabody, Mass.: Hendrickson Publishers, Inc., 1987), 34, calls ministries the purposes for which God gives the gifts. "Only in different kinds of service exists the legitimization of charismata."

sians 4:11, where the gifts listed are persons, and Romans 12:6–8, where we seem to know which gifts we have and are exhorted to exercise them to the fullest possible benefit. The verbs of 1 Corinthians 12:30 are present tenses, which may imply that some people are regularly used in certain gifts. Some regularly minister gifts of healing, some regularly minister in various kinds of tongues, some regularly interpret the tongues.[17]

The second view is that every member of the body of Christ needs to be open to whatever gifts God may grant. Certainly, when one opens himself to ministering a gift once, it becomes easier for him to have faith to minister that gift again. But the whole range of gifts can be used creatively in any ministry situation. Christians need to be active in their ministries, and the Spirit will anoint them with the gifts. Every gift is potentially available to any believer, though God will use the whole body of Christ to minister the range of gifts. For example, a word of wisdom can be manifested by a deacon as well as by an apostle.

In this view, no one possesses the gift, but all possess a ministry. Because someone has given a prophetic word does not necessarily mean he has a prophetic ministry. Nor does one instance of a person casting out a demon mean he has a deliverance ministry. However, because of the kind of ministries that some people have, they may well be expected to exercise certain gifts more often than other people might. Even so, the gifts are added to the ministries. For "the origin of a *charisma* never lies in the person, but in God's grace which surrounds him. It is essential to bear in mind this origin whenever the gift is considered or experienced."[18]

Paul's word for "spiritual gift" is *charisma*. He uses *domata* for spiritual gifts only when quoting Psalm 68:18 in Ephesians 4:8. *Charisma* is not used in the context of something Christians have permanently. Rather the emphasis is on the giver, the wonderful nature of the gift, and God's purposes in distribution.

---

[17]Stanley M. Horton, *What the Bible Says About the Holy Spirit* (Springfield, Mo.: Gospel Publishing House, 1976), 218.

[18]Arnold Bittlinger, *Gifts and Graces: A Commentary on First Corinthians 12 to 14* (Grand Rapids: William B. Eerdmans, 1967), 20.

On the other hand, Luke's word for gift, *dorean*, focuses on that deposit we receive when we are filled with the Holy Spirit (Acts 2:38; 8:20; 10:45; 11:17). Paul also refers to that experience as a deposit (Ephesians 1:14). Thus, the initial infilling of the Holy Spirit is spoken of as a possession, but the exercise of gifts depends upon the continuous distribution by God.

Favoring the view that no one possesses the gifts is 1 Corinthians 12:7–11, where the Holy Spirit continually gives gifts to the Church according to God's sovereign will. None are said to have the position of tongues speaker in the church. And although all may prophesy, not all are prophets. Healings can come through the prayers of elders, two agreeing together, or through the body of Christ, not just through one who has a gift of healing.

The church in Acts did not seek specific gifts and then develop ministries. In the process of ministry the gifts flowed freely. In fact, even ministries changed. Some who were chosen to serve tables became evangelists. Others, such as Epaphroditus at Philippi, became special helpers (see 12:28) in Paul's ministry. John the apostle became the key pastor of the church at Ephesus. Paul, who helped pastor the church at Antioch, became the apostle.

The ambiguity stems from Paul's mixing his terminology. He calls everything gifts (or graces). We are aware of the gifts God has given us and are responsible to exercise them for the greatest benefit. Yet God continually gives the gifts. Somewhere between the view that the gift defines the ministry and the gift enhances the ministry lies the actual nature of the gift.

So do people find their gifts and then develop their ministries? Or do people move into ministries and discover the gifts following? Probably the answer is yes to both questions. The issue here, due to Paul's freer terminology, is not a theological one, but a practical, functional one.[19]

For example, "working" ("operations," KJV) is from the Greek word for power that emphasizes final results (*energema*). Different

---

[19]"For Paul, the relationship between *charisma* and ministry was always integral. *Charisma* without ministry denies the purpose of charismatic endowment and ignores its grace character. Ministry without charisma denies the dynamic which makes ministry effective and ignores its gift character." Schatzmann, *Pauline Theology*, 90.

results may occur whenever gifts are exercised, depending, for example, on the time, circumstances, and people. Paul and Peter exercised similar gifts in different contexts. One was a pioneering apostle, preaching to Gentiles who had little or no background in the Hebrew-Christian heritage. The other was an apostle to the Jews and a leader in the Early Church who probably did little pioneering (except, of course, his ministry at Pentecost and at Cornelius's house). One used the gifts primarily for evangelistic purposes, the other primarily for establishing the Church.

The Holy Spirit grants us gifts of special power and anointing. Ministries are formed by the Son as He shapes us into His image; we find our place of service in Him. The Father oversees the final results of the operation of gifts and ministries. Yet these are not clear-cut divisions; overlap occurs. For example, in 12:6 "different kinds of working" are attributed to the Father, but in 12:11 "these are the work of one and the same Spirit." The unity and diversity of the Godhead are marvelously interwoven.[20]

The word *diaireseis* ("different kinds") in 12:4–6 should be translated "distributions." It is from the same Greek word used in 12:11 for "gives" *(diaroun)*. God is our source. The church of Jesus Christ is to reflect the diversity in unity that characterizes God himself. The rest of this chapter and the next will reflect this truth. The Church is a diversity, yet must act in unity. The Church is one, yet must demonstrate its diversity.

Paul, however, may have had another motive in using the word. The root word may mean "to tear apart, to split up." Paul may be hinting at the divisions among them over the very gifts that God distributes. Perhaps he does a similar thing in 12:25, where, in ministering *charisms* in the Body, he says no *schism* should occur. He has already mentioned the divisions *(schismata)* in 1:10 and 11:18. The Church in unity is a reflection of the glory of God. We work the way we do because God works the way He does.

Unity is seen in the last phrase of 12:6, "all of them in all men." The first "all" refers to the whole category of spirituals: gifts,

---

[20]In 12:4–6 Paul's variety in the use of conjunctions *(de* in 12:4; *kai* in 12:5, and a combination of *kai* and *de* on 12:6) shows this emphasis on unity and diversity.

ministries, and operations. The final "in all men" refers to the body of Christ. This is a glorious statement. God operates the gifts; no person can produce them. Yet God chooses to work through every member of the body of Christ. This is specifically shown in the following verses.

1 Corinthians 12:7–11
Many Gifts, One Spirit

[7]Now to each one the manifestation of the Spirit is given for the common good. [8]To one there is given through the Spirit the message of wisdom, to another the message of knowledge by the means of the same Spirit, [9]to another faith by the same Spirit, to another gifts of healing by that one Spirit, [10]to another miraculous powers, to another prophecy, to another distinguishing between spirits, to another speaking in different kinds of tongues, and to still another the interpretation of tongues. [11]All these are the work of one and the same Spirit, and he gives them to each one, just as he determines.

The Spirit gives and initiates the gifts. Each person seeks only to be an agent of the Spirit's manifestations. Paul does not say all the gifts are given to any one person, or given once for all time.[21]

---

[21]Some have used Romans 11:29 to argue that since God's gifts and his call are irrevocable, once we have received the gifts we possess them. That is not the context of Romans 9 to 11, however. Archibald T. Robertson, *Word Pictures*, vol. 4 (Nashville: Broadman Press, 1931), 399, explains that *ametamelata* ("without repentance," KJV, or "irrevocable," NIV) means "not being sorry afterwards." The emphasis is not *ametanoeton* (Romans 2:5), meaning "to change one's mind." See also Walter Bauer, *A Greek-English Lexicon of the New Testament and Other Early Christian Literature*, 2nd ed., trans. F. Wilbur Gingrich and Fredrick W. Danker (Chicago: University of Chicago Press, 1979), 45. The passage speaks of God's love for Israel and His ultimate purpose and vocation for all nations. See C. K. Barrett, *Romans*, vol. 6, Harper's New Testament Commentaries (N.Y.: Harper & Row, Publishers, Inc., 1957), 225; Matthew Black, *Romans*, The New Century Bible Series (Grand Rapids: William B. Eerdmans, 1973), 148, and many others. Clearly, Paul does not refer to individual ministries and gifts. He does not say once a person has been called to be a deacon, he will always be one, or that if a person has exercised a message of wisdom, he will always exercise that gift and only that gift. Roles change and needs change as the body of Christ matures and faces new challenges.

God continuously gives, purposefully and specifically, according to His will (12:11). Paul uses different pronouns to emphasize the variety.[22]

The baptism in the Spirit is not primarily a qualifying experience but an equipping experience. It enables Christians to do the job more effectively. The person who is fully yielded to the Holy Spirit will find a greater dimension of ministry than could be realized without the infilling. But this does not negate the importance or ministry of anyone who has not yet experienced this blessing.[23] That would defeat the principle of Body ministry. Such persons, however, should be encouraged to claim the promise of the Holy Spirit. Gifts are given to every member. As we yield to the Holy Spirit, we are further empowered for service.

Traditionally three categories have been logically derived from the nine gifts listed in 12:8–10. The "message of wisdom," "message of knowledge," and "distinguishing between spirits" suggest a revelation (or mind) category. "Faith," "gifts of healing," and "miraculous powers" suggest a power category. And "prophecy," "tongues," and "interpretation of tongues" suggest an utterance category.

This division is convenient (and I find no basic disagreement with it). However, Paul does not seem to be making these distinctions.

---

[22]Verse 7, *ekato*—each one

verse 8, *men*—one

verse 8, *allo*—another of the same kind

verse 9, *hetero*—another of a different kind

verse 9, *heni pneumati*—one Spirit

[23]Although many scholars seek to use passages within 1 Corinthians 12–14 to say that not all at Corinth spoke in tongues (e.g. 1 Corinthians 12:30–31; 13:8; 14:5), this is not at all convincing in the light of the experiences of the Book of Acts (2:4; 10:44–46; 11:16; 19:6–7), Paul's valuing of this gift (Acts 19:2; 1 Corinthians 14:5, 13–18), and the different purposes of the private use of tongues and the congregational use of tongues. It is possible that there were Corinthian believers who had not yet spoken in tongues, or who were inquiring seekers (14:16,23), or some who had been forbidden to speak in tongues because of the problems at Corinth (14:39). To insist that not all could or would speak in tongues devotionally is an argument from silence, the weakest form of argument. In any case, the gifts are distributed to every person.

Rather, through the use of the Greek word *heteros,* "another of a different kind," at the beginning of 12:9 and at the latter part of 12:10, he seems to make a functional division.[24]

The "message of wisdom" and "message of knowledge" are for teaching (see 1 Corinthians 14:6–12). "Faith," "gifts of healing," "miraculous powers," "prophecy," and "distinguishing between spirits" are for ministry to one another and to the world (see 1 Corinthians 14:26–40). And "tongues" and "interpretation of tongues" are for worship (see 1 Corinthians 14:13–19). (See figure 2.)

GIFT	TYPE	REFERENCE
Word of wisdom Word of knowledge	Teaching	1 Corinthians 14:6–12
Faith Healing Miracles Prophecy Discerning spirits	Ministry to church and world	1 Corinthians 14:26–40
Tongues Interpretation	Worship	1 Corinthians 14:13–19

Figure 2. Gifts: A Functional Division

The intervening word for "another" that Paul uses is *allos,* "another of the same kind." Thus, the gifts within each category are somehow related to each other. Some commentators do not believe that Paul actually intended a distinction here between *heteros* and

---

[24]In the context, both *heteros* and *allos* refer to different persons. Is Paul therefore referring to different personalities who are more open to exercising certain gifts? Possibly. Yet, his intimate connection between gifts and members in 12:12–27, where members of the Body even speak to each other and perform key functions in the Body, his emphasis on God setting persons and gifts in the Body as He desires (12:18,28ff.), and his comparison of the different functions of the gifts in 1 Corinthians 14—all suggest the different functions that *both* persons and gifts have in building up the whole Body. Paul may be showing that each person should be aware of his function in the building of the Church.

allos, but simply uses different words to emphasize again the variety of gifts and persons within the church. A study of the usage of these words in Pauline writings, however, will lead to a different conclusion. Paul usually uses *heteros* to mean another of a different kind.[25] Even within the passage itself it is used to refer to other tongues, a language other than that which is one's own. Further substantiating the idea of a functional division is 1 Corinthians 12:12–27. Is not Paul talking about the different functions of the gifts in his analogy between believers and the human body?[26]

I suggest the first category relates to teaching gifts. Both Gee and Riggs say these are gifts a Spirit-led teacher may use most fre-

---

[25]Paul uses *heteros* a minimum of thirty-two times. In each instance the most natural interpretation would be "another of a different kind." Examples of this follow: "you who pass judgment on someone else" (Romans 2:1), "you, then, who teach others" (Romans 2:21), "if she marries another man" (Romans 7:3), "another law at work in my members" (Romans 7:23), "nor anything else in all creation" (Romans 8:39), "and another, I follow Apollos" (1 Corinthians 3:4), "one man over against another" (1 Corinthians 4:6), "has a dispute with another" (1 Corinthians 6:1), "receive a different spirit" (2 Corinthians 11:4), "a different gospel" (Galatians 1:6), "in other generations" (Ephesians 3:5), "also to the interests of others" (Philippians 2:4).
Although one may not make an absolute distinction between *allos* and *heteros* in every Pauline usage, one can readily see that *heteros* provides a distinction that enriches the meaning in most usages.

[26]Both Fee and Carson propose that if grouping is legitimate at all, it is based on the use of *heteros*. Fee says wisdom and knowledge are placed in the first category because they were held in such high regard at Corinth, the next five are in a second category because of a supernatural gifting, and the last two are in the third category because tongues and interpretation are the "problem child" and its companion gift. The first and last divisions have to do with problems at Corinth. Fee, *First Corinthians,* p. 591. But I see the middle five gifts also as a problem to the Corinthians with an overrealized eschatology. Faith, healings, miracles, and distinguishing between spirits might be related to such a theological emphasis. Only prophecy might be spared. I conclude that Paul not only solves a problem, but he teaches an overall perspective on the purposes of gifts.
Carson thinks the first category may be linked with the intellect, the second category may be associated with special faith, and tongues and interpretation may be in a separate category. But he goes on to say too much overlap remains: Cannot prophecy produce intellectual results? Cannot faith be used in uttering a word of wisdom? He then decides no real categories exist. Carson, *Showing the Spirit,* 37. Some propose that different types of persons are more readily used in certain gifts, an observation few would find fault with. However, such an observation does not answer the question of the uniqueness of each category of gifts.

quently. "When one gives forth the word of knowledge under the power of the Holy Spirit in a way that imparts the knowledge to others, he is operating in the gift of teaching."[27] The Corinthian teachers were boasting that their wisdom and knowledge in spiritual matters were superior to that of other Corinthians' and superior to that of even Paul's.

First Corinthians 14:6–12 emphasizes the importance of clear communication of gifts so the church might be edified. The context of teaching is broader than only formal teaching opportunities. Every counseling situation, evangelistic outreach, prayer meeting, and church business meeting can be a blessed learning experience. Even the exercise of tongues and interpretation can be instructional for the church. Tongues usually exalt the attributes and workings of God, and the exercise of these gifts can serve as a model to others of this type of spiritual manifestation.

The next five gifts seem to be more powerful and spectacular than the others. (The first mentioned in this category is faith; the other four gifts are linked to it, according to most commentators.) Even the distinguishing between spirits is usually accompanied by certain actions, such as casting out the evil spirit(s) that is discerned. The question is, Why would prophecy be here rather than under the next grouping? Certainly prophetic utterance is related to most, if not all, of the gifts in this category and is powerful in and of itself. Prophecy, however, is horizontally directed; tongues is usually vertically directed. Everyone may prophesy; the gifts in this category are the responsibility of the whole body of Christ. These gifts are horizontally directed in ministry to Christians and to the world.[28]

---

[27]Ralph M. Riggs, *The Spirit Himself* (Springfield, Mo.: Gospel Publishing House, 1962), 116.

[28]In Paul's letters, he did not clearly state the function of the gifts as directed toward the world. His primary emphasis seems to be the gifts in the church. Yet one needs to look only to Jesus' use of the miraculous and the recording of the miraculous in the Book of Acts to know that the Early Church expected and exercised gifts of the Spirit in relationship to winning the world. Schatzmann, *Pauline Theology,* 91, says "The relationship between the Holy Spirit and the gifts he bestows seems to demand the concession that both relate to the community of believers and to the world."

The last two gifts in this list, tongues and interpretation, belong to a different category of worship. Tongues are essentially devotional in character. When one speaks in tongues he speaks to God, edifies himself, prays, sings, praises, gives thanks, and speaks the wonderful works of God.[29] The purpose of tongues and interpretation should not be confused with the purpose of prophetic messages. Often the gifts of tongues and interpretation are used in what should be the manifestation of the prophetic gift. Some take the position that tongues are always devotional and any interpretation should reflect that. Although such a definitive position on this gift may not be warranted, the emphasis of Scripture is on the devotional aspect of tongues.

Pentecostals have said that tongues and interpretation are equivalent to prophecy. Does this mean that that combination of gifts is *the same as* prophecy or a ministry gift *as valid as* prophecy? Why would God use two other gifts to do the work that one gift in proper exercise should accomplish? Tongues and interpretation are a ministry gift *as valid as* prophecy because of congregational understanding and edification, but its primary purpose is praise of the wondrous works of God.

Although tongues is not primarily for revelation, knowledge, prophecy, or a word of instruction (14:6), we should not limit God. After all, praise or a Spirit-anointed exhortation to worship can lead one to a *revelation* of the nature of God, to *know* Him better experientially, to be *instructed* through learning how to exercise the gifts, and to set free *prophetic* gifts. In fact, tongues can be useful in all four of the functional categories of 1 Corinthians 14: teaching, worship, signs, and body ministry.

But Paul's emphasis to the Corinthians, who were overzealous about tongues, was make room for the many other gifts that communicate in the understood language. The gift of tongues is most directly useful in worshipping God, encouraging others to worship, and as a sign to the unbeliever. Gifts in the understood language, however, are more useful in teaching, actual conversion of unbelievers, and ministry to believers. They are also useful in wor-

---

[29]See 1 Corinthians 14:2,4,14,15,16, and Acts 2:11 and 10:4.

ship. First Corinthians 14 contrasts tongues with gifts in the understood language. Churches need more freedom with gifts in the understood language. There is less limitation on them than on the exercise of tongues and interpretation in the congregation. Free exercise of such gifts helps us see the special function that tongues have for the congregation.

(For other Scriptural evidence to confirm this categorizing of the gifts, see the discussion of 1 Corinthians 14, chapter 4. Each category is the essential topic of a paragraph of that chapter.[30] Also, in 1 Corinthians 13:8–9, categories of teaching, Body ministry, and worship are represented by knowledge, prophecies, and tongues, respectively.)

If we carefully examine the practical essence of these categories, we will see why Paul used them to teach the Church about its life and purposes. All categories are necessary.

If a church has great teaching and worship, but the ministries are carried out by only a few people, others will not have the opportunity to grow. Thus the potential of training a great army to reach the lost will be diminished. This church is leader-style centered and worship-style centered. Using a formulaic breakdown— T = teaching, W = worship, M = ministries—my point would look like this:

$$T + W - M = \text{lack of discipleship and outreach}$$

If the church has great teaching, developing people for ministries, but does not experience a full expression of worship, then it has

---

[30]Note Martin's outline of the chapter in Martin, *Spirit and Congregation*. He identifies three of the same categories that I do. He sees the main aim of prophecy as teaching (14:1–12). Praising and prayer are worship. The last category is akin to my category on ministry to the saints and to the world. Prophecy can be used strongly in a teaching function though it may have other uses as well, in worship and in Body ministry. Paul's use of prophecy in 1 Corinthians 14 is as a representative of all anointed utterances in the known language. The focus of 1 Corinthians 14 is on clear communication, whatever the category. Paul speaks of a whole church who may prophesy. He cannot be implying that all of them are teachers; although it is true that 14:6–12 focuses on the teaching aspect of the prophetic gift, Paul will show how prophecy is used in other ways as well.

missed one of the most important reasons for assembling. For in celebration we can see beyond our adverse circumstances to God. He is the source of our unity and mission. We seek to fulfill His plan. But without His strengthening visitation, stress and discouragement overtake the Body. Thus

$$T + M - W = \text{no celebration}$$

A church that has everyone taking part in a ministry and has much freedom in worship may look good for a while, but its lack of solid teaching will ultimately allow divisiveness, self-asserted leadership, and every type of wrong doctrine and practice. (That is why Paul says he does not want the Corinthians to be ignorant about spiritual gifts.)

$$M + W - T = \text{disarray and wildfire}$$

If this categorization and analysis of the gifts are correct, then all the gifts are necessary in the ministry of the Church, but for essentially different purposes. (Overlap in function will be discussed in the commentary on 1 Corinthians 14, chapter 4.) All three of these categories must function in a balance for a thriving, growing congregation. At times, one category may have more emphasis than another, but ultimately all three are necessary.

In 1 Corinthians 14, we find a fourth category that Paul did not yet include in 12:8–10, namely, gifts serve as signs. Church growth scholars have pointed again and again to the Pentecostal-charismatic movement as the most powerful force in Christianity today. In spite of the movement's flaws, signs and wonders are a key to church growth around the world. Gifts are not meant to be contained within the walls of a church building. There we learn. Then we go forth and minister to others. The gifts themselves have a built-in *go* structure.

THE PREACHING AND TEACHING GIFTS

Let us examine the gifts more closely. Throughout the Bible, knowledge and wisdom refer primarily to God's character, His ways, and His eternal purposes. God's supreme plan revolves around Christ's dying on Calvary for our sins, so these gifts, one way or another, will point to and reflect that glorious plan of God for His people.

A Message of Wisdom

All true words of wisdom will reflect God's plans, purposes, and ways of accomplishing things. Proverbs urges us to make the pursuit of God's wisdom our highest priority. Teaching, seeking divine guidance, counseling, and addressing practical needs in church government and administration may offer occasions for a word of wisdom. Because of its practical nature, this gift, rather than prophecy, is the gift for guidance.[31] It teaches people to grow spiritually as they apply their hearts to wisdom and make choices leading to maturity. If we lack wisdom, we are exhorted to ask God for it rather than for another gift (James 1:5).[32] (Note, however, the gift is not a bestowal of wisdom but a message of wisdom and those ministering this message are not necessarily wiser than others.)

Some examples in Acts include the decision to select seven deacons to serve tables (Acts 6:1–7), Stephen's debate at the Synagogue of the Freedmen (Acts 6:8–10), the need to baptize Cornelius's household immediately for the sake of the Gentile believers (Acts 10:47), the decision of James at the Jerusalem Council concerning requirements for the Gentile believers (Acts 15:13–21), Paul's use of Roman citizenship to publicly vindicate the Christian cause (Acts 16:35–40), and Paul's decision to go to Jerusalem whatever the personal cost (Acts 21:12–14).

Although some may say that it is the pastor who needs wisdom

---

[31]I have discussed personal prophecy as having a preparatory or confirmatory, but not an initiatory, role in the New Testament in the Introduction. Guidance must be based on God's wisdom.

[32]Most commentators—Calvin, Godet, and Alford among them—describe a word of wisdom as using knowledge practically. Lange, Hodge, and Osiander go further, proposing that such wisdom must be equal to the gospel, the whole system of revealed truth, including the aims and purposes of God, the plans and operations of salvation, and the entire scheme of redemption. That is, wisdom's object is to lead men to Christ and to teach them to become more like Christ.

and it is the teacher who needs knowledge, such distinctions cannot be so clearly made. Ephesians 4:11 may seem to make the pastor-teacher one position. On the other hand, some occasions require a pastor to assume a tutorial role and some occasions require a teacher to assume a pastoral role, because both shepherd people.

Generally speaking, knowledge tells us what, wisdom tells us how. We need both from God. Donald A. Carson, however, says that Paul's use of the terms "wisdom" and "knowledge" in 1 Corinthians defies clear distinction.

> In light of [1 Corinthians] 2:6ff., "wisdom" can be essentially doctrinal and the word of wisdom can be the fundamental message of Christianity; in light of 8:10–11, knowledge can be immensely practical.[33]

The Corinthians apparently spoke of "an eloquence or superior wisdom" (2:1, cf. 1:17). Our faith should not rest in such human wisdom (2:5). That human wisdom rejected the gospel, as well as Paul's ministry. God, on the other hand, gives a message of wisdom. Jesus promised His disciples "words and wisdom that none of your adversaries will be able to resist or contradict" (Luke 21:15). Although Peter exhorts us to "Always be prepared to give an answer to everyone who asks you to give the reason for the hope that you have" (1 Peter 3:15), God can also give wisdom for special situations beyond all our preparation. Jesus spoke of unpremeditated wisdom to face the persecutions ahead.

A Message of Knowledge

The Corinthians believed strongly in wisdom and knowledge. The Greek philosophers greatly influenced Greek thinking about knowledge. Plato thought that ignorance was the cause of all the hurts and failures of mankind and governments. If people were only enlightened, they would live and act properly: "To know is to do." The Corinthians of Paul's day used knowledge to support their liberated views of eating food sacrificed to idols (which caused

---

[33]Carson, *Showing the Spirit*, 38. So also Fee, Barrett, and Bruce.

weaker Christians to stumble). But Romans 7:14–25 directly con-
tradicts Plato's belief that right knowledge leads to right behavior.
Paul observed that the good that a person wanted to do, he was not
able to do. Neither did Paul agree with the Corinthians' pride in
and wrong use of knowledge.

The Spirit's gift of knowledge has to do with teaching the truths
of the Word of God.[34] The manifestation of this gift would not be
the product of study as such, but God's special word through the
teacher, helping to communicate a scriptural truth needed by the
church. Gee described it as "flashes of insight into truth that penetrated beyond the operation of their own unaided intellect."[35] It is
often dropped into the midst of a prepared lesson in such a way as
to bring the truth home to those listening.

This gift may be manifested in a more supernatural way as well.
God shared his secrets with the prophets (e.g., when it would rain,
the enemy's plans, the secret sins of kings and servants). Sometimes
God reveals to a person someone's sin or special need or His own
activity on someone's behalf.[36] These are facts only God can know.
So when this happens, the attention should be given to the beautiful
truths of the gospel, to God's transcending knowledge, and to how
we should respond to those truths, rather than to the messenger's
personal charisma.

---

[34]Donald Gee, *Concerning Spiritual Gifts* (Springfield, Mo.: Gospel Publishing
House, 1949), 27–34, 110–19, and Horton, *What the Bible Says*, 271–72. Calvin,
Alford, Morris, Pulpit, Hodge, Meyer, and a host of Pentecostal writers would
agree with this definition. Hodge, Osiander, and MacGorman add the dimension
of a special ability to communicate that truth in such a way that believers may
appropriate it readily.

[35]Donald Gee, *Spiritual Gifts in the Work of the Ministry Today* (Springfield,
Mo.: Gospel Publishing House, 1963), 29.

[36]Howard Carter, *Spiritual Gifts and Their Operation* (Springfield, Mo.: Gospel
Publishing House, 1968), 27–36, Harold Horton, *The Gifts of the Spirit* (London:
Assemblies of God Publishing House, 1962), 51–64, L. Thomas Holdcroft, *The
Holy Spirit: A Pentecostal Interpretation* (Springfield, Mo.: Gospel Publishing
House, 1979), 148–150, and William MacDonald, interview by author, 30 October
1987, Baguio City, Philippines. MacDonald favors these supernatural uses of the
message of knowledge. Gee, *Gifts in the Ministry Today*, 31–32, and Horton,
What the Bible Says, 271–72, favor the teaching and preaching aspects of this gift.

Some examples of these gifts in Acts include knowledge of Ananias and Sapphira's deception and Paul's declaration of a judgment of blindness upon Elymas. This gift is joined with the working of miracles in Acts 3 when Peter and John pray in faith for the lame man. And in the Book of Revelation John records special words for specific congregations.

In placing these gifts in the categories of preaching and teaching, we must not limit them to church worship or classroom experiences. On whatever occasions these gifts are exercised, they show that Christ is present and in charge of the situation to develop or redeem it for His glory. The manifestations of these gifts reveal the character of God and his workings among people. In the time of the Old Testament the application of God's wisdom to the practical issues of life was so highly valued that the wisdom movement arose (Job, Proverbs, and Ecclesiastes being a part of that movement). Today, more than ever, the church needs people who have been touched with God's wisdom to teach us God's will in each situation.

MINISTRY TO THE CHURCH AND TO THE WORLD

Through the use of the Greek word *heteros* in 12:9, Paul begins the category of gifts that minister to the Church and to the world. All believers should be open to the whole realm of gifts. Yet not many will take part in preaching-teaching ministries nor will all exercise gifts of tongues or interpretation of tongues in the church. Many may find that this second category of gifts is the place where they may begin. All may readily use these gifts in their ministries: Believing God for special challenges or needs, praying for the sick, claiming miracles, speaking prophetic messages, and discerning whether an activity is of God or demon-inspired—all are responsibilities of the whole body of Christ. As the Holy Spirit manifests these gifts through us, we grow, the Church grows, and the world is touched with the power of the gospel. It is no wonder that faith heads this category.

Faith

The gift of faith is a miraculous faith for a special situation or opportunity. It is not saving faith or faithfulness that develops as a fruit of the Spirit. The vibrant, active Christian is more likely to see this gift in action as he claims God's power for present needs. Fervent prayer, extraordinary joy, and unusual boldness accompany the gift of faith. It can include special ability to inspire faith in others, as Paul did on board the ship in the storm (Acts 27:25). Faith characterizes this whole category of gifts.

The Early Church saw this gift in action. Instead of praying for relief from persecution, they asked for boldness to proclaim the gospel. Faith claims the initiative rather than seeks retreat. It is God's option between human presumption on the one hand and unbelief on the other. Hebrews 11 lists many persons of faith who did not think of preserving themselves but rather of fulfilling God's purposes. This is not a selfish faith, but one that dares to believe that God has a will for his people's needs now. Such faith accompanies every true manifestation of the Spirit. Ministering any gift is a faith proclamation that Christ is on the throne and that God's Word is being confirmed.

Two examples of the gift of faith in operation are Elijah's confrontation of the prophets of Baal (1 Kings 18:33–35) and Jesus' healing of the demon possessed son (Matthew 17:19–20).

Gifts of Healing

In Acts, healings occurred dramatically to people before their conversions. Most of those healed did not even know of Christ's redemption. After witnessing the miracles, many were saved in a new responsiveness to the gospel.

In the Greek manuscripts three sets of plurals may be noted in verses 9–10: "*gifts* of healings," "*works* of power," and "*distinguishings* of spirits" (as margin notes of the NASB indicate). Evidently no one has *the* gift for healing. These gifts are given to cover specific cases at specific times.[37] Sometimes God heals sovereignly

---

[37]Nearly all the commentaries except Wesleyan agree with this position. Charles W. Carter, *1 Corinthians*, The Wesleyan Bible Commentary Series (Peabody, Mass.: Hendrickson, Publishers, Inc., 1986), 200, considers medical science the gift of healing. Calvin assumed of this gift, "Everyone knows what is meant by

and at other times He heals according to the faith of the sick person. In a manner of speaking, the one who prays for the sick person does not receive the gift; the one who receives the gift of healing is actually the sick person. The one who prays is only the agent. In any case, God alone must receive glory.

Healing is intrinsic to God's name, nature, and work. God is the God who heals *(Jehovah-Ropheka)*. From His wilderness covenant to protect His people from the diseases visited on their Egyptian captors (Exodus 15:26) to the Early Church's praying in the name of Jesus (Acts 3:16), through faith in His name complete healing came. Jesus said, "You may ask me for anything in my name, and I will do it" (John 14:14). All the blessings the Church enjoys are a result of Jesus' atonement for our sins at Calvary. Indeed, the very existence of the Church, to say nothing of gifts to equip it, derives from the Savior's having paid the price for our redemption.

The basic question is, Does God will to heal everyone? What about those who are not yet healed? Many of them are faithful Christians, dedicated to the Lord and not hindered by sin in their lives. Paul left Trophimus sick at Miletus (2 Timothy 4:20). Timothy apparently had a weak stomach and frequent illnesses (1 Timothy 5:23). And whatever the nature of Paul's thorn in the flesh, it was not God's will to relieve him of it.

It is God's will to heal, unless He has for the immediate time and circumstances a higher will. Hebrews 11 gives many examples of Old Testament saints who faced suffering, persecution, and death for the glory of God. They followed the example of the Master, who, for the joy set before Him, endured the Cross, laying aside His present comforts. God honored that sacrifice. And His highest priority is that we become conformed to His Son.

A person's salvation and spiritual development are, ultimately,

---

this." John Calvin, *First Corinthians* (Grand Rapids: William B. Eerdmans, 1960), 262. Lenski emphasizes that these healings are not wrought by the will of the person concerned. Rather, the Spirit gives him a special word first. Richard Charles Henry Lenski, *The Interpretation of St. Paul's First Epistle to the Corinthians* (Columbus, Ohio: Wartburg Press, 1937), 502. Many contemporary scholars view gifts of healing as Messianic works bestowed upon the Church as part of the Messianic Age.

of higher value than his physical healing. Further, through one's suffering, others may come to Christ. Let us not assume that pain, problems, trials, and suffering are necessarily evil and, therefore, out of God's will. God can turn all such adversities to His advantage. Healing for the body is available, but if it's not immediately forthcoming, the sick person should not be discouraged. Rather, we should look to God for the best, for only He can see whether a greater work may be done through a gift of healing than through a physical infirmity.

Someone aptly said, "Healing is the removal of every obstacle to the Cross." May we begin to glimpse the fullness of the Cross! God may seek to build depth of character, develop Christlikeness, and use a situation to bring others to himself. Then we will also see the great power and glory that are His. He has the power of the universe at His disposal. His kingdom will come, and His will shall be done. The issue is, What will be of greatest glory for the kingdom of God in a given situation? For sickness the normal answer would be healing. But God may be working a greater miracle. Only eternity will tell.

God cares about making people healthy emotionally as well as physically. But not enough emphasis has been given to this aspect of healing. Although some may receive instantaneous healing of their emotions, probably most such healings take place over time as the afflicted one is ministered to in love by fellow Christians; this kind of healing takes place best in the context of a healthy, caring, interacting body of believers. It is not solely the responsibility of the sick to have faith or of the evangelist or pastor to have faith. Together we have faith, and together we set the climate of love and acceptance so that the healing may flow.[38] In the body of Christ are power and strength to meet the needs of the struggling member. This is the incarnational aspect of healing.

---

[38]See the Appendix, for a fuller exposition on healing as well as an evaluation of the current scholarly perspectives. Also, L. Thomas Holdcroft's *Divine Healing, A Comparative Study* (Springfield, Mo.: Gospel Publishing House, 1967) provides a good study. One of the most insightful current writers on the subject is Francis MacNutt. His books *Healing* (Notre Dame: Ave Maria Press, 1974) and *The Power to Heal* (Notre Dame: Ave Maria Press, 1977) are invaluable.

To believe in healing is not to deny the possibilities of dying. We must remember that ultimate healing is in heaven (Revelation 21:4–5). Some have lived fulfilled lives and are ready to begin the greatest part of God's plan for them. It may be in God's timing to take some home. We must be sensitive to what God is saying in each situation of the "sickness unto death" (John 11:4). Our obligation to the dying is to encourage them to seek God's perfect will for them. For some it may be an immediate healing. For others it may be heaven.

Miraculous Powers

To emphasize the power of God that accomplishes its intended results, Paul combines two Greek words (*dunamis,* active, dynamic power, and *energema,* effectual results) that have been variously translated: "working of miracles" (KJV), "effecting of miracles" (NASB), "miraculous powers" (NIV). Miracles are not human interpretations of natural events; neither are they a suspension or an interruption of the natural order. God's realm is beyond human comprehension. He does not have to change His procedures or laws in order to help us. Therefore, we say that miracles interrupt the natural order *as we understand it.*[39]

Miraculous powers is a broader category than gifts of healings. Miracles may have to do with providing protection, giving provision, casting out demons, altering circumstances, or passing judgment. The Gospels record many miracles, all in the context of the manifestation of the messianic kingdom, the defeat of Satan, the power of God, and the person and work of Jesus. The Greek word for "miracle" in John emphasizes its sign value to point to belief.

The Book of Acts emphasizes the continuation of that work in the Church. When Peter was miraculously released from prison, the church was encouraged. When Paul prayed for the sick, many were healed, and multitudes believed upon the Lord. Ananias and Sapphira fell dead as a result of the miraculous judgment of God. Elymas

---

[39]An excellent discussion of miracles is given by C. S. Lewis, *Miracles, A Preliminary Study* (New York: The MacMillan Company, 1952).

the sorcerer was struck blind. Paul was miraculously protected from the snake at Malta.

Prophecy

In 1 Corinthians 14 the term "prophecy" encompasses the many Spirit-anointed gifts expressed in the speaker's/hearers' (i.e., known) language. Paul is referring to the giving of Spirit-inspired, spontaneous messages, not the preaching of sermons. A basic relationship between revelation and prophecy exists: The Spirit illumines us to see the unfolding progress of the kingdom of God; the secrets of a person's heart are revealed; the sinner is put under conviction (1 Corinthians 14:24–25). The Old Testament prophets spoke about what people must do in terms of justice or righteousness. Even predictive prophecy was generally given to precipitate righteousness.[40] This is true of the New Testament as well. Peter Hocken says that prophecy "is always in some way a declaration of God's purpose in His Son."[41]

Any believer may exercise the gift of prophecy. Ideally the one who prophesies is a regular part of the local body of Christ, or is at least known to them by reputation. We are exhorted to publicly judge prophecies, because error, misuse, or the admixture of human opinion could slant the prophecy in the wrong direction. The lack of such evaluation may actually allow the prophecy to cause confusion. If it is accepted without discernment, people may experience disastrous consequences. Then, other Christians, fearing similar results, may avoid any exercise of this gift. It is far better that Christians ask more rather than less—or worse yet, no—questions about prophecy. With evaluation of the prophecy, everyone may learn and benefit from it.

Distinguishing between Spirits

Distinguishing between spirits ("discerning of spirits," KJV) is

---

[40]The rule of interpretation for Greek scholars is that the apocalyptic indicative is followed by the prophetic imperative. Simply put, description of the future tells us how we must live today.

[41]Peter Hocken, "Jesus Christ and the Gifts of the Spirit," *Pneuma* 5 (Spring 1983): 12.

a difficult gift to understand. Many scholars identify it as the companion gift of prophecy. Just as speaking in tongues should be followed by interpretation, prophecies must be followed by evaluation or *discerning* (14:27–29).[42] The same sequence is found in 1 Thessalonians 5:20–21 with prophecy and testing. Although all believers are to exercise discernment and test the spirits, not all have this gift. L. Thomas Holdcroft says,

> By means of this gift, human natural senses are supplemented by appropriate divine powers, so that humans are able to relate in understanding in the spirit world. The gift of discerning of spirits does not enable one to discern people; it is not "discernment" in the abstract, but simply what it purports to be: the discerning or analytic classification and judgment of spirits.[43]

Most commentators say this gift distinguishes between the operations of God's Spirit, evil spirits, or the human spirit, but Holdcroft's emphasis on recognizing evil spirits is well taken. In spiritual warfare it is important to know who the real enemy is. We have tests of truth to guide us in evaluating the human spirit: We can apply biblical teaching, watch the person's life, call for the confirmation of others in the body of Christ, and test his utterance for its edifying value. We need the gift of distinguishing between spirits to help us not only to know what we cannot know otherwise, but also to do something about it—for that is the implication of such knowledge. Thus, distinguishing between spirits can become both a safeguard against Satan's attack as well as a weapon for his defeat. Knowledge alone can lead to spiritual pride on the one hand or incapacitating fear on the other. But this gift allows us to utilize all

---

[42]Fee, *First Corinthians*, 596–97; Carson, *Showing the Spirit*, 40; Horton, *What the Bible Says*, 277; Charles Kingsley Barrett, *A Commentary on the First Epistle to the Corinthians* (San Francisco: Harper & Row, Publishers, Inc., 1968), 286; F. F. Bruce, *First and Second Corinthians*, The New Century Bible Commentary (Grand Rapids: William B. Eerdmans, 1971), 119. Shatzmann (*Pauline Theology*, 41–42) argues against limiting distinguishing between spirits to being a companion gift to prophecy and for applying it to all the gifts, especially discerning the demonic.

[43]Holdcroft, *Holy Spirit*, 150.

the gifts to work against Satan and then make a full, free proclamation of the gospel.

Related to distinguishing between spirits is the issue of whether believers can be demon possessed. Three basic positions are taken on this. The first position holds that behind every wrong attitude or emotional expression is a demon. Jealousy, insecurity, or selfishness, for example, represent spirits that must be exorcised. This view confuses the many ways the word "spirit" is used in the Bible. For example, "spirit" may refer to an attitude, the animating principle in a human being, that which is different from physical matter, a mood, breath, angels, demons, or the Holy Spirit. Thus, when Paul speaks of a "spirit of timidity" (2 Timothy 1:7), he is not referring to the demonic.

The second position says that demons may dwell in the carnal nature of believers. Unger relates experiences in Asia where people have grown up in animism, which teaches people to yield to demon power.[44] Those who are converted may manifest many of the same symptoms of possession after conversion as before. Unger appeals to Romans 7, proposing that demons may live in the sin nature of the Christian if he so yields himself. Thus, Christ lives in the person's spirit and the demon lives in the person's sinful nature.

Those holding position two argue that, biblically, "demonized" is used to describe everything from attack to possession. For them, the question is a pragmatic one: Is the person actually delivered from his problem, habit, or wrong thoughts? This view says the fight must not be about semantics or terminology, but about victory for that person.

The strength of this view lies in its openness to spiritual warfare. The Western world in general, and Western theologians in partic-

---

[44]Merrill F. Unger is one of the major proponents of this view. See his *New Testament Teaching on Tongues* (Grand Rapids: Kregel Publishers, 1971) and *Demons in the World Today* (Wheaton: Tyndale, 1971). In the second book, he speaks of Christians in China manifesting the same symptoms of possession. He also views tongues speaking as demonic, yet considers Pentecostals Christians. See also C. Fred Dickason, *Angels, Elect and Evil* (Chicago: Moody Press, 1975), 187–92.

ular, has been preconditioned to rationalize away the spirit world.[45] Asians, Africans, and Latins, on the other hand, readily accept the miraculous and the demonic in all of life's activities. This view focuses on the dramatic, miraculous element of the healing process.

However, any position that holds that demons may inhabit believers has inherent dangers. First, neither the Western nor Eastern view of the spirit world is totally correct. In Jesus' day many Jews thought Jesus was demon-possessed (Mark 3:20–35). This was their preconditioning and worldview.

Second, some become preoccupied with personal deliverance as the method of fighting Satan. But to assume that most problems are demonic is simplistic and harmful. If the manifestation of certain symptoms imply possession, then every time those symptoms recur in a person, he will believe he has the demon again. He will spend his life fighting demons rather than growing in the grace of God.

Third, the Bible is not as preoccupied with deliverance ministry as today's zealous practitioners of such a ministry might imply. Discerning of spirits was used to keep the Church holy (Acts 5), to challenge occultism (Acts 8), and to evangelize new territories (Acts 16). And though the Gospels contain general references to the healing of those who were demonized, they contain only five detailed discussions of possession (one of which is the accusation brought against Jesus).[46]

Fourth, the view that demons can possess believers does not do justice to God's great work of redemption and our deliverance from darkness to light. Our experiences must be based upon sound the-

---

[45]Rodney L. Henry, *Filipino Spirit World* (Manila: OMF Literature, Inc., 1986), 132, shows the need to recognize the spirit world, inasmuch as most churches have ignored this dimension so understood by Filipino people. In proper balance, however, he says we must recognize different causes of sickness. Medically caused problems must be dealt with as physical problems, and "the church needs to confront the spirit-world only when the spirit-world is the cause." But he warns the Filipino church, "If the church is going to help its people stop going to the out of church spirit-world practitioners, then it should get serious about the ministry of healing."

[46]Mark 1:23–28; 3:20–35; 5:1–20; 7:14–30; 9:17–29 and their parallel passages in the Synoptic Gospels are the five detailed discussions of possession. Mark 3:20–35 contains the occasion of Jesus' being accused of being possessed.

ology. Theology may be enhanced by, but not built upon, experience.

Fifth, although Satan may use a person's occultic background to deceive and depress him, this is not proof of possession or even control. The believer may simply need to claim his victory.

A third position on whether Christians may be demon possessed states that demons may oppress but never possess believers. This does justice to God's work of grace, redemption, and deliverance in Christ. In this warfare Christ is the Victor. The issue is, What constitutes salvation? If repentance and salvation is genuine, then possession is not the issue.

Instead of always identifying the source of the Christian's problems as demonic control, we need a better understanding of repentance and spiritual warfare. Those with wrong attitudes, lack of forgiveness, emotional hurts, and occultic backgrounds need deep soul-searching repentance, disowning allegiance to the enemy.[47] It is crucial that we apply God's power to our problems and combat the ways Satan uses them against us.

Admittedly, some believers may be susceptible to psychological suggestion or demonic attack because of having a weaker personality structure or being previously involved in animistic or occultic practices. Hours of counseling may not effect change in such lives. So observers might jump to the conclusion that these believers are possessed.

The key word in this discussion, however, may be neither "possession" nor "oppression," but "bonding." Psychologists and sociologists speak of bonding relationships in families and groups. Babies have a bonding relationship with their mothers. People from

---

[47]Keith and Linnet Hinton, "Conversion Patterns in Asia," *Evangelical Missions Quarterly* 25 (January 1989), 42–43, suggest the need for genuine repentance by those having backgrounds in Asian religions. They need to thoroughly repent of forbidden practices and allegiances, confessing and renouncing pagan objects and power one by one. Even in ministry to inquirers in a resistant Hindu area, successful strategies include binding the witchcraft, deities, spirits, and powers of charms in the homes of inquirers; praying for the opening of the eyes of the inquirers; and praying against hostile relatives or neighbors who would hinder conversion. Then they pray for the sick and see God's power demonstrated. This approach has worked equally well in sophisticated Singapore.

pagan backgrounds may have a bond to the past that must be broken. This would explain why idols and books related to the magical arts were burned in Ephesus. These believers had to break with their past and defy Satan publicly. This may be why Paul spoke at length on the subject of eating meat offered to idols (1 Corinthians 8–10). Weaker brothers bonded to their pagan past may not have understood another's liberty to go to feasts at heathen temples. Deliverance may be called for that does not require expelling demons, but rather claiming victory over the past with its evil habits and thoughts that put one in bondage.[48]

Included in that type of deliverance must be solid Bible teaching, aggressive prayer, control of the thought processes (1 Corinthians 10:4), exercise of the power of God and the will to love (2 Timothy 1:7), Christian counseling, focus on heavenly matters (Colossians 3:1), spiritual growth (Philippians 3:14), support of one another (1 Corinthians 12:26), and surrender of the matter to the glory of God (2 Corinthians 12:7).

In true cases of demon possession, a person has surrendered his will to demons. If the will were not involved, then he could truthfully say, "The demon made me do it—I can't help it." That is, no moral responsibility could be assigned to a demon-possessed person. But we all have a will and are accountable to God. Those who are possessed project a new personality and voice, experiencing an obliteration of their own personalities for a time. Deliverance is absolutely necessary in these cases.

WORSHIP GIFTS

Tongues and Interpretation of Tongues

Tongues and their interpretation are taken together because the effectiveness of the gift of tongues for the congregation is dependent upon being interpretated. Some say that because these two gifts are listed last they are the least in importance. Such a

---

[48]I am grateful to Rick Howard, pastor in Redwood City, California, for these insights shared at the 1986 Assemblies of God Missionary Fellowship meetings in the Philippines.

conclusion is unsupportable. All five gift lists in the New Testament have the gifts in a different order. Others suggest that because tongues is the problem gift at Corinth, Paul leaves it until the last so that he can then focus his attention on it.[49]

One may ask, Why do we need two gifts that must accompany one another? The answer lies in the nature of tongues. The Holy Spirit touches our spirit. We desire to praise God. We find liberation to exalt God's goodness in our lives. One may be exalting God over a great theological truth about His character, His redemptive work, or His special care of us. "Anyone who speaks in a tongue does not speak to men but to God. Indeed, no one understands him: he utters mysteries with his spirit" (14:2). The challenge from the speaker to the Body in his utterance in tongues is, "Let God touch your spirit the way He has touched my spirit!" Hocken says, "If the gift of tongues is fuller praise of God, the reception of this gift necessarily means a deeper knowledge of God."[50]

When the interpretation allows the congregation to understand what is being said, they are encouraged to worship. So even though tongues has this horizontal dimension, its purpose is to lead the Body to (vertical) worship. Praise more readily follows the gift of tongues and interpretation than it does the gift of prophesy. Prophetic utterances may exhort, edify, or comfort; they are more instructional.

Furthermore, we should realize that interpretation is not translation. Thus, the gift of interpretation may be expressed differently from one person to the next in the congregation. Nevertheless, the thrust of the exaltation or prayer in tongues would be the same. The interpretation is subject to being judged because it is in our own words, and we use our own familiar phrases and vocabulary.[51]

The only basic difference between the phenomenon of tongues in Acts and in 1 Corinthians is purpose. The tongues in Acts were

---

[49]John Peter Lange, ed., *Commentary on the Holy Scriptures,* vol. 10, *Romans and Corinthians* (Grand Rapids: Zondervan Publishing House, 1970), 257.

[50]Hocken, "Gifts of the Spirit," 7.

[51]R. E. McAlister, *The Manifestations of the Spirit* (Toronto: Gospel Publishing House, n.d.), 20.

for self-edification and personal enduement. They did not need to be accompanied by interpretation. The Corinthian situation related to blessing others in the congregation, making communication necessary.

Let us summarize Paul's teaching on the gifts thus far. Both God and man have a part in the gifts. The gifts are incarnational. The role of the Trinity not only reflects God's part, but also models the concept of unity in diversity.

The Holy Spirit distributes gifts according to His creative purpose and sovereignty. The word "determines" (12:11—*bouletai)* is in the present tense and strongly implies a continually creative personality. From beginning to end, God is in charge.

Although three functional categories for gifts have been proposed, these categories cannot be considered mutually exclusive. It is important to know the essential purpose of each gift so that it may be exercised to its greatest effectiveness, but a gift in one category can be useful in other categories as well. Further, different personalities express gifts differently in a variety of ministries.

2

1 Corinthians 12:12–31

1 Corinthians 12:12–14
True Unity Allows Diversity

¹²**The body is a unit, though it is made up of many parts; and though all its parts are many, they form one body. So it is with Christ. ¹³For we were all baptized by one Spirit into one body— whether Jews or Greeks, slave or free—and we were all given the one Spirit to drink. ¹⁴Now the body is not made up of one part but of many.**

The word "body" is used seventeen times in 12:12–27. Most Greek philosophers had a low view of the physical body (e.g. Socrates, Plato). Paul did not. Although his analogy of the body and its interdependence was common to Stoic as well as Jewish thinking, Paul was not averse to using analogies from other philosophies and religions if it suited his argument. Jewish thought expressed the idea of corporate personality and one voice speaking for all. For example, Adam was representative of the human race, and Abraham, Moses, and Isaiah's "Servant" were representatives of God's people. Paul's thinking, however, went a step further: This body has many members that speak; Paul's focus is on diversity.

Paul's conversion experience on the Damascus Road greatly influenced his concept of the Church as the body of Christ. As Paul sought to persecute the young church, the Lord identified himself with it when He answered Paul, ''You are persecuting me'' (Acts 9:5, *Jerusalem Bible*). Thus, when Paul spoke of recognizing, or discerning, the Lord's body at Communion, he was referring to the

Christian church (1 Corinthians 11:23–24,27,29).[1] The wrong way of taking Communion was in being insensitive to the needs of the weak, sickly, and dying members. The greatest indictment against the Christian church was that its members failed to wait for one another (1 Corinthians 11:33), submit to one another (Ephesians 5:21), or care for one another (Philippians 2:4). Who would want to join such a community? Paul further identifies Christ as the head of this Body (Colossians 1:18). This vital interrelationship of head and body shows Christ as the source of life and authority over this Body.[2]

Paul uses "body" in the sense of an extension or expression of one's personality. The body of Christ is the primary vehicle through which Christ works on earth. At the same time, the universal Church finds its best expression in each local situation. (Most uses of "church" in the New Testament refer to the local church or local churches. The clear exceptions to this are Matthew 16:18; Ephesians 1:22, 3:10, 5:23,27,29,32; and Colossians 1:18,24.) God intends to accomplish His perfect will through His people in a given locality and region.[3] This is why Paul expresses the importance of unity. The Body is not to be depreciated—not as a whole, not as individual members—for the Body is of Christ. We must not try to compare

---

[1]Depending on the context, "body" (*soma*) may refer to Christ's church or the individual believer. For example, in 1 Corinthians 6:19 "body" is one's individual physical being; in 1 Corinthians 11:27,29, "body" is both Christ and the Church. "Temple" (*naos*) may refer to the dwelling place of the Holy Spirit in individuals and in the Church. For example, in 1 Corinthians 3:16–17 "temple" refers to the Church; in 2 Corinthians 6:16 "temple" is the whole Church and the principle is applied to the practice of individual believers.

[2]Ralph Martin, *The Spirit and the Congregation: Studies in 1 Corinthians 12–15* (Grand Rapids: William B. Eerdmans, 1984), 23.

[3]Bauer, 240–241, also includes the following references under definition four of *ekklesia*, the church universal: Acts 9:31; 1 Corinthians 6:4, 12:28; Philippians 3:6; and 1 Timothy 5:16. Yet all of these references could refer to a local church or group of churches in one region. One cannot make these specific cases refer to the universal Church. For example, one cannot infer from 1 Corinthians 12:28 that Paul (or anyone else) is an apostle to the universal Church, or even to all Gentile churches, or that all churches must have an apostle over them. Thus, the only true references to the universal Church come from Matthew 16:18, Jesus' promise to build the Church, and Ephesians, Paul's exalted view of the Church, and its parallel epistle, Colossians.

this Body with any human organization or even another community of believers, but with Christ himself (see 1 Corinthians 12:12).

We cannot be sure whether Paul was answering an early Gnosticism, an antagonistic Jewish element that claimed Jesus was not the Christ, or a super-spiritual group who felt they had arrived (even to the point of not needing a resurrection body). In any case, all of Paul's possible opponents receive their answer here. To the Gnostics Paul would say that one cannot separate Jesus the human being from Christ the divine spirit. There is nothing evil about the body, because the body is compared with the Christ. To the disbelieving Jews he would say that God became the incarnate Messiah. There is no other Christ outside of Jesus. Jesus is the Christ, the son of the living God. To the super-spiritual Paul would say this Body, the Church, is still prone to weakness, suffering, carnality, and diversity of perspective. To all, Paul would say that the Church has not yet arrived in its glory. At the same time, its diversity is not negative, but reflects the way God himself works.

One of the greatest statements in all Scripture is found in 1 Corinthians 12:13. Jew and Gentile, slave and free, are all one in Christ. Every barrier, racial, cultural, or economic, has been bridged by Jesus Christ. All enter the fellowship the same way. It is not family name or background, mystical experience or philosophical reasoning, but simply the work of the Holy Spirit that regenerates us.

The stress is on the words "one" and "we all" in 12:13: "*We* were *all* baptized . . . into *one* body, . . . *we* were *all* given the *one* Spirit to drink" (emphasis added). But what do these words mean? Many interpretations have been offered. Four main streams of interpretation are summarized here:

1. The reference is to water baptism and the Lord's Supper, because the terms "baptized" and "given to drink" are related to these ceremonies. It is easy to understand why the Protestant reformers leaned toward this interpretation, particularly where it refers to all believers being given drink, rather than just one, specifically, the priest. Evidence for this dual interpretation, however, is not strong. Augustine, Luther, and Calvin held this position. For con-

temporary interpreters holding this position, it may represent a reading of one's church background into the Bible.

2. Some have suggested a heretical teaching of a group at Corinth: Everything Christ provided was given to the enlightened at the point of baptism—indeed they need never get sick, suffer, or die! The millennium had arrived at the point of this special baptism.[4] In that case, one might construe Paul's use of the term "baptism" in direct opposition to them, for this baptism places all in the body of Christ, not just an enlightened few. There are not two kinds of water baptism, one to enlighten the few and one for lesser Christians.[5] This position implies that baptism was the prerequisite or necessary corollary to becoming part of the body of Christ, that something happens through the Spirit at baptism.

However, assuming the presence of this problematic teaching at Corinth does not mean the same problem was at Ephesus (see parallel passage, Ephesians 4:4–6). Baptism here could just as easily refer to being placed in the body of Christ. Paul would then be saying to this group, "It is not water baptism that initiates you into the spiritual mysteries, but being a new creature in Christ."

When Paul discussed baptism in Romans 6, the issue is identification with Christ, not water baptism. (Note particularly the "we" in Romans 6:1–5,8. We serve God in the context of community. It is not just your special baptism or mine, but our identification with Christ.)

3. Spirit baptism incorporates believers into one body. At salvation every believer receives this baptism because it was given to the Church at Pentecost. Those holding this view understand "drink" to mean "drenched" or "flooded" and identify synonymous parallelism in 12:13a and 12:13b. Therefore, all believers are both baptized into the body of Christ and made to drink of the one Spirit.

---

[4]Gnostically-oriented concepts. The debate about whether Gnosticism had penetrated the New Testament church continues. But even if no such penetration occurred, clearly teachings existed then that inadvertently formed the basis for the beginnings of Gnosticism, which later infiltrated much of the Western church.

[5]See Martin's discussion on 1 Corinthians 15 in *Spirit and Congregation*.

A variation of this view includes water baptism as the outward sign of that incorporation.[6]

4. There is a second experience in the Holy Spirit. Most Pentecostals see 1 Corinthians 12:13 as primarily a reference to salvation. But they also see John the Baptist referring to a different baptism, a baptism in the Holy Spirit and power (an experience described extensively in Acts).[7]

Some see Paul discussing a second experience here: 12:13a referring to salvation (baptized by one Spirit into one body) and 12:13b referring to a separate experience of empowering in the Holy Spirit ("all given the one Spirit to drink").[8]

Further, 1 Corinthians 12:13a can be translated as instrumental (see also 12:3,9): "We were all baptized *by* one Spirit into one body." The Holy Spirit baptizes us into the body of Christ and makes all the blessings of Calvary available to us.

Dunn argues against this. The other six usages of *en* in the context of water and Spirit baptism do not use the *en* as instrumental, "by," but as locative, the element "in [which]" one is baptized. However, in these six references (to John the Baptist's statement), a *differ-*

---

[6]Ibid., 24; F. F. Bruce, *First and Second Corinthians*, The New Century Bible Commentary (Grand Rapids: William B. Eerdmans, 1971), 121; Donald A. Carson, *Showing the Spirit: A Theological Exposition of 1 Corinthians 12–14* (Grand Rapids: Baker Book House, 1987), 42–49, as also most other evangelical scholars. Although Pentecostal scholars on the whole would not interpret 12:13 as relating to the baptism of the Holy Spirit, many would accept this verse in both its parts as relating to salvation.

[7]Horton, *What the Bible Says About the Holy Spirit*, 215–216. See also Stronstad's position in the following footnote.

[8]See for example, Harold Hunter, *Spirit-Baptism: A Pentecostal Alternative* (Lanham, Md.: University Press of America, 1983), 39–42, and Howard M. Ervin, *Conversion-Initiation and the Baptism of the Holy Spirit* (Peabody, Mass.: Hendrickson Publishers, Inc., 1984). Against this, see Roger Stronstad, *The Charismatic Theology of St. Luke* (Peabody, Mass.: Hendrickson Publishers, Inc., 1984), 10. Stronstad believes that in Paul baptism in/by the Holy Spirit refers to salvation and that in Luke (i.e., Luke-Acts) it speaks of empowering. Whatever one may understand 1 Corinthians 12:13 to mean, Pentecostals and many Luke-Acts scholars think the term "baptism in the Holy Spirit" refers to more than salvation in Luke-Acts passages.

entiation between water baptism and Spirit baptism is made (Matthew 3:11; Mark 1:8; Luke 3:16; John 1:33; Acts 1:5; 11:16), and Spirit baptism is not related to, or equated with, salvation. Rather, the contexts show an empowering, a judging and cleansing, and a setting apart for service. For this, Christ immerses believers "in" the Spirit. In the only other Pauline usage of *en* as related to baptism, the Israelites were baptized unto Moses "in" the cloud and "in" the sea. This one usage has nothing to do with salvation, water baptism, or empowering, and should not be used to dictate how 1 Corinthians 12:13 is to be interpreted.

What of the translation of *en* as "in" instead of "by"?[9] The passage would then read, "In one Spirit we were all baptized into one body." Would this not imply that all have been filled with the Spirit? This could only be inferred if one assumed the phrases "we were baptized" and "we were made to drink" are in synonymous parallelism. Then the second line means the same as the first line. But if "we were made to drink" is an additional statement about the outpouring of gifts after baptism, then Paul is using synthetic parallelism. Being baptized and drinking one's way into the body of Christ is "more than a curious mixing of metaphors."[10] Howard Ervin argues the drinking of the Spirit is not to be associated with salvation, but with the fullness of the Spirit. The parallelism of these verses also parallel Paul's own spiritual experience: first salvation on the Damascus Road, then the filling of the Spirit after Ananias comes. In the first-century church the experience of an enduement of power after the experience of salvation was the norm. It is not surprising to hear Paul say that they were all made to drink of the one Spirit.

---

[9]J. A. Robinson, *St. Paul's Epistle to the Ephesians* (London: Clark, 1922), 203–04, in discussing the issue of instrumentality ("by") or sphere ("in"), says that Ephesians 5:18 applies to both. The Holy Spirit is "at once the Inspirer and the Inspiration." He points to the new community of believers who are the dwelling place of God *by* His Spirit (Ephesians 2:22), the revelation of the mystery of the new community to the apostles and prophets *by* the Holy Spirit, and the prayer life of the Christian (Ephesians 6:18), being filled *with/by* the Holy Spirit (Ephesians 5:22) and sanctified *by* the Spirit (Romans 15:16). So also, he sees both sphere and instrumentality in 1 Corinthians 12:13.

[10]Ervin, *Baptism of the Holy Spirit*, 100.

The major points of the passage may be summarized as follows: There is to be no exclusiveness in the body of Christ. The basis of unity is that we are sinners saved by Jesus Christ, free to experience every blessing available from Him. No one was to look down on others, or to look down on himself. Paul placed all the Corinthian Christians in the same category. Fee makes the point that "one body" is really the goal of their experience in Christ.[11] We are to move toward unity of Jew and Greek, slave and free; we cannot take it for granted or assume its existence. We are the body of Christ now, but we are moving toward full maturity. True unity is achieved through the Spirit of God.

Paul understood salvation as a call to service: the infilling of the Spirit a natural consequence of salvation. There is no need for great delay between salvation and empowering. Paul does not make a distinction between the experience of the two events, though they have a distinction of purpose. Indeed, the experience of Peter at Cornelius's household shows that salvation and being filled with the Spirit can happen at the same time. For Paul, the whole of the Christian life should be characterized by a fullness of the Spirit (Ephesians 5:18).

Paul concludes this section with another emphasis on diversity (12:14).[12] This verse serves as a transition: From all members sharing the same spiritual experiences (12:12–13), Paul moves on to speak of one Body and many members exercising gifts (12:15–20). Any group who thought themselves superior to others would do well to understand this lesson of diversity.

1 Corinthians 12:15–20
All Members of the Body Are Vital

15If the foot should say, "Because I am not a hand, I do not belong to the body," it would not for that reason cease to be part of the body. 16And if the ear should say, "Because I am not

---

[11]Gordon Fee, *The Epistle to the First Corinthians,* The New International Commentary on the New Testament (Grand Rapids: William B. Eerdmans, 1987), 606.

[12]NIV includes 12:14 in the following section; however, the Greek text includes all of 12:12–26 in one paragraph.

an eye, I do not belong to the body," it would not for that reason cease to be part of the body. [17]If the whole body were an eye, where would the sense of hearing be? If the whole body were an ear, where would the sense of smell be? [18]But in fact God has arranged the parts in the body, every one of them, just as he wanted them to be. [19]If they were all one part, where would the body be? [20]As it is, there are many parts, but one body.

The issue of interpretation in these verses is whether Paul uses the analogy of the body to refer to gifts or persons. The context is gifts, but the analogy is to members of a body. Is the problem that of persons having a superiority complex and consequently exalting their gifts? Do the others feel they are inferior because of less spectacular manifestations?[13] The emphasis is on the need for a diversity of gifts, rather than the exalting of one or two gifts. Yet, superiority and inferiority complexes have to do with persons, not gifts. It may be that 12:15–20 refers to gifts and 12:21–26 refers to persons; however, the distinction is not clear-cut because the same terminology of the body is used.[14]

We may conclude the following from this passage: Paul is not speaking of maturity in the Body and stronger or weaker Christians. His primary emphasis is on diversity and unity.

Diversity may make some gifts appear more important than others. Nevertheless, all are necessary. At the same time, persons who think of themselves as superior may be despising others or neglecting them (as in the celebration of the Lord's Supper in 11:17–34). The gift in itself is not inferior or superior. Who exercises the gift and how it is exercised affect how it is perceived by others.

Paul shows the fallacy of the logic some use concerning gifted persons. The Greeks knew deductive logic well and could easily spot an error in thinking. It is evident that the foot does not have to be the hand, nor the ear the eye, to be a part of the body. In fact, a body needs a diversity of members. The Corinthians magnified tongues over other gifts. Christians tend to magnify one gift

---

[13]Martin, *Spirit and Congregation*, 20–21; and Carson, *Showing the Spirit*, 46–47.

[14]Fee, *First Corinthians*, 609.

or ministry as *the* work of the church. They may believe only certain pastors, missionaries, or evangelistic organizations do *the* work of Christ. But are not all necessary to a healthy Body?

The identical phrases of 12:15 and 16 are more literally translated, "It is *not* for this reason *not* of the body." Neither *saying* I am not a hand or an eye, nor the fact that I *am* a foot or an ear instead of a hand or an eye, makes me less a part of the body. No member should feel inferior and less useful than others, for he was designed for his function by God. The last phrases in these two verses are questions intended to push the Corinthians' logic to its absurd conclusion.

In 12:15–20 members that appear to be inferior compare themselves unfavorably with those members that seem to be superior. The foot gets little attention compared to the hand, and the ear is seldom noticed when compared to the eye. Normally, we observe the eyes or hand gestures. Paul shows his sense of humor in describing the monstrosity that would result if one member were the whole body (12:17). He pictures a large eyeball coming into the assembly declaring that he is the body of Christ. Following the eyeball would be an ear declaring he is the body of Christ. Again, how absurd!

Verse 21 reverses this argument. The apparently superior member looks down on the seemingly inferior member. The eye does receive more notice than the hand, and the head more than the feet. But public attention is no indication of real usefulness in the Body. In fact, if one member is out of service, the other members are handicapped.

> The discontent of the lower members and the scornfulness of the higher are alike signs of a selfish individualism, indifferent to the welfare of the Body ecclesiastic. Dissatisfaction with one's particular charism or contempt for that of another is disloyalty toward *Him* and distrust of His wisdom.[15]

---

[15]George G. Findlay, "St. Paul's First Epistle to the Corinthians" in *The Expositor's Greek Testament,* ed. W. Robertson Nicoll (London: Hodder and Stoughton, Ltd., n.d.), 891.

Paul summarized this argument in 12:18. God put the Body together according to His will and for His glory. We must not look down on God's design. He is sovereign. Where He places us, we grow best, and the church is edified. This is not to deny that we may function like a different member at a different stage of the church's life, for we may grow into other ministries. Early Church deacons Stephen and Philip are good examples of this. John Mark grew from secretary and assistant to evangelist and theologian.

1 Corinthians 12:21–26
The Place of the Weaker Member

²¹**The eye cannot say to the hand, "I don't need you!" And the head cannot say to the feet, "I don't need you!" ²²On the contrary, those parts of the body that seem to be weaker are indispensable, ²³and the parts that we think are less honorable we treat with special honor. And the parts that are unpresentable are treated with special modesty, ²⁴while our presentable parts need no special treatment. But God has combined the members of the body and has given greater honor to the parts that lacked it, ²⁵so that there should be no division in the body, but that its parts should have equal concern for each other. ²⁶If one part suffers, every part suffers with it; if one part is honored, every part rejoices with it.**

No one should isolate himself or consider himself superior. Neither should the rest of the Body disregard one of its members or his gift, for this hurts the whole Body. Rather, we should learn to respond to and encourage all to exercise their ministry gifts. We must recognize the importance of apparently weaker members. Members may differ in function, authority, and influence, but not in intrinsic value. Outward appearances are deceiving. A finger or toe helps in coordination and balance much more that we realize. The gifts are not given on the basis of whether the vessel is stronger or weaker, but on the basis of the grace of God and people's needs. Basic modesty dictates that we clothe, pamper, and care for the less honorable parts of the body (12:23). We should also care for every member of our family in Christ.

The strong adversative "but" *(alla)* (12:22,24,25) contrasts God's design with carnal, divisive thinking. The Corinthians neglected the weaker brother out of selfish pride, *but* ("on the contrary") God says the weaker members are indispensable (12:22). We give greater honor to those parts that we think are less presentable, *but* God has combined us (12:24). The word "combined" implies that God "mixed, blended, and united" believers through mutual adjustments in their lives and through interaction with one another. The Corinthians tended to be schismatic, or divisive, *but* God tells believers to have equal concern for one another (12:25).[16]

Empathy means suffering and rejoicing together. It is an in-depth sharing of life because we belong to His family. The carnal tendency is to rejoice over those who suffer and suffer over those who are honored. It is easy to say that others are suffering because they have sinned. Jealousy may arise when others are honored ahead of us. Sometimes it seems the wicked prosper and Christians struggle. Real empathy disregards selfish feelings and considers what benefits others. Paul says "in humility consider others better than yourselves" (Philippains 2:3). This liberates us to become all we were meant to be and to set others free to fulfill their potential.

Empathy tells the believer not merely to focus on himself or his gift. Frequently the main question the sharer asks is, What is my gift? Or, Is this truly from God? But the real questions—before, during, and after the ministry of the gift—should be, How may the church benefit by that ministry? Are needs truly being met? Are others encouraged? Is God glorified instead of people? Thus, through sensitivity to the Holy Spirit and the needs of others, individuals may become unobstructed avenues of blessing for the whole church.

> The gifts are not, in the first place, given to the one who ministers them, but to the one who is ministered to. It is, for example, the sick person that recovers, who receives healing as a gift, not the one who lays hands on him and prays for healing.[17]

---

[16]Walter Bauer, *A Greek-English Lexicon of the New Testament and Other Early Christian Literature,* 2nd ed., trans. F. Wilbur Gingrich and Fredrick W. Danker (Chicago: University of Chicago Press, 1979), 773.

[17]Arnold Bittlinger, *Gifts and Graces: A Commentary of First Corinthians 12 to 14* (Grand Rapids: William B. Eerdmans, 1967), 63.

Thus our focus should be on needs and ministries, not on the gifts and those who exercise them.

1 Corinthians 12:27–31
Enabling Gifts and Ministry Gifts

27Now you are the body of Christ, and each one of you is a part of it. 28And in the church God has appointed first of all apostles, second prophets, third teachers, then workers of miracles, also those having gifts of healing, those able to help others, those with gifts of administration, and those speaking in different kinds of tongues. 29Are all apostles? Are all prophets? Are all teachers? Do all work miracles? 30Do all have gifts of healing? Do all speak in tongues? Do all interpret? 31But eagerly desire the greater gifts.

First Corinthians 12:27 concludes the body analogy and begins the listing of gifts. It is one of the most profound verses in 1 Corinthians. The emphasis is on the plural "you," for all Christians make up the body of Christ. Paul appeals to the Corinthians' highest motives. These schismatic believers had a higher calling than divisiveness. Given their party spirit, legal problems, immorality, doctrinal differences, issues of meat offered to idols, and misuse of the gifts, the Corinthian church would have been written off by most people. Nevertheless, Paul still says to them, "You are the body of Christ." Carnal as they were, God wanted to use them.

Paul's list, following verse 27, is not comprehensive.[18] Gifts can be divided into two basic categories: enabling gifts, as in Ephesians 4:11, and ministry gifts, as in 1 Corinthians 12:8–10. The enabling gifts are given to enable persons to set others free for their ministries. The ministry gifts are sovereignly distributed to meet specific needs. The first three gifts listed in 12:28 are enabling gifts and the last five are ministry gifts. Anyone ministering in the first three could conceivably minister in the last five. God appoints them in the

---

[18]Other gifts are mentioned in 13:1–3; 14:6,26; Romans 12:6–8; Ephesians 4:11; 1 Peter 4:10–11. The idea of more than nine gifts is not uncommon in Pentecostal circles. Ralph M. Riggs, *The Spirit Himself* (Springfield, Mo.: Gospel Publishing House, 1962), 117, lists all the above passages and 1 Corinthians 1:5,7; 2 Corinthians 8:7; and 1 Thessalonians 5:19–21 as "other references to the gifts of the Spirit."

church. The word "appoints" has the idea of personal desire (aorist middle): God did it for himself. He has a plan of reconciliation for the whole creation. The church plays a vital part in this, but people cannot do this work in the best of their strength. God must impart supernatural power.

The key question in 12:28 is, Does the word "first" answer the question of *rank of importance* or *historical order* in the establishing of the church?[19] Are apostles first in importance, and tongues least?

Throughout the whole chapter Paul has described how every member of the body of Christ is equally important through receiving the same salvation, experiencing the same spiritual blessings, and receiving the gifts by God's sovereignty. Though our roles and responsibilities may differ, no member can assume an attitude of superiority or inferiority toward the other. Would Paul then conclude by saying the apostles were most important? Actually, the problem at Corinth was that some were exalting some personalities, positions, and gifts over others. Paul would only be adding fuel to that fire of controversy if he were listing the gifts in order of importance. A carpenter does not say a hammer is more important than a saw. Each tool is vital in its proper time and function.

Furthermore, it is difficult to understand how each gift is of less importance than the previous one on the list. For example, are miracles more important than healings or administrations? If gifts are given through grace, then how are Christians supposed to seek the greater ones? Interestingly, the numbering ends with the third gift. Paul does not establish an ecclesiastical or gift hierarchy either in this passage or in Ephesians 4. If he did in Ephesians, then evangelists would be over pastors.

Paul answers the question of *when* for the first three gifts. The apostles appeared first because no other congregations besides the one in Jerusalem existed. The need for prophets and pastors was yet to come. After Pentecost, the Church grew spontaneously. There was no church history to rely on, no New Testament, no written direction for church goals or emphases. The prophets met this need by bringing the immediacy of God's word to the churches. They

---

[19]Fee, *First Corinthians*, 620–21.

served in a foundational role in the building of the Church (Ephesians 2:20). Then, as numbers were added to the Church, more stability was needed. Pastors gave care and direction to local congregations. All the ministry gifts were present throughout to equip the Church for its ministry. It was truly the Church on the growing edge.

The temple system and priesthood had become ineffective because of a preoccupation with roleplaying, power politics, economic gain, and tradition. One reason the New Testament church grew was its ability to be relevant to real issues. It was organized for growth. Paul lists the gifts this way to show the practical task-orientation of the Church. The Church must be built. The world must be reached.

The church is a *go* structure.[20] If improperly organized, the organization itself may be the biggest obstacle between the church and the needy world and, therefore, between the church and its ministry. Hundreds of creative ministries could be developed if the church were structured for it.

Solid teaching allows the move of God maximum results. It protects from wildfire, yet allows the full expression of God's revelation. It encourages diversity in ministries and builds stability, conviction in the authority of God's Word, and tolerance about less important matters.

Teaching develops a philosophy and methodology of ministry. Many people get frustrated because they do not know how to perform their ministries properly. Then they quit because they feel they have failed. To do God's work, we must learn to do it God's way.

But good organization and good teaching are not ends in themselves. They are only means to the end. The growing edge for the Christian is in seeking to be Christlike, reaching lost souls, and moving with the Spirit of God. In pursuing God's kingdom, we reach our potential.

Three enabling gifts begin this list. Each of them shall be discussed, as well as the gift of evangelist that is listed in the parallel

---

[20]Others who were called apostles were Barnabas (Acts 14:14), Junia, Andronicus (Romans 16:7), possibly James, the Lord's brother (Galatians 1:19), Titus, and Epaphroditus (2 Corinthians 8:23; Philippians 2:25). This is not to suggest they all served as apostles in the same sense as the Twelve or Paul. But they obviously had very important ministries in the growth of the young church. They too were "sent ones" with a mission.

passage of Ephesians 4:11. These four enabling gifts broadly cover the range of enabling gifts. Most forms of enabling ministries, however creative, can readily fall under one or more of these four gifts (an example of this is seen below in the difference between the original apostles and other apostles). But lack of definition in these areas has led to misuse, misunderstanding, and even heresy. Also, because I have already discussed the other ministry gifts in chapter 2, here I shall discuss only the two additional ministry gifts in this list: helps and administrations (12:28).

APOSTLE

The word "apostle" is used eighty times in the New Testament. All but ten uses are found in the writings of Luke and Paul. The term is applied once to Jesus in Hebrews (3:1). It means "one sent forth," signifying a special mission. Because Luke followed mainly the activities of Peter and Paul, we have little information about the other apostles. The rest were scattered and Acts only hints at the many churches outside the circuits of Paul. A precise definition of "apostle" is therefore difficult because most of our understanding comes from Paul alone, and it does not seem that all the apostles had the same ministries or authority that Paul had.[21]

The criteria for apostleship was (1) having seen the risen Lord and (2) having done a foundational work (Acts 1:22; 1 Corinthians 9:1–2; 15:7–9; Ephesians 2:20). None today can claim to be a part of the foundation of apostles and prophets in the same sense as those of the New Testament era. No one today can write Scripture or claim infallibility. Likely Paul's use of the term "apostles" in 12:28 is not exclusive to the Twelve, for elsewhere in his writings he uses the term to refer to others sent out on a special mission.

Peter and Paul are the best-known of this first group. Their ministries were as different as their personalities. Paul pioneered in new areas, planned strategy, and developed evangelistic teams. God worked miracles through him, particularly for evangelistic purposes. Peter's mission was establishing the Christian testimony in Jeru-

---

[21]Ronald Y. K. Fung, "Function or Office? A Survey of the New Testament Evidence," *Evangelical Review of Theology* 8 (April 1984): 36.

salem, helping the church move in the proper direction, and reconciling Jewish and Gentile believers with the Jerusalem church (Acts 8, Samaria; Acts 10–11, Cornelius). We know of no churches he pioneered. Paul wrote almost half the New Testament; Peter wrote two epistles. Paul was a theologian and an aggressive defender of the faith; Peter was an exhortational preacher.

Does the church have apostles today? Although the New Testament period did feature specialized ministries, scholars agree that "church organization was still fluid," that there was no such thing as "*the* New Testament church order."[22] The Bible's focus is on the function of ministry, not the role. Paul lists only three enabling ministries here, leaving it open-ended. Many other enabling ministries could develop. Although today no one in the church serves in the same sense as the first-century apostles, one may well be a pioneer missionary or key enabler who knows how to impart his ability, vision, and wisdom to others. Such broader authority comes because of one's calling, effectiveness, wider ministry, and function. However, self-proclaimed apostleship or prophethood is full of danger: Pride, the creation of a personality cult, manipulative authority, and extremes in doctrine have often accompanied such self-promotion. Accountability for leaders was paramount in the New Testament church and must be so today.

PROPHET

Prophetic ministry in the Old Testament was in essence similar to that of the New Testament. Prophets spoke when anointed by the Spirit of God to call people to repentance, restoration, and righteous living. Luke carefully showed the continuity between Old Testament and New Testament prophecy. Matthew showed how the Old Testament prophecies were foundational to Jesus' ministry and fulfilled only in Him. The same Spirit is at work in both Testaments. Old Testament prophets spoke of a day when greater revelation would dawn and the anointing of God would come on all people.

---

[22]Ronald Y. K. Fung, "Ministry, Community and Spiritual Gifts," *Evangelical Quarterly* 56 (January 20, 1984): 19. "While the Pauline lists of *charismata* refer to function and not offices, *charisma* may be associated with office and office should not be separated from *charisma*."

Some differences, however, must not be overlooked. Most Old Testament prophets arose to bring a disobedient people back to the law of Moses: The prophetic period occurred mainly because of the spiritual compromising and apostasizing of the kings of Israel and Judah.

Because of Israel's political enemies, local deliverers, or judges (e.g., Samson, Gideon, Deborah), were not adequate for uniting and leading the entire nation. Israel clamored for a king like those of other nations. Representing the last of the judges and the first of the prophets who arose with the monarchy was Samuel. Such spokesmen arose to call kings and religious leaders to repentance and God's people back to a right relationship with Him. Their positions became more formalized than their predecessors. Some were associated with the priests in the temple worship, others were writing prophets, and some were in kings' palaces. Several had disciples ("sons of the prophets," e.g., Elijah and Elisha). Other key figures of Israel's history were also called prophets: Abraham, Moses, and Aaron.

More often than not, a prophet's calling was a lonely one. False prophets countered with opposing prophecies. Consequently, formal tests of true prophets were given by God, such as, Did they speak in the name of the Lord (Deuteronomy 18:20–22)? Did their messages agree with Moses' teaching (Deuteronomy 13:1–5)? Were their prophecies fulfilled? For Old Testament prophets spoke primarily in the context of Israel as the people of God.

The New Testament inaugurated a different setting for the prophet. The coming of the Spirit represented the coming of the Messianic Age, the end times. New Testament prophets spoke on the basis of the authority of the risen Christ, who, having begun God's kingdom by His incarnation, had it validated by His resurrection. Given the message of redemption for a dying world, all God's people are now a prophetic people; the Spirit has come upon all flesh. Prophets stand against this backdrop of the prophetic people of God. Their role is to keep the immediacy of God in the church, proclaiming the kingdom of God to believers as well as unbelievers until Jesus comes again.

Although every Christian in the New Testament era had the opportunity to exercise a prophetic gift, a special group were set apart as prophets because of their recognized ministry (12:28,29; Ephesians 4:11; Acts 13:1; 21:9). But many scholars do not believe it was a formal position, simply that those who prophesied regularly were prophets.[23]

Prophets proclaimed a message of exhortation, edification, and comfort to the Church and a message of salvation, grace, and judgment to the unbeliever. The apostle John exercised both an exhortational function and a predictive function in Revelation. Agabus ministered predictively in Acts 11:28 and 21:10–11. When prophets spoke, their messages were driven home by the reality of the truth. At the same time, their messages had to be tested for adherence to God's Word, clarity, and sensitivity to the church and world situations.

Wayne Grudem identifies two types of prophecy. The first type was unquestioned, on the level of biblical inspiration, and accepted because of who the prophets were. If one assumed they were God's words, the prophecy was beyond question and had to be obeyed. The second level of prophecy needed full evaluation and was not considered on the level of biblical inspiration. This type of prophecy was present even in the interbiblical times, though prophecy on the level of biblical inspiration had ceased until the time of the Messiah. Josephus, Philo, and the rabbis accepted this second level of prophecy as valid, but in need of evaluation.

This is not to say that the biblical writers were accepted without question. This may have been true many years after their deaths, but Moses, Samuel, Jeremiah, and all the prophets were challenged in their day. Truth must always be tested by the life and authority of the messenger as well as by his words. However, once the canon was tested and accepted, unquestioned faith was placed in it. Grudem states:

> [I]f the prophet claimed to be speaking God's words, another sort of evaluation takes place. There are only two possibilities,

---

[23]Fung, "Ministry, Community and Spiritual Gifts," 19.

and there is no middle ground. The question becomes, "Are these God's words or not? If so, I must obey. If not, the prophet is misrepresenting God and must be put to death" (so Deuteronomy 18:20). Once his words are accepted (by whatever means) as God's words, they have a different status and are beyond challenge or question.[24]

This first level of prophecy belongs only to the Bible, which is inspired and authoritative. It occurred for writers of the Old and New Testaments. This type of prophecy is no longer needed because God's written revelation for mankind is as complete as necessary. John warned that no one add to or take away from his book of prophecy (Revelation 22:19), a warning that may very well extend to the whole Bible (2 Timothy 3:16). The apostles and prophets who formed the foundation of the church (Ephesians 2:20) are no more; the essential revelation of Jesus Christ has been presented (Hebrews 1:1–2).

The second level of prophecy is what Paul discusses in 1 Corinthians and what we encounter today. It was prophecy that everyone could participate in—including its evaluation. The prophecies of Agabus and others about Paul's arrest in Jerusalem had to be evaluated.

The guidelines for the church today must be the same as those held throughout the New Testament era. Believers do not seek to bring people back to the law of Moses, but to lead people to the risen Christ and the truths of the kingdom in Christ. The basis for testing is both testaments, the whole Bible, and the sensitivity of all the prophetic people of God. The gift of prophecy speaks to both believer and unbeliever. It has exhortational and predictive functions. Some Christians have the unique, specialized enabling ministries of a prophet, though not necessarily formalized to a role. None write Scripture today inasmuch as the first-century apostles are no longer here to validate and approve such writings. All prophecies need evaluation.

---

[24]Wayne Grudem, *The Gift of Prophecy in 1 Corinthians 12–14* (Lanham, Md.: University Press of America, 1982), 271ff.

EVANGELIST

The evangelist is not mentioned in 1 Corinthians 12 except as he may fit under the role of an itinerant teacher. Basically an evangelist proclaims the good news to sinners. The Gospel writers are called evangelists because they proclaimed the good news. Although all believers are to witness, not all have the gift of the evangelist. Apollos was a powerful, itinerant teacher-evangelist, mighty in Scriptures. Epaphras was the evangelist of the Lycus Valley, having pioneered churches at Colossae and Laodicea. Philip the deacon became an evangelist, doing both personal and public evangelism.

As an enabler, the evangelist has a twofold function: first, to mobilize the saints in evangelism and, second, to develop methodology to reach beyond the church to the lost. Unlike the apostle, who must be accountable to the church at large, the evangelist works under the guidance and direction of local churches. He is accountable to a local body of believers who have confirmed his calling. Not necessarily eloquent, he has learned to be an expert communicator of the good news, making the Bible practical and relevant to sinners. Although the apostle may do the work of an evangelist as one of his functions, the evangelist's role is more narrowly defined as proclaiming the good news.

TEACHER

The ministry of the teacher is closely related to the role of the pastor (Ephesians 4:11). Jerome said, "Whoever is a shepherd must be a teacher."[25] Likewise, while not every teacher is a pastor, every teacher needs a pastor's heart. The teacher teaches the depths of Scripture to equip the saints for their ministries. He seeks to develop individuals for effective service and full maturity. He counsels, teaches, exhorts, and imparts of himself in such a way that others will not only be receivers of the message, but senders of the message as well. Every Sunday school teacher or Bible teacher is an undershepherd working with the pastor of the church. The emphasis of

---

[25]Jerome, in Bittlinger, *Gifts and Graces*, 70.

the teacher is expounding the Word of God; the emphasis of the prophet is an immediate word from God.

Some may have had both the role of the prophet and the teacher, as at Antioch (Acts 13:1–2). But between the two, major distinctions can be observed. Biblically, the prophet spoke more from an immediate revelational perspective. He may have been educated or uneducated. He spoke what God impressed on his heart. His challenge was to bring people back to God's priorities. His ministry appears more charismatic and spontaneous. The teacher, on the other hand, is gifted to do studied expositions of Scripture, building carefully one truth upon another, looking to the welfare and nourishment of the spiritual needs of believers.

A confusion of roles exists. Leaders try to be all things to all people and effectively bless only a few. Those with other ministries, who should be followers, often try to be leaders or try to do ministries not given to them by the Lord. If each enabler can do his task well, placing each member in his appropriate ministry, the church may develop its full potential.

HELPS AND ADMINISTRATIONS

Helps and administrations in 12:28 are additional to the lists of 1 Corinthians 12:8–10, Romans 12, and Ephesians 4. Likely "helps" means those who show mercy and special kindness to others. "Administrations" implies the giving of guidance and counsel to the community or to an individual.[26] Ralph Martin identifies the people who exercise these gifts as deacons and overseers, respectively.[27] In a narrow sense, they could be considered enabling gifts, setting others free for greater ministries. Yet these two terms should be left in a general sense because the ministries they identify often fall outside established positions and may relate more to the personal ministry of an individual.

---

[26]Fee, *First Corinthians*, 621–22.

[27]Martin, *The Spirit and the Congregation*, 33. Also, Archibald T. Robertson, *Word Pictures in the New Testament*, vol. 4 (Nashville: Broadman Press, 1931), 174.

THE BEST GIFTS?

Seven rhetorical questions conclude the discussion on the distribution of gifts (vv. 29–31), for the Greek requires a negative answer to each question. Conceivably one person could be used in all the gifts, but it is not probable, practical, nor would it be healthy for the body of Christ. God gives as He determines. One does not do the work of all. Christ apportions the gifts in respect to one's place and function in the Church and in one's ministry to the world.

The key question of this passage is, What are "the greater gifts"? The answer depends on one's understanding of the Greek verb, translated "desire" (KJV, "seek"), in verse 31. Most translators take it to be an imperative, Paul's commanding the Corinthians to seek the greater gifts. His reference to greater gifts, then, would be to those gifts (exercised in love and communicated with clarity) meeting the need of the congregation. This view, however, assumes the existence of greater and lesser gifts. In this context, the Corinthian believers were to seek to be apostles, prophets, and teachers.

But Paul does not evaluate gifts so that we may assign a rank to them. For example, in his comparable lists in Corinthians (12:8–10) and Ephesians (4:11), "prophecy"/"prophets" is sixth and second, respectively. Neither is he referring to love as the greater gift, as some have taught; the word is "gifts"—plural—and "love" is singular.

Furthermore, how does the Spirit distribute according to His sovereignty and plan (1 Corinthians 12:11) if we are told to seek the greater gifts? If helps comes before administrations, for example, are we all to seek the ministry of helps first? Then the church may lack in other areas. Though we may tell God which gifts we desire, we are not qualified to determine which gifts our church needs most. What we can do is be loving, open, and growing—available for God's use according to *His* desire.

The issue is clear in 1 Corinthians 13—it is the *way* in which we exercise the gifts that is crucial. The gifts themselves are only tools of ministry. Love is the fruit of the Spirit by which the tool is best utilized. Spirituality is not measured by giftedness in the New Testament. The truly spiritual person looks after orphans and widows in their distress, keeps pure, reconciles the weaker member, bears the burdens of others, doesn't look down on others, and reflects Christlikeness. In other words, he acts in love.

Some commentators construe 12:31 as an imperative that the Corinthians were using on one another, rather than one Paul was using on them. That is, Paul has been answering their questions throughout this epistle: questions on morality (7:2), food sacrificed to idols (8:1), spiritual gifts (12:1), etc. It is possible one (or more) of them brought up the issue of greater gifts. He would understand Paul as writing, "[You say,] 'Desire the greater gifts,' " and covering the question by saying greater gifts is not the issue, but gifts shared in love (12:31 to 14:1).

The difficulty with this view, however, is that the immediate context contains none of the usual signals Paul gives elsewhere in this epistle ("concerning . . . we know that . . .") to show he is replying to their questions or quoting their comments. And discounting such signals, one can identify a Corinthian error in anything Paul writes and come out with one's preferred interpretation. This view, thus, poses a weak option. A strong variation of this position, however, can be seen in the next view.

Recent scholars propose that the verb "desire" can be either in the imperative mood or in the indicative mood. The spelling is the same. If the verb is indicative, the translation would be, "You are eagerly desiring . . ." In this case, Paul is indicting the Corinthians for desiring greater gifts when the real issue is the manner in which the gifts are ministered. This is clearly the intent of 14:12—They should not be selfish, but direct their zeal for gifts into helping others. They should be content with God's sovereignty in the apportioning of gifts to fulfill His purposes and plans, not egotistically parading their gifts or envying the gifts of another (12:11,18).

At the same time, "desire" in 14:1 is clearly imperative, but does not include the word "greater" of 12:31. When Paul gives the command in 14:1 and again in 14:39, he encourages the desire for gifts, but not necessarily greater ones. The issue of 1 Corinthians 14 is the intelligibility of gifts, not their relative value.[28]

---

[28]Gerhard Iber, "Zum Verstaandnis von 1 Corinthians 12:31," *ZNW* 54 (1963): 43–54. Other scholars holding this view include Martin, *Spirit and Congregation,* 35, and Bittlinger, *Gifts and Graces,* 73.

The diversity of gifts and the Church itself as a unity in diversity are manifestations of the nature of God. God has set each member of the body in the rightful position and has blended ministries and personalities together. All gifts are vital, but serve best in the functions intended. We are all equally important. We all need each other. In weakness and in strength, Christians together are the body of Christ.

Does anyone have all the gifts, or does everyone have the same gift? No. Should we seek the greater gifts? No. We should seek "the most excellent way," the way of love, to manifest the gifts God gives.

3

1 Corinthians 13

Chapter 13 of 1 Corinthians provides the ethical base of the argumentation of the entire epistle. Love must be the motivation for all Christian actions, whether facing issues of morality, lawsuits, church discipline, personal liberty, or methodology in worship. We must especially recognize how it is integral to chapters 12 and 14. Because of the diversities of gifts, ministries, and members (1 Corinthians 12), Paul points to the need for love in exercising gifts (1 Corinthians 13). No one has all the gifts, or even one gift in its fullness. The greater way is not love in distinction to gifts, but love in exercise of gifts. The fact that gifts apart from love are ineffective is reemphasized in parallel passages in Romans 12:9–21 and Ephesians 4:25–32. The Holy Spirit through Paul gave us a "poetic rhapsody composed in praise of . . . some attribute regarded as divine."[1] Love is the key attribute of God's character in action and should become the norm of our behavior.

---

[1]Ralph P. Martin, *The Spirit and the Congregation: Studies in 1 Corinthians 12–15* (Grand Rapids: William B. Eerdmans, 1984), 42. First Corinthians 13 may not technically be a song, but powerful prose. See Charles Kingsley Barrett, *A Commentary on the First Epistle to the Corinthians* (San Francisco: Harper & Row, Publishers, Inc., 1968), 299, and Gordon Fee, *The First Epistle to the Corinthians,* The New International Commentary on the New Testament (Grand Rapids: William B. Eerdmans, 1987), 626. Archibald T. Robertson, *Word Pictures in the New Testament,* vol. 4 (Nashville: Broadman Press, 1931), 176, calls it a prose poem. On the other hand, Ralph Martin argues strongly that hymnic qualities and all the marks of a liturgical composition are here, especially in stanzas 1 and 3 (1 Corinthians 13:1–3, 8–13). The middle stanza reflects the style of the wisdom school of Judaism. See 1 Corinthians 15:55–57, Philippians 2:6–11, and 2 Timothy 2:11–13 as examples of songs Paul writes or applies to his arguments (pp. 41ff.).

1 Corinthians 13:1–3
Love: The Indispensable Quality

¹**If I speak in the tongues of men and of angels, but have not love, I am only a resounding gong or a clanging cymbal. ²If I have the gift of prophecy and can fathom all mysteries and all knowledge, and if I have a faith that can move mountains, but have not love, I am nothing. ³If I give all I possess to the poor and surrender my body to the flames, but have not love, I gain nothing.**

These verses contain a series of three "if-then" clauses.[2] Though the word "then" is not in the Greek, it is understood. Paul suggests that one might even be able to express each of the gifts to the ultimate degree. We see this in the following expressions: tongues of men *and* of angels, all mysteries, all knowledge, all faith, all I possess.[3] The gifts in normal usage are partial expressions of God's mind. We manifest a word of wisdom, a word of knowledge, a discerning of spirits, a healing.

If Paul is taking each gift to the ultimate degree, it follows that speaking in tongues is usually a human language. Luke reported tongues at Pentecost as human. Paul spoke of tongues at Corinth in the same way. Tongues could be interpreted and regulated, had a valid place in gift ministry, involved communication with God and people, were a sign to the unbeliever, and were desirable for all believers. These purposes far exceed anything pagan worshippers

---

[2]Note Paul's appeal to the sanctified reasoning processes of the Corinthian believers through parallel statements in these chapters. Typical of Hebrew writers is the use of parallelism. Over one fourth of the Old Testament uses parallelism.

[3]George G. Findlay, "St. Paul's First Epistle to the Corinthians" in *The Expositor's Greek Testament,* ed. W. Robertson Nicoll (London: Hodder and Stoughton, Ltd., n.d.), 897, speaks of prophecy "in its widest range, and faith at its utmost stretch."

Also, the definite article before knowledge and faith emphasizes the gifts in their entirety. See F. Blass, A. DeBrunner, and R. W. Funk, *A Greek Grammar of the New Testament* (Chicago: University of Chicago Press, 1961), 144. Donald A. Carson, *Showing the Spirit: A Theological Exposition of 1 Corinthians 12–14* (Grand Rapids: Baker Book House, 1987), 58; and Fred Fisher, *First and Second Corinthians* (Waco: Word Books, 1975), 210, see the phrase "and of angels" as hyperbole, taking tongues to the greatest possible extent.

saw in their ecstatic speech (purposes that hardly accord with the belief of some commentators that Paul condoned ecstatic experiences from the Corinthians' pagan backgrounds.)

"Tongues of angels" probably describes a total freedom of communication with God.[4] The Corinthian believers had an overrealized eschatology that caused some among them to feel they had already arrived spiritually. Thus, they denied the need for a resurrection body (1 Corinthians 15), promoted sexual abstinence among married people (1 Corinthians 7), ate at pagan temple festivals (1 Corinthians 8–10), disregarded some of the church at Communion (1 Corinthians 11), and thus caused a factious spirit because of their assumed superiority (1 Corinthians 3).[5]

Paul's response is that spirituality is not measured by manifestations, but by love. Chapter 13 is no rhapsodic digression on love; it is an integral corrective for the situation at Corinth.

Ministry apart from love brings negative results: The one who voices tongues without love gives them a hollow ring (13:1). Possessing prophecy, knowledge, and faith gifts in their entirety doesn't increase our intrinsic value to God (13:2). Giving away everything out of any motive other than love brings no special blessing from God (13:3). Volumes have been written about the meaning of *agape* love. The meaning of the word cannot be found in the Greek itself. It was rarely used before the Septuagint translation and the New Testament era. The sacrificial death of Jesus gives the word its content. *Agape* is God's selfless, giving, purposeful, creative love directed toward us. He loves us, not for our worth, but out of the abundance of His nature. The Christian must reflect this love to the world. We love others, not because they are lovely, but because Christ's love dwells in us.[6]

---

[4]In interbiblical literature the daughters of Job are heard speaking in angelic prayer speech to praise God. *Test. Job,* 48–50.

[5]Fee and Martin predicate their teachings about these passages on a Corinthian perception that they had already arrived in the *eschaton.* The "not yet" was "now."

[6]Some of the best discussions on love are found in Anders Nygren, *Agape and Eros* (New York: Harper & Row, Publishers, Inc., 1969); Markus Barth, *Ephesians: Translation and Commentary on Chapters 4–6,* vol. 34A, The Anchor Bible Series (Garden City, N.Y.: Doubleday and Co., Inc., 1974); C. S. Lewis, *The*

The present Christian discussion on love revolves around the meaning of the second greatest commandment. What does it mean to love our neighbor as ourselves? Humanistic psychology emphasizes the need to love self first before one is able to love others. Christians must beware of the possible selfishness in this approach. There is truth to the idea that from a basis of healthy self-esteem we are able to reach out to others. But if humanism's focus on self-fulfillment and self-actualization becomes paramount, we miss the biblical emphasis on service to neighbor and humility before God. The New Testament perspective is that in loving our neighbor, we are loving ourselves. We are made complete in unselfish relationships.[7] This love is not a selfish, sensual type of love, as may be expressed by the word *eros*. Anders Nygren sees an irreconcilable difference between *eros* and *agape:*

> Eros is acquisitive desire; agape is sacrificial giving. Eros is an upward, agape a downward, movement. The first is man's way to God; the second is God's way to man. Eros is egocentric, though a sublime self-assertion; agape is unselfish, self-giving love. Eros seeks to gain immortal life; agape lives the life of God and is willing to lay down its life for the beloved.[8]

In 1 Corinthians 13, *agape* love is set in the context of a methodology of exercising gifts (13:1–3), an interdependence in the Body (13:9—if our sharing is "in part" ["partial," NEB; "incomplete," Phillips; "imperfect," RSV], then no one shares the whole; there-

---

Four Loves (New York: Harcourt, Brace and Jovanovich, 1960); and more recently, Lewis B. Smedes, *Love Within Limits: Realizing Selfless Love in a Selfish World* (Grand Rapids: William B. Eerdmans, 1978). The latter work is one of the most insightful, therapeutic essays on 1 Corinthians 13.

[7]The best current discussion on *agape* may be found in Barth's *Ephesians* commentary, when he analyzes Ephesians 5:22–23. In the midst of his discussion on the husband-wife relationship, he shows how love of neighbor is integral to loving oneself fully.

[8]Nygren, *Agape and Eros*, 210. Whether there can be a relation between *agape* and *eros* is not in the scope of this book. Barth, *Ephesians*, 716, believes *eros* can be redeemed by *agape*. In other biblical contexts *agape* is used with other meanings: for example, "Demas loved the world" (2 Timothy 4:10) and "Do not love the world" (1 John 2:15).

fore we need the sharing of the other members), a concentration on the importance of others (13:4–7), the final Judgment Day (13:10,12), and the temporality of everything but love (13:8–13).

The three categories of gifts in 12:8–10 are represented in 13:1–3: teaching (mysteries and knowledge), ministry (prophecy, faith, giving, martyrdom), and worship (tongues). (Also, the traditional categories of utterance, revelation, and power gifts can find representation here.)

"Gong" (*chalkos*) could refer to a number of metals—gold, silver, copper, brass, bronze—but there is no evidence, prior to Paul's use here, of the word being used to identify an instrument of worship. The word has been used by the Early Church fathers to describe the material for making idols. And some forms of this word occur in descriptions of pagan worship.[9] Nevertheless, the meaning of this term is ambiguous. The cymbal was a loud percussion instrument used in Jewish temple worship.[10] In the pagan cults they were used "to excite the worshippers."[11]

But even if gifts are exercised to their ultimate degree, that does not indicate the spirituality or worth of the individual participating. People are only instruments. Love is the ethic and motivation of the truly spiritual person.

"Mystery" in the New Testament primarily refers to what was once hidden and is now revealed in Christ. The greatest mystery is that of redemption and how Christ perfects His will through the church.[12] Paul's use of "mystery" was clearly different from the

---

[9]Walter Bauer, *A Greek-English Lexicon of the New Testament and Other Early Christian Literature,* 2nd ed., trans. F. Wilbur Gingrich and Fredrick W. Danker (Chicago: University of Chicago Press, 1979), 875.

[10]2 Samuel 6:5; 1 Chronicles 13:8; Psalm 150:5.

[11]Ralph P. Martin, "A Suggested Exegesis of 1 Corinthians 13:13," *The Expository Times* 82 (1970–1971): 120. Barrett, *1 Corinthians,* 300, says the noise "may have been intended to call the god's attention or to drive away demons," but "its probable effect was to excite the worshippers."

[12]In Corinthians the word *musterion* (most often translated "mystery") is used in several contexts. Here it is something that needed to be fathomed, or understood. In 1 Corinthians 2:6–7 it is a special message beyond the wisdom of this age. In 1 Corinthians 14:2 it is the content of an utterance in tongues to God. In 15:51 it is the truth of the coming of the Lord.

mystical secrets that only certain initiated ones in the pagan cults knew. Every member of the body of Christ could know and understand these mysteries. Yet none of us understands all mysteries. They "are secrets, things undiscoverable by human reason, which divine revelation alone can make known. And the gift of prophecy was the gift of revelation by which such mysteries were communicated; see 14:30. All mysteries . . . refer to *all the secret purposes of God relating* to redemption."[13]

Paul's references to "faith that can move mountains" in 13:2 (see Matthew 17:20–21; Mark 11:25) and giving to the poor in 13:3 (see Matthew 19:21; Luke 12:33) reveal his acquaintance with Jesus' teachings. It can well be said that Jesus Christ is central to this chapter. He gave *agape* its meaning by dying on the Cross. One could write "Christ" in place of "love" in this chapter without missing any meaning.

God's characteristic of patience with a disobedient people is well-established in the Old Testament and restated in 1 Corinthians 13:4. Only His love never fails. Only He knows fully. Love is the eternal nature of God.

The gift of giving is an addition to the list of gifts (13:3). If Paul is not referring to a gift here, why would he use this example? A paraphrase of this verse might be, "If I make a practice of dividing all my food into separate portions and carefully placing them in the mouths of the poor but have not love, I gain nothing." The rabbis taught much about giving to the poor, but even they were prohibited from giving over twenty percent of their possessions per year.[14] Jesus talked about selling one's possessions and giving to the poor. But here again Paul is pressing his illustration to the extreme: It was not until after the first century that Christians sometimes sold themselves into slavery to meet the needs of the poor.[15]

A textual question arises in the phrase, "deliver my body to be

---

[13]Charles Hodge, *An Exposition of the First Epistle to the Corinthians* (New York: Robert Carter and Brothers, 1857), 267.

[14]H. L. Strack and P. Billerbeck, *Kommentar zum Neuen Testament aus Talmud und Midrasch,* (Munich: C. H. Beck, 1965), vol. 3, 451; vol. 4, 536–558.

[15]Note Matthew 19:21. Also see Clement in his *Letter to Corinth,* Grant-Graham transl. (New York, 1965), 55:2, on selling oneself into slavery.

burned/that I may boast'' (NASB and note): In the Greek a spelling difference of one letter makes the word either "burn" or "boast."[16] If the word is "boast," then the sharer of the gift may have the wrong motive of drawing attention to himself and seeking his own benefit. But boasting is not necessarily a negative action for Paul. He speaks of his converts as his "boast . . . in the day of the Lord" (2 Corinthians 1:14), "the crown in which we will glory" (1 Thessalonians 2:19). The word "burn," however, does seem more fitting to the internal argument of the passage and makes a more forceful statement. The objection to this reading is that at the time of the writing of 1 Corinthians martyrdom by fire was not yet the experience of the Church.[17] But Paul may not be speaking of martyrdom. He may simply be saying that "even in giving my life in sacrifice to the most painful of deaths, apart from love, I gain nothing." With either reading, the point is the same and the result is the same.

1 Corinthians 13:4–7
Love Liberates!

⁴Love is patient, love is kind. It does not envy, it does not boast, it is not proud. ⁵It is not rude, it is not self-seeking, it is not easily angered, it keeps no record of wrongs. ⁶Love does not

---

[16]Papyrus 46, the Sinaitic (Aleph), Alexandrine (A), and Vaticanus (B) codices, and Nestle-Aland *Novum Testamentum Graece*, 26th ed., support the reading for "boast." The Ephraem Codex (C) and the Codex of Beza (D) support the reading for "burn." Westcott and Hort's translation, Robertson, *Word Pictures*, 177; Fee, *First Corinthians*, 633–34; and Fisher, *First and Second Corinthians*, 211, agree that the reading should be "boast." The external textual evidence agrees. Barrett, *First Corinthians*, 302–303; F. W. Grosheide, *Commentary on the First Epistle to the Corinthians* (Grand Rapids: Wm. B. Eerdmans, 1955), 305, Harold Mare, *First Corinthians*, Expositor's Bible Commentary Series (Grand Rapids: Zondervan, 1976), 268, and Martin, *Spirit and Congregation*, 45, accept "burned" as original and more fitting to the internal argument.

[17]The first recorded martyrdom by fire was in A.D. 60–64 under Nero. Fee, *1 Corinthians*, 634, says "one does not 'give over one's body' to martyrdom; rather, such is taken from one." Although martyrdom is defined as "choos[ing] to die for the sake of religion" (Origen), the terminology of "giving over one's body" is not normally so used.

delight in evil but rejoices with the truth. ⁷It always protects, always trusts, always hopes, always perseveres.

In this second stanza, all fifteen verbs picture continuous action. Some verbs describe attitudes, others describe active involvement on behalf of others. Love is a life-style directed at reflecting the nature and glory of God. It does not consist only of once-in-a-while acts of mercy: Note especially 1 Corinthians 13:7 where Paul uses "always" four times to express love's continuous behavior. Love in this passage is directed primarily to horizontal relationships. Note the clustering of phrases in five groups by the NIV, bringing major ideas together.[18]

This is not just a noble soliloquy on love. Paul attacks the Corinthian problem produced by pride. It had caused division in their midst and opposition to Paul. The only answer would be for each Christian to manifest Christlikeness.

Two words for "patience" are used, at the beginning and at the end of this stanza. The first, *makrothumia,* refers to a great capacity to be patient with people who repeatedly wrong you. It means to be long-tempered. The Christian seeks to control his temper and take the time to understand others. We are patient to ascertain what is best for others as well as what is best for us; certainly God is patient with us. The second word is *hupomones,* translated by the NIV as "perseveres." It means to be patient in circumstances, to bear up under the load. We need to be patient with both people and circumstances.

Adverse circumstances and adversarial people are inevitable, but how we face them is determined by the love within us. Selfish love seeks to find comfort and accommodation in the easiest ways possible. However, to seek to avoid and eliminate the suffering may

---

[18]These verses can be dealt with in two ways. RSV sees seven couplets incorporating Hebrew poetic parallelism. The first, sixth, and seventh couplets are affirmative; couplets two to five (beginning with "does not envy") are negative.

NIV, GNB, and Phillips cluster "does not envy, does not boast, is not proud" as one triplet and "is not rude, is not self-seeking, is not easily angered" as another triplet, with "keeps no record of wrongs" as a summary statement of the latter. No major issues are affected with either breakdown. The NIV breakdown clusters the natural ideas together.

be an unwise shortcut. Smedes says, "When I turn off suffering for the sake of my pleasure, I turn it off too soon."[19] God's love challenges us to confront it. On the other hand, too many of us tend to accept evil and suffering as God's will for our lives. We must hate the evil, the sickness, the hurt, within us. To persevere is to neither run nor resign, but to resolve the problem in Christ.

Love shows kindness *(chresteuetai).*[20] Instead of using an adjective like he does in Galatians 5:22–23 *(chrestotes),* Paul uses an active verb to describe this aspect of the fruit of the Spirit. Practical love reaches out to others. Early Christians saw the relationship between this word *(chresteuetai)* and Christ *(christos),* whose very nature is to show kindness.[21] Jesus' greatest act of kindness was at Calvary. Kindness is a unilateral action, demanding no reward or response from others. It comes from a disposition of graciousness.

Kindness seeks to redeem and reconcile (Romans 2:4). Superficial kindness is not the focus here. What may seem kind now may be permissiveness, overlooking the problem. True kindness may require repentance of the other person or firmness in a given situation. Kindness seeks the greatest long-term good for another. Just as the blessed peacemaker seeks permanent peace rather than temporary tranquility, the kind person desires what Christ would desire for the other person.

First Corinthians 13:4 speaks of envy, boasting, and pride. They are invariably connected. To envy means to use zeal for selfish reasons. The Corinthians were zealous for gifts (1 Corinthians 12:31; 14:1,12). Zeal is not wrong when love is the motive, but when the desire for self-exaltation is present, jealousy is the result. We should

---

[19]Smedes, *Love Within Limits,* 6.

[20]Paul seems to tie kindness and patience together: in Galatians 5:22 as fruit of the Spirit, in 2 Corinthians 6:6 in service, and in Colossians 3:12 as spiritual clothing. God is like this, full of mercy and slow to anger.

[21]Not only do *chresteuetai* and *christos* sound similar, prompting an immediate association, but the root verb *chresteuomai* ("be kind" or "show kindness") is found only in Christian writings. The third person singular form is found in 1 Corinthians 13:4, its only occurrence in the New Testament. The noun and adjective forms are used in the Septuagint and the New Testament primarily to describe God's nature, though an occasional reference to human kindness does occur.

rejoice when others are being used of God. In fact, we should be delighted when others surpass us in their development. This means they are being discipled to accomplish God's work and liberated to find their full potential in Christ.

Love does not draw undue attention to the one manifesting the gift, or to the gift itself. The goal is to build the body of Christ and encourage life-changing behavior. In contrast to this loving goal is the attitude of "pride" (NIV), or being "puffed up" (KJV); this describes an arrogance in one based on presumed superiority to another. At Corinth they were divided among themselves and against Paul. Some boasted of deeper revelations and knowledge. Pride caused them to be puffed up.[22]

C. S. Lewis, speaking of pride as "essentially competitive" and leading to "every other vice," called pride the Great Sin.[23] Since the Garden of Eden humanity has succumbed to Satan's temptation that "you will be like God" (Genesis 3:5). Even atheistic French philosopher Jean-Paul Sartre pointed out that the greatest human folly is the attempt to be God.[24] Pride is really a problem of insecurity. That is what drives a person to envy what others have and to lift himself up. A secure person does not need to exalt himself. Christ will exalt him in due time. Christ, on the other hand, was willing to empty himself. He was secure in His equality with the Father and was willing to be abased on our behalf (Philippians 2:5–11). *Eros* tends to self-preservation, *agape* to self-giving.

Three more characteristics of Corinthian Christian behavior are clustered in 13:5—rudeness, self-seeking, and anger. To be rude reflects an insensitivity to others, a shameful behavior. Rudeness insists that its own way is right and others are wrong. Love must consider the feelings of others and their sense of self-respect. Misusing the Lord's table, being improperly attired, flaunting religious

---

[22]1 Corinthians 4:6,18–19; 5:2; 8:1.

[23]C. S. Lewis, *Mere Christianity*, 4th ed., rev. and enl. (New York: MacMillan, 1952), 109.

[24]Jean-Paul Sartre, *No Exit and Three Other Plays* (New York, Vintage Books, 1946).

superiority, claiming personal rights, and responding to the evil of others in anger were problems that needed to be confronted.

Love is not self-seeking. Paul says, "Do nothing out of selfish ambition or vain conceit, but in humility consider others better than yourselves. Each of you should look not only to your own interests, but also to the interests of others" (Philippians 2:3–4). Those who look upon others as a means to their own ends become easily frustrated; instead of practicing forgiveness, they keep a record of wrongs.

The believer's goal, however, must be what benefits others and the kingdom of God, even if occasionally he feels wronged. He should always value others as persons whom Jesus came to redeem. The believer must be willing to be wronged, to even give up what belongs to him, if it will be for the greater good of God's kingdom.[25] Although a person naturally wants to be proven right, vindicated, he ought to be more concerned about what people think of God, not his own small reputation. God's name and glory matter completely. The Christian must learn how to distinguish between those things that hurt him personally and those things that hurt the cause of Christ. Jesus said that all kinds of evil spoken against Him personally would be forgiven, but not that spoken against the Holy Spirit. If a person deliberately defies the Spirit of God and denies all that is good and holy and just, he cuts off his own salvation. Jesus was not thinking of His own vindication but of the salvation of humanity.

Although we are not to be self-seeking, neither are we to disparage ourselves. A person who has a poor self-concept will seek pity, advantage, and attention, or retreat to a point of inaction, although he may go so far as to call this behavior self-denial. Knowing who we are in Christ liberates us to love God, neighbor, and self in an eternal sense. Kindness and humility free us for our God-ordained potential of service. We do not have to waste time and energy exalting ourselves and protecting our position.

Pride and self-seeking are lesser problems if we realize who we are in God's sight. After many years of ministry, Paul relays his

---

[25]1 Corinthians 10:24,33.

insight in the pastoral epistles. One of the most vital is the first of the five "trustworthy sayings" found in those epistles:

"Here is a trustworthy saying that deserves full acceptance: Christ Jesus came into the world to save sinners—of whom I am the worst. But for that very reason I was shown mercy so that in me, the worst of sinners, Christ Jesus might display his unlimited patience as an example for those who would believe on him and receive eternal life" (1 Timothy 1:15–16).[26]

He was not saying that he continued to live in sin. But the closer he came to God, the more he realized his present sinfulness. In realizing his sinfulness he could begin to realize the grace of God. This is liberation for ministry. Someone may object to this, saying we are no longer sinners but saints. True, we have been set apart and sanctified for His service. But for Paul, a saint is a marvelously redeemed sinner. He lives his life completely on the grace of God.[27]

For a person to be easily angered is to feel the world is at odds with him, out to get him. He seeks to protect what ground he has, experiencing a deep irritation within. A sense of frustrated unfulfillment settles in. Everyone becomes his enemy. On the other hand, the Christian stands on a solid foundation, reaching out to others, knowing that God is for him and no one can stand against him. He knows even enemies have needs and can be loved. God can use an enemy's actions to strengthen the believer. Archimedes claimed that if he had a foundation to stand on outside of this world, he could move the world with the lever. This may not be scientific possibility,

---

[26]The other "trustworthy sayings," not discussed here, are found in 1 Timothy 3:1; 4:9–10; 2 Timothy 2:11–13; Titus 3:5–8.

[27]Robertson, *Word Pictures,* 564, notes the present tense in 1 Timothy 1:15. In 1 Corinthians 15:9 he calls himself the least of the apostles because he had persecuted the church. He is less than the least of all God's people (Ephesians 3:8). It was not a false modesty, but a liberating truth that God's grace was everything in his life. See also, J. N. D. Kelly, *A Commentary on the Pastoral Epistles* (Grand Rapids: Baker Book House, 1963), 54–55; Homer A. Kent, *The Pastoral Epistles* (Chicago: Moody Press, 1962), 89; and J. H. Bernard, *The Pastoral Epistles* (Grand Rapids: Baker Book House, 1980), 32–33. Bernard also mentions other saints, e.g., Ignatius of Antioch, Augustine, and Bunyan, who increasingly saw their sinfulness as they approached the holiness of God.

but it is a spiritual possibility: We have a firm foundation in Jesus Christ; with God's perspective on problems, we can move our world.

Some, because of a cultural background, a family situation, life's tensions, or biochemical makeup, find it easy to become angry. God knows all about our emotions, yet He still loves us. We can confess our anger to God and begin to mature in love. Paul is realistic: He does not say *we* are not easily angered (or provoked) but that *love* is not easily angered. Someone has said, "The love of God will not lead you where the grace of God will not keep you." God can sustain His children emotionally whatever they're up against.

Love keeps no record of the wrong. This phrase likely reflects Zechariah 8:17: "Do not plot evil against your neighbor." The word *logizetai* means to calculate carefully. But to keep a record of wrong only makes us smaller people inside.

On the other hand, some glibly say forgive and forget. However, besides being unrealistic, such advice is psychologically impossible to practice. Rather than keeping score of wrongs, pursuing a deeper understanding can help a person recognize the other's good motives—which should be given the benefit of the doubt. And even when the motive is wrong, the grace of God can help us past it. It is on the basis of greater understanding, clearer communication, and the grace of God that we can truly forgive. And when resolved properly, a misunderstanding or hurt can become the basis of a deeper interaction and love between offended persons.

Although the goal is forgiveness and reconciliation, what if that is not possible? Do we simply suppress the hurt? No, we must learn from it. Whether or not we've been intentionally offended, Christ can work it out for our good. Indeed, He can use another's evil to develop our Christian character. Ultimately we will see the benefits of the painful situation. And if we refuse to live in the pain of the past, then we are freed to live in the present and for the future. It is an act of the spirit, mind, and will to choose God's way rather than listen to our emotions demanding that the score be evened. Charles Kingsley Barrett says, "What then does love do with evil? the final answer must be that it takes evil upon itself, and thus disposes of it."[28] We act like God did, "reconciling the world to himself in Christ, not counting men's sins against them" (2 Corinthians 5:19).

Pain is inevitable. Rather than avoid it, the issue ought rather to be how to handle it. Keeping a record of wrongs is not the way. It makes one suspicious, guarded, hostile.

Verse 6 says, "Love does not delight in evil but rejoices with the truth." It is a distorted pleasure we enjoy in thinking that we are superior, or that by criticizing another we make ourselves look good. Every person has strengths and weaknesses. We see shortcomings in others because we want to. Sometimes we are glad when others meet calamity. We feel they are suffering because they sinned. But love does not rejoice at the shortcomings, evils, injustices, or calamities of others.

On the other hand, matters of right and wrong, good and evil, do exist. When we accept evil, or resolve to live at peace with it, we delight in the evil. Ultimately evil and good relate to the warfare between the devil and God. The opposite of *the* evil is *the* good. No one is good but God. The evil must be replaced by nothing less than the authority and presence of God. The contrast is clear in Psalm 1. We may choose the way of the wicked, or choose to delight in the law of the Lord.

Jesus is the truth. Our joy is in the full truth of God prevailing, even if we find ourselves wrong on an issue. Truth is more than facts. From the facts alone we may prove ourselves right. Christ's truth will change our lives, help us forgive, and stimulate our desire for Christ's blessing the lives of others. Truth sets us free (John 8:32). Christians look to the day when His truth prevails, the devil is defeated, and God is glorified in everything.

Paul couples truth with love. In Ephesians 4:15 he encourages his readers to "speak the truth in love" (NEB). Love apart from truth leads to permissiveness. Truth apart from love can be judgmental. We need truth in love for healing and reconciliation. We need love in truth for edification. Because Jesus is the truth He is

---

[28]Barrett, *First Corinthians*, 304.

the standard by which love is tested. Because He died on Calvary, He is the example of how love is exercised.

To contrast with evil, one might think that Paul would use the word *righteousness:* "Love does not delight in evil but rejoices with righteousness." But when Paul uses the word, it carries meanings related to justification and salvation, a right standing before God—which is not Paul's point here. His contrast, like the Psalmist's, is between the way of evil and the way of truth and how such behavior affects those around us.

Verse 7 gives four basic attitudes of love that lead to positive, healthy change in any human situation. First, love "always protects." The verb *stego* ("protects") can mean one of two things: To throw a cloak of silence over what is displeasing in another person, or to bear up under, to endure.[29]

Those favoring the first interpretation see 1 Peter 4:8 as further amplification, "Love covers a multitude of sins." Love will not eagerly broadcast another's faults. This cannot mean sin will be overlooked, however, for sin may fester as a disease and hurt the Body. Love does not tolerate sin but reaches out to the sinner, discreetly handling the sin. To confront it wrongly may build barriers. Love finds a way to provide an acceptable solution.

The focus of the latter position is the bearing up under the problem or need. It relates to the noun form of the verb, the idea of pillars bearing up a roof. True endurance accepts the other's personhood and worth just as it is. Such an attitude seeks to compensate for another's weaknesses and develop them into strengths, to set free the gifts in that person. Love seeks to affirm the positive in a person whenever possible. All of Paul's other uses of *stego* have the idea of loving, supportive eagerness to help. This meaning also seems to fit best in this context.

---

[29]Bauer, *Greek-English Lexicon,* 766, prefers the idea of covering up, allowing for the bearing up, or enduring, as a possible meaning. Joseph H. Thayer, *A Greek-English Lexion of the New Testament* (Grand Rapids: Baker Book House, 1977), 586, and James Hope Moulton and George Millgan, *The Vocabulary of the Greek New Testament* (Grand Rapids: William B. Eerdmans, 1972), 587, argue for the bearing up, or enduring, citing all of Paul's other usages in 1 Thessalonians 3:1,5 and 1 Corinthians 9:12.

Eastern philosophy is tolerant and accepting of other people but in a passive way. "Let everyone sweep the snow from his own doorsteps, and do not worry about the snow of your neighbors," is a saying among the Chinese. And Confucius said, "What you do not wish others to do to you, do not do to them." Jesus stated this in positive terms: The Christian goes the extra mile. We all know how we like to be treated. We should take the initiative and treat others the same way. Biblical love means active acceptance of others, desiring to include them in fellowship. Although this love teaches us not to be judgmental, it does not allow us to be virtual isolationists, indifferent to others. It casts us in the role of helping others fulfill their potential.

Second, love "always trusts." Faith must be expressed in a person to draw out the best in him. Paul does not speak of blind acceptance of all statements and dreams of other people. But often we emphasize the negative because of our own personal shortcomings: We blame, we despise, we slander. We become suspicious of motives. People need people who believe in them. We must try to put the best interpretation on people's actions. Because all people are made in God's image, tremendous potential lies within every human being. How much greater potential lies within believers, saved and filled with the Holy Spirit!

Relating this truth to the gifts, we must assume the best motive for the one sharing. Where carnality is evident, appropriate discipling must follow, but the weakest Christian has great potential in the Lord's service. What appears as pride may be the immature, yet sincere, sharing of a gift. In such cases, simple instruction would help greatly. Condemnation may be interpreted as personal rejection. Somebody had faith in us, and helped free us for ministry. Let us set others free.

Third, love "always hopes." As faith without works is dead, so faith without hope is short-lived. I love my children as they are, but I also have hopes they will mature and grow. Growth takes place in a dynamic husband-wife relationship or any other healthy relationship as well. God loves us just as we are, but He also has a plan for our lives. On the human level, love without hope is frustration. It is God's glorious hope that gives direction and meaning to our faith.

Some glibly say to their friends, "I believe in you." The Christian is able to say, "I believe in you, that the image of Christ is being formed in you!" Paul was confident that what God had begun in the Philippians would be completed (Philippians 1:6).

Love itself provides great hope. God's love provided an eternal plan for our lives. The love we have for others gives them hope. No matter how betrayed or devastated by the ravages of life, people can feel accepted in the family of God.

Fourth, love "always perseveres." Such an attitude is necessary for change. This stanza began with patience with people; it concludes with patience in situations. To let circumstances overrun us is not patience. The picture is not of one groaning underneath the load, but of one aggressively carrying the load *(hupomones)* as a stout-hearted soldier. What a freedom when a person can commit a matter to God! The pure in heart will see God at work in all situations: past, present, and future.

Paul could even praise God in a Roman prison—though other believers criticized him, tried to stir up trouble, and sought to take advantage of the situation at his expense. Nevertheless, he rejoiced that, through his chains, the gospel was being advanced, more were boldly preaching the Word, and God was glorified (Philippians 1:12–18). Ultimate results are in His hands. Wait on Him to do His part. Our prayer then becomes, "Let me be clay in the potter's hands. Use me as an instrument of your redemption in this situation." We can seek transformation and victory regardless of the trial, whether it includes people or circumstances.

Perseverance and hope are interrelated. "Hope animates and is nourished by endurance."[30] Because we have the blessed hope of His coming, we can face all manner of difficulties. Smedes reflects on the combination of courage and patience in this word. We need both. "Courage alone wastes its power by settling only for total victory now; patience alone would eventually accept evil as our inescapable destiny."[31] Romans 5:2–3 says we rejoice in tribulation

---

[30]Findlay, *1 Corinthians,* 900.

[31]Smedes, *Love Within Limits,* 130.

as well as in hope. Romans 5:1–5 pictures a cycle of Christian maturing that starts with hope and ends with hope. (See figure 3.)

God uses sufferings to produce perseverance in us. This, in turn, develops character. The word "character" in Greek is from *dokimos*, referring to that which is tested and approved. Our experiences will be positive if we have the endurance to see God's hand bring the victory. Then we will grow in greater assurance of hope in the glory of God. If we can rejoice in both hope and tribulations, indeed, nothing can stand against us. (See James 1:4–5; Romans 12:12.)

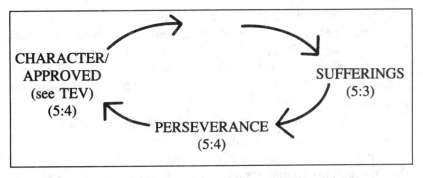

Figure 3. A Cycle of Christian Maturation

Through God's love in us, we can accept people for who they are, have faith in what God is doing in them, see the hope of God's image worked out through their lives, and patiently await God's outcome. Our families and churches would never be the same if we allowed God to release His love through us. For just as God sees the best in us and seeks to develop it, so we are to see the best in others and draw it out of them. This is the truth of 1 Corinthians 13:7.

1 Corinthians 13:8–13
Love Never Fails

⁸Love never fails. But where there are prophecies, they will cease; where there are tongues, they will be stilled; where there is knowledge, it will pass away. ⁹For we know in part and we

prophesy in part, ¹⁰but when perfection comes, the imperfect disappears. ¹¹When I was a child, I talked like a child, I thought like a child, I reasoned like a child. When I became a man, I put childish ways behind me. ¹²Now we see but a poor reflection as in a mirror; then we shall see face to face. Now I know in part; then I shall know fully, even as I am fully known. ¹³And now these three remain: faith, hope and love. But the greatest of these is love.

Paul now shows how gifts must be exercised in light of "perfection." Gifts are only tools, means to God's goals for His church. Because of the temporal and partial nature of gifts (they are for us only while we are on this earth and no one person—only the Holy Spirit—is the container and dispenser of all the gifts), love must be the guiding principle for exercising them until the return of Jesus Christ.

Some interpret "when perfection comes" (13:10) to mean gifts were needed only for the first century, i.e., until the completion of the Bible, which was in A.D. 96. This view has three difficulties:

First, the context doesn't even hint that Paul is referring to a completed canon or even a perfect Church. The Church will not reach its final state, without spot or wrinkle, until the coming of the Lord. So Paul can only be talking about the Judgment Day.

Second, in the parallelism of the passage, when perfection comes, we shall see face to face and shall know fully. Neither of these things has happened yet, and again can be fulfilled only at the coming of the Lord.[32] When tongues cease, so will the gifts of knowledge and prophecy.[33]

Third, although Scripture was theoretically complete by A.D. 96,

---

[32]The argument that the Greek middle verb *pausontai* means tongues will cease of themselves and that the active verb *katargethesontai* means prophecies and knowledge will pass away—that is, that Paul is deliberately demeaning tongues in comparison to prophecy and knowledge—is not in view here. Nor is Paul answering a question about which of the three gifts will stop first. He *is* making a comparison: between the partial and the complete. Both Fee, *First Corinthians,* 643–44, and Carson, *Showing the Spirit,* 66–67, effectively answer this argument.

[33]Obviously only the gift of knowledge, not knowledge in general, is referred to here. If all knowing ceased, so would our existence. Yet there is a future knowledge of God (1 Corinthians 13:12).

practically speaking, the whole canon was neither collected nor made available to the church at large until the invention of the printing press and translations into the vernacular. Even today many nations and tribes have not yet received God's Word. What does this mean for the position that a completed Bible means no more gifts? It would imply that the gifts should operate in language groups that have received only a witness of the gospel and not a complete translation of the Bible—a curious, if not absurd, thought.[34]

In 13:9–12 three "now-when" phrases are seen in parallel form. Each "now" refers to partial knowledge and its impartation in this age. Each "when (then)" refers to the day of full understanding, when we shall see Him face to face.

However, 13:11 contains a "when" that refers to childhood days. Three possible interpretations of the word "child" follow: "Child" may refer (1) to the church now that needs maturity, (2) to this present age as the age gifts belong to, or (3) to practices that should be put aside now.

The first view, that Paul refers to the Corinthian believers as children needing maturity, is weak. Paul does not normally describe the Church as a child, though the Corinthians acted childishly. The childish behavior of the Corinthians belonged to the world of non-believers![35] For Paul, there is a Christian way of behavior and a

---

[34]Ronald A. N. Kydd, *Charismatic Gifts in the Early Church* (Peabody, Mass.: Hendrickson Publishers, Inc., 1984), 87, documents carefully how the gifts were very widespread in the church, not only in the first century, but through A.D. 200. It was only after people began questioning the gifts in the third century that manifestations began to diminish.

[35]1 Corinthians 3:1 has often been used to support the idea that carnal Christians behave in a certain way. Actually, the contrast through the first three chapters is between those perishing and those being saved (1:18), the wisdom of this age and God's wisdom (1:20–31), human eloquence and the Spirit's power (2:1–5), the revelation of this age and the revelation of the Spirit (2:6–16), and the worldly and the spiritual (3:1–23). The Corinthian Christians were not reverting to carnality as a middle stage between non-Christian and spiritual Christian. They were actually reverting to non-Christian methodology and attitudes! Paul exhorts Christians to know they fully belong to Christ and should act that way.

Modern interpreters may confuse Hebrews 5:11–14 with 1 Corinthians 3:1, but Hebrews is addressing Christians of Jewish background reverting to Jewish practices, not to pagan practices. Neither can the (positive) analogy of 1 Peter 2:2 to sincere, newborn believers drinking milk be compared to this rebuke of the worldly

non-Christian one. When we are saved we become adult children of God, responsible for our calling and privileges. Maturity is not the issue of this passage.

As for the second view, that "child" refers to the age that gifts belong in, it seems weak because Paul declares that he has become an adult and has put away childish things. Besides, the word for child is "infant." Are the gifts for the infant age in contrast to being for the adult age? If so, the natural conclusion would be to try to put away childish things as one matures to adulthood.

The third view is that Paul is again confronting the carnal, selfish, childish approaches of the Corinthians. The gifts are not childish, but the ways they were being exercised were.

Now we are adults. An adult should think through issues, then speak. Literally 13:11 says, "When I have become a man, I have abolished the things of the infancy period." The perfect tense of each verb indicates it has happened, and the results should be apparent: I should behave like it. Now we are adults, but not perfected. We know and share in part. The intrinsic nature of the gifts indicates they are only for the present age, so Christians should exercise gifts Christianly and maturely, not as non-Christians behave, but in light of the judgment day of Christ.[36] This is the most likely interpretation of this verse.

The gifts are only tools, the means to an end. Prophecies, tongues, and a word of knowledge are mentioned here as samples of three categories of gifts: ministries, worship, and teaching. All gifts are only temporary. Only love never fails. In heaven the questions will

---

wise Corinthians. Newborn, spiritual believers will have rid themselves of malice, deceit, hypocrisy, envy, and slander (1 Peter 2:1), the very sins the Corinthians were guilty of!

Note how negatively Paul uses the word *nepios* (translated "child" in 1 Corinthians 13:11): Romans 2:20—the legalizer is a teacher of infants (*nepion*); Galatians 4:3—when we were children (nepioi), we were in slavery under the basic principles of the world; Ephesians 4:14—we will no longer be infants (*nepioi*). This position is in contrast to Colin Brown, ed., *The New International Dictionary of New Testament Theology*, vol. 1 (Grand Rapids: Zondervan Publishing House, 1975), 281–283; and Bauer, *Greek-English Lexicon*, 537.

[36]To put it another way, the Christian should live in the tension of the now and the not yet rather than in the tension of his pre-Christian days and after he becomes a Christian (the before and the now).

not be, What gifts did you manifest? How many sermons did you preach? What group did you belong to? The issue will be the glory of God as it is perfected in and through His people. We need to ask the right questions now.

We see only partially (13:12). Paul refers to the famous Corinthian bronze mirrors, the finest in his day. The issue is not so much distorted vision as indirect vision. One looked through (*dia*) them, because the image appeared to lie on the farther side. Barrett makes the analogy with Alice in *Through the Looking Glass,* where the virtual image produced by a mirror's surface appears to lie on the farther side.[37] To "see in a glass" may refer to prophetic revelation. There is no lessening or obscuring of the revelation, only that one day we will have direct experience of seeing God face to face.[38]

Paul says we see in a riddle (lit., "enigma"). The reference is to Numbers 12:6–8, where God *speaks* to Moses "face to face, clearly and not in riddles" (v. 8; see also Deuteronomy 34:10). Communicating to other prophets God used visions and dreams. What the prophets said often had to be explained. This is the state of our insight now as compared with the full, direct knowledge when we see Christ face to face.

This future revelation is greater than that which Moses received on Sinai. When Moses saw God face to face, God's glory was upon Moses' face as he came before the people of Israel. Moses had to cover his face. Paul gives two reasons for the covering. First, it was too glorious to behold. Second, it was a glory that would fade (2 Corinthians 3:7–18). We are able to behold the unfading glory of God with the veil taken away (2 Corinthians 3:17–18). Even so, we look indirectly in a mirror. One day we will see face to face and fully understand. Now, no matter how distinct the message, our understanding is limited.

---

[37]Barrett, *1 Corinthians,* 307. See also Brown, *Dictionary of New Testament Theology,* vol. 2, 756, and Fee, *1 Corinthians,* 647–648. This is in opposition to NIV and most commentators, who translate "we see but a poor reflection."

[38]Gerhard Kittel, *Theological Dictionary of the New Testament,* trans. and ed. Geoffrey W. Bromily, vol. 1 (Grand Rapids: William B. Eerdmans, 1964), 178–180, has a full discussion of the usage of the word *esoptron,* "mirror," among Jewish rabbis and Philo as clear prophetic vision.

Paul places himself at a future standpoint, looking back at the point of his present condition (13:12).[39] One day we will know Christ exactly as He now fully knows us. The word "just as" is always used by Paul to mean "exactly as."[40] There will be no distortion, ambiguity, or indirectness in heaven. The word for "know" in 13:12 *(epignosis)* suggests full knowledge. Here Paul may be directing his comments to those who claimed special revelations from God. He says that only in heaven will we have full knowledge. Paul does not refer to the measure of knowledge, but the kind of knowledge: None of us will know as much as God, but the kind of knowledge must be heavenly in and of itself (i.e., revelational).

The conclusion of the matter is found in 13:13. Faith, hope, and love will abide throughout eternity. But why is love the greatest of the three?

First, faith and hope are means to the end. We are saved by faith. That is our first step toward God. Then we live by the strength of the blessed hope. Faith and hope should lead us toward the goal of perfecting our love relationship with Jesus Christ. "Love is the end in relation to which the two other virtues are only means, and this relation remains even in the state of perfection."[41]

Second, faith and hope are eternally a part of love. But if faith is "being sure of what we hope for and certain of what we do not see" (Hebrews 11:1), why will we still need faith in heaven? And if "hope that is seen is no hope at all" (for "who hopes for what he already has"), why will we need hope in heaven (Romans 8:24)?

Faith is simple trust and surrender to the rulership of God. It is the eternal mark of our relationship with Him. In heaven we will not speak of great or small faith, strong or weak faith. We will glory in God's faithfulness to His plan and His people. Our faith here at best is partial. It will be complete there.

Hope here is marked by uncertainty and anxiety, which are not inherent to the nature of hope itself. Hope can grow even now.

---

[39]"I was fully known" (Greek aorist passive).

[40]P. C. Spicq, *Agape in the New Testament,* vol. 2 (St. Louis: n.p., 1965), 102.

[41]Frederic L. Godet, *Commentary on First Corinthians,* vol. 2 (Edinburgh: T. and T. Clark, 1886), 262.

James 1:2–4 shows how trials develop perseverance and perseverance develops maturity and completeness. From a point of maturity we are able to recognize God's sufficiency in our lives. In Hebrews, Christ is spoken of as giving us a greater revelation than that of angels, Moses, Abraham, the Old Testament priesthood, the tabernacle, and sacrifices. On the basis of this greater revelation we have a greater hope. Hebrews 2:1–4 exhorts us not to ignore so great a salvation.

In heaven hope changes to enlarged anticipation. Our glorified bodies will provide greater capacities for comprehending God. Our minds will not be static, but will explore the vastness of the glories of God's universe and truths of His kingdom. Blessed anticipation! Still, we will not have all knowledge, for then we would be God. Faith and hope are unchangeable qualities of an eternal relationship.

Love will be based on a fuller knowledge and a greater ability to communicate love. We will not need to hide within our personalities, since we all will genuinely know one another. With greater knowledge comes better communication and greater hope in God and in one another. We will grow to love more deeply and effectively than ever before. Love incorporates both faith and hope.

> The permanent essence of the creature is to have nothing of its own, to be eternally helpless and poor; every instant it must take possession of God by faith, which grasps the manifestations which He has already given, and by hope, which prepares to lay hold of His new manifestations. It is not once for all; it is *continually* that in eternity faith changes into vision and hope into possession. These two virtues, therefore, abide to live again unceasingly.[42]

As wonderful as relationships in heaven may be, how does this truth of the integration of faith, love, and hope apply on earth? One cannot say, "You may have faith, I will have love." All three must work together in each person. Using a mathematical formulation again, let us see the absurdity of cutting up the three qualities.

What if a husband were to say to his wife, "I have faith in you, and I have great hope for our relationship, but I have no love for

---

[42]Ibid., 261.

you''? One can imagine the exasperation, the dryness, and the desperation of such a marriage. A church with sound doctrine, mighty exploits of faith, and a strong anticipation of the coming of the Lord still needs love to hold it together. Galatians 5:6 speaks of a faith activated by love.

Faith + Hope − Love = No lasting relationship

Again, if the husband were to say to the wife, ''I have faith in you and I love you dearly, but I have no hope for us,'' one can sense the despair. A congregation may claim great faith and love, but if they do not look forward to God's ultimate plan for the future, they may become preoccupied with the present. In the face of continuing tribulation they would be tempted to give up. They would be like the seed planted in shallow ground that came up and then quickly withered. It would be as if they had forgotten the great message of the second coming of the Lord. Great hope leads to great maturation and great ministries. It is Lewis's observation that

> the Christians who did most for the present world were just those who thought most of the next. . . . It is since Christians have largely ceased to think of the other world that they have become so ineffective in this. Aim at Heaven and you will get earth ''thrown in'': aim at earth and you will get neither.[43]

Faith + Love − Hope = Despair

Can the husband say, ''I love you and really have great hope for this marriage, but, frankly, I cannot have faith in you''? Without daily trust, all the words about love are but wishful thinking. It becomes an emotional relationship, the spouses hoping that somehow the marriage will work out. A church may have a correct doctrine of the last days and the members may have a love for each other, but if they practice no faith in God through the daily obstacles, hope will become easily discouraged. Further, if members of the

---

[43]Lewis, *Mere Christianity*, 118.

body of Christ have no faith in each other, the distrust, criticism, and suspicion will tear the church apart.

Love + Hope − Faith = Wishful Thinking

The relationship of faith, hope, and love to the gifts of the Spirit becomes very clear. God may use the very person we would pass over (see 1 Samuel 16:6–7). He may be a new Christian or one with a personality quirk; he may not be known as the most spiritual—but he gives an utterance. Do we then say, "Thank You, Lord, for the gift, but please use another person next time"? Do we say to the one expressing the gift, "I love you and have hope for you, but please sit on the back pew"? We cannot deny anyone his proper place and ministry in the body of Christ.

On the contrary, Christians should thank God for the one sharing the gift as well as the gift itself. Some try to qualify the value of the gifts by whether a mature or immature vessel is used, but love allows each gift to do its part in building the body of Christ. Even a weaker vessel may powerfully encourage the church. That draws the sharer and the rest of the church closer together. It deepens fellowship and allows our worship to be acceptable to God. We must express faith, hope, and love toward each other. This will elicit the gifts.

Third, love is an essential attribute of God (1 John 4:18). As Barrett explains it, God does not need to trust or hope. Indeed, if He did, He would not be God. "But," writes Barrett, "if God did not love he would not be God."[44] Martin translates 13:13 "So then, *these three* are what lasts: faith, hope, love. But greater than these is the love (of God)."[45] Thus, greater than the gifts God gives and the faith, hope, and love we are to exercise toward one another is the eternal, redemptive, gracious *love of God* that guides us in all we do and gives us our identity.[46]

---

[44]Barrett, *First Corinthians,* 311.

[45]Martin, *Spirit and Congregation,* 39, 56. "First Corinthians 13 is an exquisite blend of Christology, soteriology, and ethics."

[46]Ibid.

One more area needs to be discussed in relation to faith, hope, and love in today's church. My observation is that a faith group, a love group, and a hope group have all developed in reaction to real issues, but have inadvertently polarized segments of the church.

The faith group grew out of believers' reactions to the negative view of humanity and anti-supernatural bias expressed by some segments of Christianity. Christians often spoke of serving a great God, but many did nothing to actualize that potential. The faith group wanted to claim their inheritance in Christ.

The hope group grew out of believers' reaction to the superficiality they believed they saw in much of Christianity. They taught on repentance, holy living, a simple life-style, helping the poor, and preparing to face sufferings, whether economic, political, or natural. Christians must take up the Cross and follow Christ. The hope group stressed the prophetic function of the Church.

The love group reacted against the focus on human sinfulness and the legalisms that pervaded the evangelical world through the 1960s. They saw the need for total acceptance of people as they were, sinners who could be forgiven by the grace of God, and for Christians who could be open and honest with each other. They believed that only in an atmosphere of total acceptance could people be motivated to change.

Each group found fault with the other two groups. The love group saw the faith group as selfish, non-biblical, western culture bound, and presumptuous and the hope group as judgmental and loveless. The faith group looked down on the other two groups for missing the real meaning of Scripture, living beneath their privilege, and being tied to tradition. The hope group felt the other two groups had misplaced their emphases: The love group was too permissive and was not really preparing the Church for the coming trials and the faith group concentrated too much on material blessings.

The Church needs a balance of faith, hope, and love. To go to an extreme is to reject the rest of the Body. More important than being right in these matters is how we relate to other believers. Do we isolate them? Do we look down upon them? Or do we, in patience, seek to help them grow in Christlikeness? Are we willing to learn from other members of the body of Christ? Paul, addressing the church at Thessalonica, spoke of their "work produced by faith, . . . labor prompted by love, and . . . endurance inspired by hope" (1 Thessalonians 1:3). Christians need to appreciate all parts of this triad as integral to, and primary in, relationships and service to God.

Further, 1 Corinthians 12 to 13 holds at least nine reasons for love being the necessary fruit among believers.

1. Because we are all one Body by His grace, no greater and lesser members exist. We must love each other as equals (12:13).
2. God has sovereignly placed each member in the Body according to His purposes, so love will set aside complaining or boasting (12:18–24).
3. We must have equal concern for each another (12:25–26).
4. The issue is not greater gifts, but exercising gifts in love (12:31): not the manifestation of the gift in its fullest degree, but manifesting it from the right motive (13:1–3).
5. Attitudes and behavior must correlate (13:4–7).
6. Gifts are tools that one day will not be needed, but love will always be needed (13:8,13).
7. Presently, our best efforts at communication are limited. Love, however, covers our flawed efforts at communication and develops appreciation for and deeper relationships with other believers (13:9).
8. Presently, we are limited in knowledge and understanding (13:12); we need not be similarly limited in love.
9. Faith, hope, and love are interconnected (13:13).

Exercise the gifts in love. This is the supremely excellent way. When we look at the full scope of these truths we stand back in awe at the creativity of God and the potential of His people. Love liberates this potential. Barth gives a fitting summary of the three stanzas of this chapter. "It is love alone that counts, love alone that triumphs, and love alone that endures."[47]

---

[47]Karl Barth, *Church Dogmatics,* vol. 4 (Edinburgh: T & T Clark, 1958), 825. See his discussion, "The Manner of Love," 824ff.

4

1 Corinthians 14

Paul contrasts the value of tongues and prophecy in church in four categories in 1 Corinthians 14: teaching (vv. 6–12), worship (vv. 13–19), signs for the unbeliever (vv. 19–25), and ministry to the church (vv. 26–33). Situations of misuse of gifts through lack of clear communication are brought up. Paul gives guidelines firmly, practically, wisely, and tenderly. He uses the term "brothers" four times to indicate his sensitivity.[1] He includes a short discourse on the disorder caused by the women (vv. 34–35), and then concludes his discussion on gifts in 14:36–40 with a brief summary.[2]

1 Corinthians 14:1–5
Contrasting Tongues and Prophecy

[1]Follow the way of love and eagerly desire spiritual gifts, especially the gift of prophecy. [2]For anyone who speaks in a tongue does not speak to men but to God. Indeed, no one understands him; he utters mysteries with his spirit. [3]But everyone who prophesies speaks to men for their strengthening, encouragement and comfort. [4]He who speaks in a tongue edifies himself, but he who prophesies edifies the church. [5]I would like every one of you to speak in tongues, but I would rather have you prophesy. He who prophesies is greater than one who speaks in tongues, unless he interprets, so that the church may be edified.

---

[1] 1 Corinthians 14:6,20,26,39.

[2] The following expressions emphasize the context of church worship: "in the church," *en ekklesia* 14:19,28,35; "the whole church [when it] comes together," *synelthe* 14:23; "when you come together," *synerchesthe* 14:26; "as in all the congregations of the saints," *en pasais tais ekklesias* 14:33.

139

The issues of 1 Corinthians 12:31 are resolved in the parallel commands of 14:1. Desire the greater gifts? No. But go after all gifts to share them in love. The issue is not the greater gift but the greater effectiveness. "Eagerly desire" in 12:31 and "eager to have" in 14:12 come from the word *zeloute,* from which we derive the word "zealot." To be zealous for spiritual gifts is good, even though the word carried negative as well as positive connotations. Jewish zealots in Palestine, in the name of nationalism and the overthrow of Roman authority, plundered their own people. To use the gifts for selfish purposes can hurt a congregation. But Paul is not afraid of zeal, as long as it is directed to the edification of the church.

In 1 Corinthians 14 "prophecy" is representative of all anointed utterances in the understood language (a word of knowledge, wisdom, revelation, etc.). "In the spirit" (vv. 2,14,15,16) is a reference to worship and ministry in tongues.[3] The contrast is between that which is immediately understood and that which needs interpretation.

Speaking in tongues is primarily directed to God, whether praise (Acts 2:11), mysteries (1 Corinthians 14:2), prayer (1 Corinthians 14:15), or thanksgiving (1 Corinthians 14:16–17). In this chapter, Paul shows the relative effectiveness of tongues in four areas: They excel in worship, in functioning as a sign, and in body ministry with guidelines (1 Corinthians 14:26–28), faltering only in the area of teaching. The gifts of tongues and interpretation are combined to minister to the congregation, encouraging other believers to tune their spirits to the Spirit of God. The immediate result is worship from the congregation. On the other hand, nonbelievers, those rating the gifts, and those seeking love only do not understand the nature of the gifts. They may consider tongues just another foreign language

---

[3]The phrase "in the spirit" is not always used to mean speaking in tongues in Paul's writings. Further, it is not necessary in Paul's writings to conclude that all prayer in the Spirit had to be in tongues and that prayer in understanding could not be "in the Spirit." See, for example, Romans 8:26 where the Spirit prays with "groans that words *cannot* express" (emphasis added). Ephesians 6:18 says "all kinds of prayers and requests" should be "in the Spirit," implying even times of silence or prayer in the understood language.

(1 Corinthians 14:11) or the one who speaks in tongues out of his mind (1 Corinthians 14:23).

Prophecy may not result in an immediate worship response because its primary direction is horizontal: to Christians and to the world. It may demand a response of obedience or self-examination. Prophetic speaking is effective in teaching, worship, body ministry, and evangelism, but not particularly as a sign. It is, after all, in the unbeliever's own language. If, however, it happens to be a revelation of the secrets of the unbeliever's heart, then it takes on a sign value for him. (Making this distinction in the essence of tongues and prophecy helps us to exercise them.)

Paul's use of the term "mysteries" (14:2) throughout his writings refers to divinely revealed truth. That which was hidden in Old Testament times is now revealed in Christ. When we speak in tongues we declare the wonderful works of God. The greatest truth is the incarnation of Christ, which opens the door for all people to be fellow heirs of God's promises. Paul does not use "mystery" to refer to subtle, hidden truths only a select few can understand. In the New Testament, mysteries are available to the understanding of all God's people. Without interpretation, these mysteries are understood only by God.

Paul considered tongues a language. There is no justification from the Scriptural text to state otherwise. Why would Paul say "kinds of tongues" (plural) or "speak ten thousand words in a tongue" or "speak in tongues of men and of angels," if it were only ecstatic gibberish? Further, he uses the same word for "speak" *(laleo)* to apply to both tongues and prophecy in 14:27,28,29. Paul introduced the work of the Spirit to the Corinthians, Ephesians, and other congregations; he knew what genuine tongues were. Peter, not knowing the languages at Cornelius's house, could say they were filled with the Holy Spirit, just "as he had come on us at the beginning" (Acts 11:15).[4]

---

[4]The following four arguments suggest that the occurrence of tongues in Corinth was non-linguistic gibberish, carrying over from experiences of ecstasy in either their Jewish or pagan backgrounds.

A. The word *glossai* (tongue) is used in Corinthian paganism and ecstasy and

The primary purpose of prophecy is to edify others; it results in strengthening, encouragement, and comfort (14:3). Frederick Dale Bruner goes so far as to say "It is questionable if, in Paul's thought, a gift can be said to 'exist' for the individual if it is not employed for the church."[5] Although his point is well-taken one must remember that the gift of tongues can be used for self-edification. No recorded case of tongues in Acts was interpreted because the purpose was the infilling of the Holy Spirit, not ministry to the congregation. Even self-edification, however, must be directed toward building

---

could refer to such. Yet Paul values tongues. Does he affirm pagan experience? No, he says pagan idols are dumb and decries their worship, which at times exhibited the loss of self-control. Stanley Horton, *What the Bible Says About the Holy Spirit* (Springfield, Mo.: Gospel Publishing House, 1976,) 27–28, says that the case for the ecstatic prophet in the Old Testament is weak. Even assuming the possibility of ecstatic prophets is no argument for tongues being non-linguistic. In chapters 48 to 50 of *The Testament of Job*, trans. R. P. Spittler (Garden City, N.Y.: Doubleday & Company, Inc., 1983), vol. 1, *Apocalyptic Literature and Testaments*, ed. James Charlesworth, 829-866, the daughters of Job are heard speaking in tongues identified as that of angels, and Jewish rabbis thought it was real language (see James H. Charlesworth, *The Old Testament Pseudipigrapha*, vol. 1 [Garden City: Doubleday, 1983], 866). Some rabbis, likely out of patriotism, thought tongues of angels was Hebrew. Origen felt angelic tongues were superior to human language. (See Archibald Robertson and A. Plummer, *A Critical and Exegetical Commentary on the First Epistle of St. Paul to the Corinthians* (Edinburgh: T & T Clark, 1911), 288.

B. Tongues of angels in 1 Corinthians 13:1 may involve ecstasy. But Paul does not oppose tongues of angels, or suggest mere toleration of it. He lists each gift here at its zenith, its most perfect manifestation. Tongues of men implies language. The corollary is that tongues of angels implies the finest possible expression of the gift.

C. 1 Corinthians 14:7–11 speaks of no distinction in sounds, therefore implying gibberish. But, in context, Paul speaks about a Greek talking to a foreigner, i.e., a non-Greek; the language of the latter would seem to have indistinct sounds. In 14:10 Paul says all languages have meaning, and in 14:11 he describes a hearer's lack of comprehension rather than a speaker's ecstasy.

D. The need for an interpreter indicates no one understands the tongues. Therefore, critics say, the gift is different from that in Acts 2. But on the contrary, the call for interpretation presupposes language—gibberish cannot be interpreted.

O. Palmer Robertson, "Tongues: Sign of Covenant Curse and Blessing," *Westminster Theological Journal* 38 (Fall 1975): 48–49, believes there is conclusive evidence that the tongues at Corinth were languages, just as at Pentecost.

[5]Frederick Dale Bruner, *A Theology of the Holy Spirit: The Pentecostal Experience and the New Testament Witness* (Grand Rapids: William B. Eerdmans, 1970), 289–90.

up others. We are part of the larger, redeemed community and the greater good of the community must be primary.

The word "encouragement" (14:3, KJV—"exhortation") literally means "to call alongside." It means to appeal to the will and arouse it to greater earnestness in Christian living. In John 14 to 16 the noun form, *parakletos,* is used to refer to the Holy Spirit as the "one called alongside of us." When one has received encouragement in immediate revelation or as a result of victoriously passing through a trial, he is able to call others alongside himself to share in his rejoicing. It would be hypocritical to call others to a place one has not experienced.

In the Greek, "comfort" and "encouragement" are closely related words.[6] "Comfort" may relate more to mutual loving interaction and ministry to one another rather than God's comfort of us or the comfort of the hope of His coming.[7] Paul uses this word again in his first letter to the Thessalonians (2:11-12), speaking of his method in ministering to them.

Barnabas was one of the prophets at Antioch. His name is from Aramaic, meaning "son of prophecy" (Acts 4:36). Luke tells us more of his character by calling him a "son of consolation" (Acts 4:36). What a wonderful combination for a prophet of God! He could clearly speak forth God's word in love; his personality en-

---

[6]Walter Bauer, *A Greek-English Lexicon of the New Testament and Other Early Christian Literature,* 2nd ed., trans. F. Wilbur Gingrich and Fredrick W. Danker (Chicago: University of Chicago Press, 1979), 618, gives as a first definition for *paraklesis* both "encouragement" (NIV) and "exhortation" (KJV). This usage goes as far back as Thucydides (fifth century B.C.), carries on through the Septuagint and into New Testament usage. Likewise, the definition for *paramythia,* translated both by NIV and KJV as "comfort," is "encouragement, especially comfort, consolation." This dates in Greek usage to the fourth century B.C.(Plato) and carries on through the Septuagint and the contemporaries of Paul. Paul uses *paramythia* in its noun and verb forms four times in the New Testament.

[7]G. Stahlin, "Comfort," ed. Gerhard Kittel, *Theological Dictionary of the New Testament,* trans. Geoffrey W. Bromiley (Grand Rapids: William B. Eerdmans, 1964), 785. Referring to *paraklesis* and *paramythia,* Stahlin says, "Since both terms combine admonition and comfort, it is hard to draw any clear distinction between them. . . . The only possible difference is that *paramytheomai* is not used directly for God's comfort or for eschatological comfort, but always for comfort in the earthly sphere."

hanced the message and gifts of God. A consoler by nature, he was also full of the Holy Spirit. That he was a strong man is clear. When the Jerusalem church was still afraid of Saul, Barnabas built the bridge to bring Saul into fellowship (Acts 9:26–28). Barnabas, as the key leader sent by the Jerusalem church to Antioch (Acts 11:22), went to seek Saul of Tarsus as preparation for the great Gentile outreach.

At the Jerusalem Council (Acts 15), helping to determine how Gentiles would enter the church, Barnabas proved an influential voice. Building relationships was a key element of his ministry philosophy. He did not want to confront Peter on his reluctance to eat with Gentiles (Galatians 2:13), likely because of Barnabas's reconciling nature. Yet he dared to confront Paul about his disqualifying John Mark for their evangelistic team (Acts 16:37–41).

Paul may have learned from Barnabas's example, for later, when Paul had to confront the Corinthian church, he shared from great love, distress, and many tears (2 Corinthians 2:1–5). Sometimes a church or an individual needs correction. By our compassionately facing a problem early, God is able to bring healing and peace out of confusion. Then He can encourage and comfort the whole church. No matter how confrontational the message, there can be room for consolation and encouragement.

Many scholars believe 1 Corinthians 14:5 teaches that prophecy is more valuable than tongues. The issue, however, is not relative value. That is, one tool is no more valuable than another. A hammer is not more important than a saw. The eye is not more valuable than the hand. Each member of the church has his function. What is vital to fulfilling God's purposes is exercising the tool (i.e., gift) at the right time and in the right way. A gift ministered clearly and in love is always greater than a misunderstood gift.

Others say that tongues with interpretation equals prophecy, that we have, in effect, two "tools" for the same purpose. If this is so, then why would God use two other gifts to do the work that prophecy does by itself? The gift of tongues primarily leads to vertical response, the gift of prophecy to horizontal edification. Equality of gifts is not the issue, but the validity of different gifts which have diverse functions.

1 Corinthians 14:6–12
The Gifts and Teaching

(For this passage I have used my own literal translation to show the parallels more clearly. My notations are added in the parentheses.)

> [6]**And now, brothers, if I come to you speaking in tongues, (then) what will I profit you unless I speak to you, either by a revelation or by knowledge or by prophecy or teaching?** [7]**Yet lifeless things giving sounds whether pipe or harp, if they give not a distinction in the sounds, (then) how will it be known what is being piped or harped?** [8]**For especially if a trumpet gives an uncertain sound (then) who will prepare himself to the battle?** [9]**So also you, through the tongue unless you give a clear word, (then) how will it be known that which is being said, for you will be speaking to the air?** [10]**Certainly many kinds of sounds are in the world, and not one without meaning.** [11]**If therefore I know not the meaning of the sound (then) I shall be a foreigner to the speaker, and the speaker a foreigner to me.** [12]**So also you, since you are zealots of spirituals (gifts) seek that you may abound to the edification of the church.**

Paul tenderly, yet firmly, speaks to them by calling them "brothers" and by using himself as a personal example. The absurdity of the great planter of churches, discipler of leaders, organizer of Gentile churches, and missions strategist coming only with the gift of tongues is unthinkable to the Corinthians. By his life and letters, Paul emphasized the great need for teaching.

The five "if-then" propositions of this passage emphasize the need for communication in the understood language. These statements remind us of 13:1–3—without love, the result is negative. Here, without clarity, the result is confusion. Four of the gifts listed here may relate to teaching: revelation, prophecy, knowledge, teaching.[8]

---

[8]Grudem goes to great length to link prophecy and revelation as a specially miraculous gift, not primarily used in teaching. For him, teaching as a gift is natural ability in expounding God's Word. Wayne Grudem, *The Gift of Prophecy in*

Paul illustrates this truth by referring to musical instruments. Useless in themselves, the instruments are made for specific purposes. The pipe and harp had a great part in both sad and joyous ceremonies.[9] The trumpet gave direction for battle, a usage Paul emphasizes here.[10] No one would rise up to face the enemy without a clear trumpet sound. In spiritual warfare the Church cannot afford to be talking to the air.

Any gift can be misunderstood—given carnal attitudes, improper methodology, or poor timing. In the matter of tongues this is readily apparent, since the language itself is not understood.

"Foreigner"(14:11) is from the Greek word that referred to non-Greek speaking peoples, not necessarily the uncivilized. In the family of God we cannot be foreigners to one another. Rather, we need to communicate on the level of understanding. It is not enough that the sender of the message is blessed, the receiver must be able to respond to the utterance.

Some felt they were more zealous spiritually than others.[11] Some emphasized tongues over other gifts. In spite of overrealized eschatology, divisiveness, and abuse of gifts among the Corinthians, Paul does not decry zeal for gifts. He tells them to direct the zeal so that the church may excel (12:31 and 14:12).

----

1 Corinthians (Lanham, Md.: University Press of America, 1982), 139–44. Martin and Dunn define the essence of prophetic ministry as not inspiration but intelligibility and see no problem relating prophecy and teaching. J. D. G. Dunn, *Jesus and the Spirit* (Philadelphia: Westminster Press, 1975), 229, and Ralph P. Martin, *The Spirit and the Congregation: Studies in 1 Corinthians 12–15* (Grand Rapids: William B. Eerdmans, 1984), 67.

[9]Likely the Early Church did not use musical instruments, though nothing was wrong with using them. Both in the tabernacle and temple, instruments were used. Mention of instruments abound in the Psalms. Harp and trumpet are found in Revelation. Perhaps the church met in temporal quarters. Perhaps no musical program had developed. Some think the church may have avoided using musical instruments because they were used in orgiastic Greek mystery rites or in a new hostile Jewish cult. Whatever the reason, the church was flexible, not legalistic, and adapted to the best ways of reaching their world.

[10]1 Corinthians 15:24–32,51–56 pictures Christians in the fight against death and the devil, with the trumpet signaling final victory. In the worship-warfare passages of Ephesians, the word to husbands and wives is to "submit," another military term. Life's issues are to be compared with eternal values and plans.

[11]See F. W. Grosheide, *Commentary on the First Epistle to the Corinthians* (Grand Rapids: William B. Eerdmans, 1955), 344.

1 Corinthians 14:13–19
The Gifts and Worship

[13]**For this reason anyone who speaks in a tongue should pray that he may interpret what he says.** [14]**For if I pray in a tongue, my spirit prays, but my mind is unfruitful.** [15]**So what shall I do? I will pray with my spirit, but I will also pray with my mind; I will sing with my spirit, but I will also sing with my mind.** [16]**If you are praising God with your spirit, how can one who finds himself among those who do not understand say "amen" to your thanksgiving, since he does not know what you are saying?** [17]**You may be giving thanks well enough, but the other man is not edified.** [18]**I thank God that I speak in tongues more than all of you.** [19]**But in the church I would rather speak five intelligible words to instruct others than ten thousand words in a tongue.**

Worship is the theme of this section. Paul compares worship in tongues and in the understood language, and concludes the need for both. The use of tongues is valuable in worship. If we are to "enter his gates with thanksgiving and his courts with praise" (Psalm 100:4), then how helpful to begin our worship and devotional time praying in tongues!

What roles do the mind and spirit play in worship? The mind is the rational, analytical side of a person. The King James Version appropriately translates "mind" as "understanding." Spirit is the inner essence that makes a person who he or she is. When a person becomes a Christian, the Holy Spirit renews his spirit and thus changes the whole person.

Fee suggests the phrase "my spirit" should be translated "my S/spirit" to indicate the presence of divine and human aspects of praying and singing in the Spirit.[12] This is my approach in this chapter. Paul is not saying that praying in the S/spirit does not include the mind or that praying with the mind cannot be in the S/spirit. He is simply differentiating praying in tongues and praying in the understood language.

---

[12]Gordon D. Fee, *The Epistle to the First Corinthians,* The New International Commentary on the New Testament (Grand Rapids: William B. Eerdmans, 1987), 670.

It is not the case that one method of prayer is superior to the other but rather that the methods are complementary. "In the S/spirit" is a reference to worship and ministry in tongues in 14:2,14–16. Praying in tongues is primarily worship or exhortation to others to worship God. Praying in the understood language helps believers make specific requests to God and consciously apply the truths of God to prayer life. It can also be an interpretation of the praying in tongues, so all may benefit from knowing the content of the prayer. The contrast is between that which is immediately understood and that which is not.

Then why does Paul say that when praying in the S/spirit the mind is unfruitful (14:14)? Two differing interpretations of the phrase "the mind is unfruitful" will help us see the issue of this verse:

1. The speaker's mind is dormant.
2. The Holy Spirit especially touches the spirit, personality, and emotions.

The first interpretation suggests that "the human mind does not produce the language."[13] The thought here is that the Spirit totally bypasses the mind, so that neither the speaker nor the listener has any benefit, that the speaker has no idea what he is saying. Many scholars hold to this view.

Many who hold this view tend to look upon tongues as a lesser gift than prophecy and thus to emphasize the value of the rational and to deemphasize the role of the experiential in worship. But beyond this, such a position denies the concept of incarnation, assuming the mind has no part at all to play in the gift of tongues. Although the spirit may transcend the rational, it may also include it. From 1 Corinthians 2:9–15, we see that spiritual persons through the Spirit may know (2:11), understand (2:12), express in words taught by the Spirit (2:13), discern (2:14), and make judgments (2:15).

The second interpretation emphasizes divine/human cooperation. Quotes from F. W. Grosheide and Bruner may help:

---

[13]Kenneth Barker, ed., *The NIV Study Bible* (Grand Rapids: Zondervan Bible Publishers, 1985), 1753.

> When a Christian spirit speaks in a tongue the understanding is not left out. . . . The one "spirit" may not touch the other "spirit" [i.e. Holy Spirit] at all, if the "understanding" does not cooperate. . . . "Spirit" views man as a personality, "understanding" as a knowing and thinking being. . . . When the spirit is renewed the understanding is also renewed, without however changing its operation. The renewed spirit may use the understanding, but it is not compelled to do so.[14]

> The Spirit does not exhibit himself supremely in sublimating the ego, in emptying it, removing it, or in ecstasy overpowering it, extinguishing or thrilling it, but in intelligently, intelligibly, christocentrically using it.[15]

The mind is not blanked out and put into neutral, as may be the case in some Eastern religions. That being so, the mind should not be wandering around in the world of politics, sports, and schedules when worshipping God. True worship requires the mind, as well as the spirit and the body.

One should at least sense whether one is praising God for His greatness, love, care, or holiness. Of all people in the congregation, the one praising God in the S/spirit should be a step closer to the interpretation, listening to what the Holy Spirit is doing within. Perhaps this is why he is responsible to pray for the interpretation. For if no one else will interpret, he must; it is, after all, *his* expression of praise. Of course, opportunity should be given to others for interpreting the utterance, so they may have the joy of exercising gifts. Then the one giving the utterance in tongues can confirm that others are sensing the same touch of the Spirit.

Paul says he will pray and sing "with [his] spirit" (14:15). The only difference between singing and speaking in the S/spirit is the same difference between singing and speaking with the understanding: music. Singing is not more spiritual or mystical than speaking. So why do we sing our hymns and choruses rather than speak them? Because music is a powerful tool to express the depths of a person's

---

[14]Grosheide, *First Corinthians*, 325–326.

[15]Bruner, *The Holy Spirit*, 287. Bruner is not sympathetic to the Pentecostal position, but his point here is valid.

worship to God. Nations and armies have discovered the power of music in battle or in uniting people in a cause. Likewise the church has recognized that music allows a release of the human spirit to express worship to God. Worship both in the S/spirit and with the understanding are important. However, singing with the understanding, though it may follow singing in the S/spirit, does not necessarily imply that it is the interpretation of singing in the S/spirit.

Is Paul discussing private devotions or public worship here? If it is private devotions, then Paul is asking them to pray for the interpretation for private edification. Although this is not to be ruled out as personally beneficial, the primary focus in this chapter is on public worship (14:16).

Who occupies the "room of the unlearned" (KJV), or uninstructed, (idiotes) in 14:16?[16] "Room" cannot refer to a place separated from the general gathering; such an arrangement was a later development in church history. How one defines idiotes in 14:16 should be consistent with its usage in 14:23. Six possibilities of who the idiotes were present themselves:

1. Believers who do not understand the tongues. This view fits 14:16 but not 14:23. In 14:23 the whole church (thus, all believers) gathers and then others enter in. "Will they not say you are out of your mind?" This question implies a different, smaller group who come in.

2. Believers who have not yet experienced tongues.[17] Because of the excesses at Corinth, some forbade others to speak in tongues. Also, some may have been as the disciples before Pentecost, or the Samaritans before the arrival of Peter and John. The baptism in the

---

[16]For both Luke and Paul the idiotes are in a place of honor. In Acts 4:13 Peter and John are described as "unschooled" (agrammatoi) and "ordinary" (idiotai) yet could claim the healing of a lame man. Paul is not ashamed to speak of himself as "not trained" (idiotes) in relation to eloquence in Greek rhetoric (2 Corinthians 11:6). There must be a place for these people when the church gathers (1 Corinthians 14:16,23). So although idiotes is used differently in Acts, 1 Corinthians, and 2 Corinthians, idiotes are not ever to be despised!

[17]Donald A. Carson, Showing the Spirit: A Theological Exposition of 1 Corinthians 12–14 (Grand Rapids: Baker Book House, 1987), 105.

Spirit did not always occur at the point of salvation. This explanation poses the same problem as the first: It fits 14:16 but not 14:23.

3. Unbelievers in both verses. If the *idiotes* were unbelievers, then Paul is saying in 14:23, "there come in those who are unbelievers or unbelievers." This is needless repetition. However, 14:23, using both *idiotes* and *apistoi,* could be translated "unbelievers who are untutored in the faith," speaking of one group rather than two.[18] This does not solve the problem of 14:16, however. Is the non-Christian expected to say amen to all that goes on in church?

Ervin believes the *idiotes* were anti-Pentecostal, non-Christian, Gnostic novitiates who joined the Christians regularly in worship.[19] The unbeliever would then be the Gnostic teacher. Gnosticism could accept many of the teachings of Christianity and yet deny its incarnational essence. This group was therefore half in and half out of the church. They needed to be evangelized. This meaning fits both the context and thrust of 14:16 and 14:23.[20]

4. The laity who would not understand spiritual mysteries as distinguished from those in public ministries. Classical Greek distinguished private persons from trained public officials. This is a weak option because the Early Church had no such gap between clergy and laity. Indeed, all Christians were expected to minister in the power of the Spirit.

5. Believers in 14:16 and unbelievers in 14:23.[21] The contexts are seen as separate, avoiding the problem of coordinating the two verses. But Paul seems to be isolating as a separate small group or

---

[18]Fee, *1 Corinthians,* 685.

[19]Howard M. Ervin, *These Are Not Drunken As Ye Suppose* (Plainfield, N.J.: Logos Books, 1968), 201–208. How early did incipient forms of Gnosticism infect the church? Did it go back as far as the first century? Nothing in the church fathers supports this. It is possible Paul faced a Gnostic problem in A.D. 55, but not probable.

[20]Ibid. Ervin raises the possibility that these are Gnostically-oriented persons present at Communion services. Some types of early Gnosticism might not have rejected the Communion as later Gnostic positions did. They might say amen if everything were explained clearly. For Paul, the object is to reach them, not reject them.

[21]Fee, *First Corinthians,* 673, Grosheide, *First Corinthians,* 330, Charles Kingsley Barrett, *A Commentary on the First Epistle to the Corinthians* (San Francisco: Harper & Row, Publishers, Inc., 1968), 324.

individual "one who finds himself among those who do not understand" (v. 16). "Everyone speaks in tongues" (v. 23), and these others come in.

6. Inquiring persons, Christian or non-Christian, open to spiritual things and evaluating them. This interpretation seems to fit the context. It is important that all people who are open-minded and searching for truth be able to respond positively to the Holy Spirit's working. If the whole church gathers and speaks only in tongues, the seeker and the unbeliever will come in and say Christians are out of their minds. They are justifiably antagonistic when disorder prevails. In Greek religious terminology *idiotes* refers to the un-initiated but inquiring person (thus see the NIV footnotes to these verses). "The *idiotes* are neither similar to the *apistoi,* nor are they full-fledged Christians; obviously they stand between the two groups as a kind of proselytes or catechumens."[22] There must always be a place for them.

Earnest seekers should have the opportunity to see the body of Christ in its full range of activities: worship, witness, fellowship, discipline. To be able to say " 'amen' "—to find relevant the ministry gift of another—is as vital as the sharing of that gift. Clear understanding is requisite to the seeker's wholehearted response. The Bible does not relegate the gifts to a corner of the church. Rather, it promotes their proper exercise and explanation. The church gathered was witness to what the church scattered in the world should be. The church gathered learns to worship and minister in the Spirit. Acts 1 and 2 form the pattern: The church gathered discovered its mission and chose a twelfth apostle. They waited on the Lord together, searched the Scriptures, and developed a powerful unity. Then they were filled with the Holy Spirit. The church scattered gave testimony to the dynamic power and love of God.

What were the "amen" and the "thanksgiving" (14:16)? Calvin

---

[22]H. Schlier in Bauer, *Greek-English Lexicon,* 371. Schlier's view is that both 14:16 and 14:23 refer to unbelievers who have indicated an interest in Christianity. Fred Fisher, *First and Second Corinthians* (Waco: Word Books, 1975), 224, and Harold Mare, *First Corinthians* (Grand Rapids: Zondervan, 1976), 273, agree, although Mare sees possibly Christians in 14:16 as well as unbelievers.

thought these terms related to the public prayer of one person (the thanksgiving), followed by the collective response of the congregation (the amen), similar to the worship ceremony in a Jewish synagogue.[23] But worship in the Early Church, although patterned after synagogue worship, was likely more spontaneous. The "amen" could well be a response to an utterance of thanksgiving in tongues. After all, the manifestation of each gift should be open to the response and evaluation of the rest of the body of Christ. One shares, another responds, and together the congregation learns how to worship God.

From God's standpoint, praising Him in tongues is well and good (14:17). He understands our yearnings to worship Him in ways beyond our natural, limited expression. Nevertheless, "you [singular] may be giving thanks well enough, but the other [*heteros: other of a different kind*] man is not edified." The issue at church is to build up others. A slight irony is expressed here. You are blessed by it but the other, the inquirer, is not. Indeed, the rest of the congregation does not understand the utterance either. They may understand you are being blessed and rejoice over it, but for them to be blessed, interpretation must come.

Most versions of the Bible translate 14:18 in such a way that Paul appears to boast about his zealous use of tongues, in effect beating the Corinthians at their own game.

But—since the original Greek manuscripts had no punctuation—there is an alternate reading of the Greek text. If the comma is changed to a period after the first phrase, Paul may simply be making two statements: "I give thanks to God. I speak in tongues more than you all" (valid for the best manuscripts Aleph, B, D). He is responding to the one in 14:17 who boasts of giving thanks to God. Paul may be saying, "You give thanks? I do too. You speak in tongues? I do more than you, not to boast about it, but because I fully realize its value." Codex C (Alexandrinus) supports this idea. It omits "speak" entirely, suggesting a reading of "I give thanks

---

[23]John Calvin, *The First Epistle of Paul the Apostle to the Corinthians,* trans. John W. Fraser, Calvin's New Testament Commentaries (Grand Rapids: William B. Eerdmans, 1960), 293.

in tongues more than you all." It is a straightforward statement of Paul's normal practice. He was confessing his reliance upon the Holy Spirit to accomplish God's work.

For Paul, praising in tongues was a normal part of the Christian life—not an occasion for boasting. But some of the Corinthians were doing just that, boasting of their spirituality, their insights into spiritual matters, their practice of tongues speaking. Paul—apostle, missions strategist, church planter, and writer of much of the New Testament—bore the burden of the churches and the persecution of the world: He needed self-edification; speaking in tongues was a matter of spiritual survival. He argued from experience; he knew the strengthening provided by spiritual gifts. Paul would be the last to deny the purpose and effectiveness of tongues. How could anyone with insight say he was "more spiritual" than Paul? What sets a Christian apart is his ministry to others.

Fee confirms this approach to 14:17–18 by suggesting that the lack of the conjunction "that" heightens the significance of the second sentence. Thus 14:18 is actually two separate ideas, with a focus on the second idea. The meaning of 14:17–18 is, " 'When praising God in tongues you are thanking God well enough. Indeed, I do this more than all of you. But what goes on in church is another story altogether.' "[24]

Paul then moves from the three basic statements in vv. 17–18 to the greater principle, "But in the church . . ." (14:19). Paul makes the contrast with a strong conjunction, "But" *(alla)*, and an emphatic placement of "in the church" at the head of the sentence. When the church assembles, instruction for building up the whole Body is preeminent. Paul wants to instruct others *(allous*—of the same kind). This means those who understand the same language, as opposed to the "other" in 14:17 who did not. Saved and unsaved alike may hear and respond to God's words. The word "instruct" is *katecheso,* from which the word "catechism" is derived. Although formal catechism developed later in the church, Paul sought to teach basic truths at every opportunity and especially in the church service.

---

[24]Fee, *First Corinthians,* 667, 675.

1 Corinthians 14:20–25
The Gifts and Sign Value

²⁰Brothers, stop thinking like children. In regard to evil be infants, but in your thinking be adults. ²¹In the Law it is written: "Through men of strange tongues and through the lips of foreigners I will speak to this people, but even then they will not listen to me," says the Lord. ²²Tongues, then, are a sign, not for believers but for unbelievers; prophecy, however, is for believers, not for unbelievers. ²³So if the whole church comes together^A and everyone speaks in tongues,^B and some who do not understand^C or some unbelievers come in, will they not say that you are out of your mind?^D ²⁴But if an unbeliever or someone who does not understand^C comes in while everybody is prophesying,^B¹ he will be convinced by all^D¹ that he is a sinner and will be judged by all, ²⁵and the secrets of his heart will be laid bare. So he will fall down and worship God, exclaiming "God is really among you!"

Paul is sensitive to three groups of people whenever ministry occurs: believers (14:1–39), inquirers (14:16,23), and unbelievers (14:20–25).[25] Our effectiveness depends on communicating to all three groups.

Paul quotes from Isaiah 28:11–12 for background to his argument on the sign purpose of tongues. "Law" can refer to Moses' writings or to the Old Testament in general; here it is the latter.

In Isaiah two themes predominate: repentance and judgment. God desired repentance, but the Israelites hardened their hearts, feeling insulted. The Israelites, particularly the drunken priests and prophets (v. 7), were the unbelievers in Isaiah's day. They accused Isaiah of speaking to them as if they were babies just being weaned from their mother's milk. They thought they were mature, when in fact they were childish, stubborn, and rebellious. So Paul, in keeping with the context of Isaiah, rebukes a similar element at Corinth,

---

[25]William Richardson, "Liturgical Order and Glossalalia in 1 Corinthians 14:26c–33a," *New Testament Studies* 32 (January 1986): 147, points out that "Paul's over-riding concern in chapter 14 is that of missionary witness."

"Stop thinking like children" (14:20) (an excellent translation of the Greek). For they, too, were being childish in their attitudes.

Paul's command implies we can, by an act of the will, break the cycle of immature thinking about gifts. We can judge the validity and purpose of all spiritual manifestations. Tongues can be exercised properly. If we are to be "immature" in some area, it should be in malice or revenge. Infants do not know what revenge is. If they are angered, they soon get over it, bearing no grudge.

Isaiah had warned that God would judge the Israelites through foreigners, and the language of these foreigners—which the Israelites would not understand—would remind them that Isaiah had warned them of God's judgment. Every time they heard the strange language, it would be a sign of God's rebuke: "You should have accepted your accountability to God!" The fulfillment of this prophecy was the invasion of the Assyrians, speaking a language incomprehensible to the Israelites.[26]

Paul uses the Isaiah passage simply as an illustration. It is not a Joel-like prophecy of the outpouring of the Holy Spirit. The word "unbelievers" may indicate a hardened state of unbelief.[27] But such hearts may be aroused by tongues, an indication, a sign, that possibly something supernatural is going on. Prophecy then follows, exhorting the aroused hearts to repent. If they harden themselves to

---

[26]Robertson, "Tongues," 43–53. He sees the basis of this curse as beginning with Deuteronomy 28:49, repeated in the eighth century B.C. in Isaiah 28:11, and again in the sixth century B.C. in Jeremiah 5:15. The ultimate fulfillment of the curse on Israel is found in the New Testament, and particularly here in 1 Corinthians. Although one may not agree with all his conclusions, he does point out that tongues is uniquely singled out as the sign for unbelievers.

However, if tongues in the Church Age are seen as a *fulfillment* of prophecy in Isaiah 28, then one might fairly expect tongues in the New Testament to be regarded as a sign of judgment on unbelieving Jews, because Isaiah's teaching is based on the warning of Deuteronomy 28:49–50. But even Acts 2 contains no indication that tongues is construed as a sign of judgment on the Jews. Neither is judgment the context of either 1 Corinthians or Acts. The Jews never received it that way then, nor would Jew or Gentile perceive tongues as being judgment upon them today.

[27]See Zane C. Hodges, "A Symposium on the Tongues Movement: The Purpose of Tongues," *Bibliotheca Sacra* 120 (1963): 229–230, and Findlay, *1 Corinthians*, 910: "believing"—present active participle; "unbeliever"—adjective with the article (thus used as a noun), which may imply a static, confirmed unbelief.

even that, what else must God do? Tongues then become a sign of judgment on stubborn hearts.[28]

The events on the Day of Pentecost bring out the sign value of tongues. Tongues attracted a crowd. Such a crowd may have held both the spiritually alert as well as the spiritually indifferent. But then Peter's prophecy, his prophetic messsage, touched people's lives; they were "cut to the heart" (Acts 2:37).

The complexity of 14:22–24 has resulted in many differing interpretations of who the sign is for, who the unbelievers are, and whether prophecy, like tongues, is a sign. I have summarized the four basic possibilities:

1. The reverse of what is stated is really what Paul meant. Tongues are a sign to believers, and prophecy is a sign for unbelievers. Since tongues mainly bless believers, we need prophecy to reach unbelievers (J. B. Phillips translation). There is no textual basis for this. It is a novel approach to try to solve the difficulty.

2. Prophecy is a sign like tongues. If 14:22 is parallel, then the word "sign" should be added in the second statement. It should read: "Tongues, then, are a sign, not for believers but for unbelievers; prophecy, however, is [a sign] for believers, not for unbelievers."

This view generally construes Paul's reference to the Isaiah prophecy as negative. That is, since tongues are not understood and will not lead anyone to repentance, they must have a limited place in the church. Although a "sign" could be an indication of either God's favor or disfavor, we can easily see how stammering lips and another tongue were a sign of disfavor, i.e., judgment, in the Old Testament. At the same time, when prophecy was taken away (Psalm 74:9), this too was a sign of judgment, and when prophecies would abound again, this was an indication of the arrival of the day of the

---

[28]W. E. Vine, *First Corinthians* (Grand Rapids: Zondervan, 1961), 193–95; Robertson and Plummer, *First Corinthians,* 316–19; and Frederic L. Godet, *Commentary on First Corinthians,* vol. 2 (Edinburgh: T & T Clark, 1886), 712–25.

Messiah, a sign of God's favor upon His people (as in Luke 1 to 4).[29]

There are two objections to this position. First, it does not make sense to say that prophecy is a sign for believers, therefore you must prophesy to unbelievers. Second, in 1 Corinthians 14 the strength of prophecy is in the clarity of its message, not in its sign value.

3. "Unbelievers" were false teachers with a Gnostic orientation.[30] They may have refused to call the historical, incarnate Jesus their Lord (12:3).[31] They denied the need for a physical resurrection, emphasizing enlightenment and blessing in the present rather than in the future.

It could be that originally these persons were as much a part of the Corinthian church as Simon Magus was a part of the fellowship in Samaria. But then they became enamored of strange doctrines and, after gaining influence at Corinth, mixed their doctrines with Christianity.

If the "unlearned" of 14:16 is a Gnostic novitiate and the unbeliever of 14:23 is the Gnostic teacher, Paul is hoping the novitiate may still be open to the gospel, and the false teachers may be aroused to the fact that God may judge them. Neither student nor teacher must occasion false accusations about the church's discipline and worship. The word of God must be unhindered; there must be no disarray in the ministry of gifts.

4. The gift of tongues focuses on the sign aspect; the gift of prophecy focuses on content. Prophecy emphasizes the grace of God

---

[29]Grudem, *Gift of Prophecy,* 201. Fee, Carson, Barrett, and Grosheide hold this view. Bruce takes a slightly different slant, suggesting "prophecy is a sign for believers in the sense that it produces believers." F. F. Bruce, *First and Second Corinthians,* The New Century Bible Commentary (Grand Rapids: William B. Eerdmans, 1971), 133. Interestingly, Barrett, *1 Corinthians,* 324, sees prophecy as a sign of judgment to the Corinthian Christians in the same way tongues served as a sign of judgment to the unbelievers. The Corinthians shut their ears to words that revealed their faults and unfulfilled duties, preferring the speaking in tongues.

[30]Among those seeing some type of Gnosticism at Corinth are Schmidtals, Ervin, and Martin. Especially see Ervin, *Not Drunken,* 202–03.

[31]Of sixteen Pauline references to *apistos* for "unbeliever," fourteen are in the Corinthian letters. In 2 Corinthians 6:14, 11:22, and possibly 4:4 the allusion is to false teachers. Titus 1:15 refers to false teachers as the *apistos.* Some of the Early Church fathers used the word the same way and in a Gnostic context.

being extended to both the unlearned and the unbeliever for salvation. Prophecy serves to confront everyone with God's word and invite repentance. O. Palmer Robertson points out, " 'Tongues' serve as an indicator; 'prophecy' serves as a communicator. 'Tongues' call attention to the mighty acts of God; 'prophecy' calls to repentance and faith in response to the mighty acts of God."[32]

> Tongues are a miraculous sign of God's presence. They may harden some hearts and soften others. The results depend upon the responsiveness of the listeners.[33]

All gifts have *sign* value and *content* value. Healings have sign value for those observing and content value for those healed. The mere fact of tongues is a sign to unbelievers. Their content, however, is significant only if the unbeliever understands the tongue, either through interpretation or through knowledge of the language. Prophecy, on the other hand, has more content value than sign value. In fact, some prophetic utterances may go unrecognized as gifts because they are in the understood language. Prophecy can serve as a sign to the unbeliever when it specifically reveals his sins.

> Prophecy is an inspired utterance proceeding from a supernatural intuition, which penetrates "the things of man," "the secrets of his heart," no less than the "things of God" (2:10ff): the light of heart-searching knowledge and speech, proceeding from every believer, is concentrated on the unconverted man as he enters the assembly.[34]

By referring to the superscribed notations in verses of 14:23–25 (p. 155) one can observe the following: The "A" statement sets the occasion—the whole church is gathering together. The "B" or "B₁" statement discusses the option of everyone speaking in tongues or prophesying. The "C" statements assume the presence of the

---

[32]Robertson, "Tongues," 52.

[33]Mare, *First Corinthians,* 274.

[34]George G. Findlay, "St. Paul's First Epistle to the Corinthians," in *The Expositor's Greek Testament,* ed. W. Robertson Nicoll (London: Hodder and Stoughton, Ltd., n.d.), 911.

unbeliever or unlearned one. The "D" or "D$_1$" statement discusses the results. The parallels are readily seen.

The question is, Does statement "B" in 14:23 mean everyone speaking in tongues at the same time or one at a time? If the same time, then tongues in corporate worship is discouraged by Paul. If one at a time, Paul is making room for the exercise of other gifts, not wanting tongues to dominate the whole service. That Paul is not denying the value of corporate worship in tongues should be evident for the following reasons:

1. 14:23–24 present two parallel statements:

"B"—everyone speaks in tongues" (14:23).
"B$_1$" everyone is prophesying (14:24).

If 14:23 means everyone speaking at the same time, then 14:24 also refers to everyone prophesying at the same time. Obviously 14:24 cannot mean that. It must mean all may prophesy in turn. Everyone prophesying at the same time would be seen as confusion, if not lunacy. This is confirmed in 14:31. Paul discourages the domination of the whole service by teaching that those who prophesy should speak "in turn" (14:27).

2. In 14:27 Paul limits the number of times tongues and interpretation should be manifested. This further confirms that the issue here is that believers must not dominate the service with one gift.

3. In Acts 2:4; 10:44–46; 19:6, all spoke in tongues corporately in public worship settings. Although this may not be proof of a normative pattern that public worship must include tongues, neither can corporate worship in tongues be denied from a biased interpretation of 1 Corinthians 14:2, 22–25. Paul and Luke do not contradict one another.

4. The purpose of tongues is to rejoice and praise God. Tongues with interpretation will encourage others to worship God. To then deny people the opportunity to respond by worshipping God in S/spirit would seem to be a contradiction. Paul would, in effect, be saying to the rest of the congregation, "You may worship with understanding in church, but not in the S/spirit. Only two or three may be allowed that experience."

5. Paul valued the gift of tongues for worship (14:2), for self-edification (14:4), for praying in the S/spirit (14:14), for giving thanks (14:17), and as a sign to the unbeliever (14:22). He spoke in tongues more than the Corinthians did. They, however, had abused the gift: Some may have believed they were speaking in angelic languages (13:1), services may have been dominated by tongues (14:23), and speakers apparently interrupted each other to give their message in tongues, disregarding interpretation (14:27–28). But Paul appeals to their maturity. Without dampening their enthusiasm or forbidding their speaking in tongues, He gives guidelines.

6. The issue of this passage is not whether to deny worship in tongues but how to participate in worship to bless others. Thus, some who deny the efficacy of mutual worship in tongues may be doing so from a cultural perspective. For example, the Western mindset is afraid of any proposition that seems to substitute the experiential for the rational.[35] The Eastern mindset, on the other hand, has no problem with the experiential as a way of perceiving reality. In fact, the Eastern mind perceives supernatural things more readily than the Western mind.

The Pentecostal-charismatic revival around the world has not apologized for genuine celebration. It has sought wholistic worship from the entire person. The individual spirit is not suppressed for the corporate Body. Rather, it is fully utilized and controlled for that Body. Tongues have not been relegated to the prayer closet, implying a sharp distinction between public and private worship. Indeed, we learn through the model of corporate worship how to worship in private devotions. Our sensitivity to God in private devotions should enhance our sensitivity to our fellow believer's needs during public worship. Public and private worship can enhance each other because the essence of worship is the same.

The church gathered should be a promise of what Christians are

---

[35]Richardson, "Glossalalia in 1 Corinthians," 148, says, "In an era when great stress is placed on a more cerebral approach to religion, it is conceivable that Paul's counsel might easily stress the need for more 'praying in the Spirit' rather than less."

when scattered. Gathered, we learn about God's Word, spiritual dynamics, and interaction. We declare to the world: This is our life—watch us! We have things to learn, but we have nothing to hide. To unbelievers and inquirers, the believers should explain what is happening. This can be a time of instruction for all. If all understand there are mutual times to praise God, basic order should be evident.

The inquirer and unbeliever will receive the clear witness of all that happens and be held accountable by God for that. They will be judged (sunakrino—"sifted judicially, put on trial") by God. Before Him all men must be accountable for what they know and have experienced. If the church truly ministers, believers will be edified and unbelievers will be converted.

Some prophetic utterances will speak right to the heart of the unbeliever (14:24–25). It could be a revelation of either hidden sin or a spiritual hunger that has been covered with a false smugness or security. In either case, it is clearly revealed in contrast to God's love and power manifested in Christian worship services. For example, James, the brother of Jesus, seemed critical of and indifferent to Jesus during His earthly ministry; yet later James appears as a leader of the church. And his epistle, more than most of the New Testament other than the Gospels, abounds with quotes from Jesus' teaching. What seemed like a hardened heart was really a hungry heart tuned to seek truth.

After speaking generally of inquirers and unbelievers, Paul stresses that God will speak individually to the sinner so that genuine repentance can take place. " 'God is really among you' " is a reference to Isaiah 45:14, " 'Surely God is with you.' " That passage speaks of the Gentiles coming to bow before the only true God in repentance.

1 Corinthians 14:26–33
The Gifts and Body Ministry

²⁶What then shall we say, brothers? When you come together, everyone has a hymn, or a word of instruction, a revelation, a tongue or an interpretation. All of these must be done for the

strengthening of the church. ²⁷If anyone speaks in a tongue, two—or at the most three—should speak, one at a time, and someone must interpret. ²⁸If there is no interpreter, the speaker should keep quiet in the church and speak to himself and God. ²⁹Two or three prophets should speak, and the others should weigh carefully what is said. ³⁰And if a revelation comes to someone who is sitting down, the first speaker should stop. ³¹For you can all prophesy in turn so that everyone may be instructed and encouraged. ³²The spirits of prophets are subject to the control of prophets. ³³For God is not a God of disorder but of peace.

The structure of this passage helps us see important principles ("A" statements). Notice two if-then clauses which provide specific applications ("B" statements) sandwiched by the principles:

14:26	All have gifts.	^Auniversal
	All must strengthen the church.	^A₁goal
14:27	If anyone speaks in a tongue	^Border
	(then) two or at most three, one at a time and someone must interpret.	
14:28	If no interpreter is present	^B₁submission
	(then) keep quiet, speak to yourself and to God	
14:29	Exercise—prophets should speak	^A₂active exercise
14:30	If revelation given to another	^B₁submission
	(then) you should stop.	
14:31	All may prophesy	^Auniversal
	All may be instructed and encouraged	^A₁goal
14:32	Prophets in control	^Asubmission
14:32	Order reflects nature of God	^Abasis

These are more than corrective guidelines. They are positive principles to encourage the exercise of gifts. Three times Paul uses "all" to refer to the whole church (*pantos* 14:31). The tenor of these verses indicates total church participation. The basis of the gifts is to reflect the very nature of God (14:33). Thus the goals are to strengthen the church (14:26) and to learn and to encourage one another (14:31). Simple guidelines on specific examples of tongues and interpretation and prophecy are given. There is a proper time and place for everything (14:27, 28,30). We may even be silent so that others will learn to exercise gifts, or so that we will not cause confusion (14:28,30). But by all means exercise the gifts and have them evaluated by others in the meeting (14:29).

The word "has" (14:26) is repeated before each gift in Greek to stress that everyone, potentially, has a contribution to make. So that many can share in the service, no one gift should predominate. Then the focus is on what God is doing rather than on what man is doing. Note the contrasting parallel of 14:23 and 14:26. Rather than tongues dominating the whole service, a wide variety of gifts are to be ministered.

"If the whole church comes together and everyone speaks in tongues . . ." (14:23).

"When you come together, everyone has a . . . [different gift]" (14:26).

The phrase "edify [strengthen] the church" is a theme that runs throughout this chapter (14:4,5,12,17,26; see also 14:23). Paul's emphasis is on practical results.

As has been noted, Paul limits tongues and interpretation to "two— or at the most three" (14:27). After all, if a congregation is sensitive to the Spirit at all, two or three exhortations to worship should be quite sufficient. If the congregation is not sensitive, no number of messages in tongues and interpretation will do. But this guideline should not be legalistically applied. For example, a person may lose count of how many times an utterance in tongues has been given, or a new Christian—in the excitement of what God is doing for him—may give a fourth utterance. This is understandable. The church should not frown on such events, but gently guide and encourage the sharing of the gifts, thanking God that others are being used. We learn together; we will make mistakes together. We will love each other into maturity in Christ.

Three categories of people should pray for the gift of the interpretation of tongues: The first is the one ministering in tongues. The second is the spiritual leadership. The third is all others who discern and confirm the meaning of the utterance.

However, the one who would exercise the gift of tongues should do so in private if he knows of no one in the congregation who has been used in the gift of interpretation: He can pray quietly to himself and to God without disturbing the service. Nevertheless, if a public utterance in tongues is given and, for whatever reason, no one else gives the interpretation, the responsibility falls on the one who gave the utterance (14:13,27–28). In the British Pentecostal Assemblies, the pastor is responsible to give the interpretation if no one else does. It is reasonable to assume that the spiritual leadership should be able to sense what God is saying to the congregation.

The one limitation on prophecy is that it should be evaluated after two or three messages. Why is this? Utterance in the known language can cover many gifts. Not all such gifts can be instantly identifiable and categorized.

Evaluation is also necessary because the gifts are incarnational. That is, God does not speak directly; He speaks through people— and people are fallible. Thus Grudem identifies two levels of prophetic authoritativeness: the "very words" and the "main ideas." For example, Scripture alone is authoritative right down to its words (Matthew 5:18). At the same time, the prophecies in Acts were authoritative in their general content. Christians had to make their own decisions after the famine was predicted (Acts 11:27–30) or guidance was suggested (Acts 21:4–14). After Paul had a vision, a collective decision was made to go to Macedonia. "We got ready . . . concluding that God called us" (Acts 16:9–10).

Proper evaluation is important to the continuing ministry of the gifts. For example, after the prophecies have been given, "others" should "judge" (KJV), or "weigh carefully" (NIV), what has been said (14:29). The word "others" is from *allos,* meaning "others of the same kind." This could mean others with a similar prophetic word or the whole of a Spirit-filled congregation. It does not likely refer to a select group called prophets. In the final analysis this evaluation must be made by all believers. And even though leadership may fear evaluating utterances because this might quench the Spirit or hurt someone's feelings, the congregation will do it nevertheless. To guard against confusion and doubt, the leadership ought to take courage and assume its proper role, leading the congregation in responsible evaluation of prophecies.

Prophecy should be evaluated in the light of Scripture, actual edification of the church, the life-style of the one sharing, and the confirmation by others who have been touched in a similar manner. No word is to blindly be accepted as authoritative. The congregation must exercise judgment in spiritual matters. God does not give private revelations only for one or two initiated persons to express. He speaks to several in the body of Christ about the same thing. Together they can confirm the validity of the utterance. Even when God speaks to individuals about specific matters, there can be safety in confirmation from mature, respected brothers and sisters in the Lord.

Part of the reason for that evaluation is to encourage others who are learning to share. If a prophet may keep silent in order to let others share (v. 30), this indicates that the words are not so important that they have to be given in any one meeting; they can wait for another time. Further, the more experienced believer may refrain from sharing if he senses others are developing in this gift, or he may function in a confirmational, responsive role, rather than an initiatory role. One who is beginning to share may stumble in his grammar or nervousness, or hesitate out of doubt that he is being used. The experienced person may say amen to the ministry of the gift. After the service he may confirm to the sharer the blessing his utterance was.

Many times God has impressed me to take the responding role, so that later I could publicly confirm what the first speaker said. This encourages the first speaker and reinforces the truth for the congregation. During all this, others who did not share can evaluate the impressions God had made on their hearts to determine if they were sensing the same word. The ministry of gifts thus becomes a learning, growing experience for all.

Mutual submission is the principle so that all may be instructed and encouraged (14:31). The word "instructed" (NIV), or "learn" (KJV), has the idea of being discipled. The noun *disciple* comes from this basic root word. We are discipled as we learn to listen to the Spirit and minister in the Spirit. Most discipleship programs are effective to a point. So that the church may achieve the full dynamic of the Spirit-empowered witness and life, we must teach our people to respond to the Spirit and minister the gifts. The church is a school of the Spirit. In the context of a loving, understanding, and affirming congregation, we learn. Then we go out to minister to a dying world.

True expressions of the Spirit unite a congregation so its members can reach maturity. That is why "disorder" (v. 33), "confusion" (KJV), is to be avoided. The Greek word refers to "civil disorder" or "mutiny." That is the one extreme. God is a God of peace. *Peace* means to "join together that which has been separated." That is the church's task, to seek reconciliation to God and to one another. This is best effected in the full operation of the gifts by a loving congregation who understand the goals of the gifts as well as their principles of operation.

1 Corinthians 14:33–35
Women and the Gifts

[33]As in all the congregations of the saints, [34]women should remain silent in the churches. They are not allowed to speak, but must be in submission, as the Law says. [35]If they want to inquire about something, they should ask their own husbands at home; for it is disgraceful for a woman to speak in the church.

Several aspects of the passage make its interpretation complex. The Nestle Greek New Testament (as NIV, NEB, and TEV) makes 14:33b apply to 14:34 rather than to 14:33a. NASB, Knox, and Moffatt hold to the traditional verse division, thus seeing 14:33 concluding the discussion on order in every-member ministry. The Greek can actually read either way. No major doctrine is at stake. By connecting 14:33b and 14:34 Paul may be laying down a principle he applies to all churches regarding women in the church. Paul does not show partiality against the Corinthian church situation. What he says to one, he says to all.[36]

---

[36]See also 1 Corinthians 4:17, "in every church"; 7:17, "in all the churches"; 11:16, "nor the churches of God"; 16:1, "Do what I told the Galatian churches to do." Paul conscientiously teaches the same way of life in every church: to

Actually 14:33b seems to flow naturally into 14:36 as a fitting conclusion to his whole argument in 1 Corinthians 14. Paul would then be saying, "God speaks through the whole Body, through His churches everywhere. You are not the only ones with revelation."

This question then arises, Does 14:34–35 belong at this point, at the end of the chapter, or not at all? Some scholars believe 14:34–35 does not belong in the original manuscripts. They think these verses were a first-century gloss inserted either at this point or at the end of the chapter to counter the issues of women's liberation.[37] Because of this passage's close relationship to 1 Timothy 2:11–15, some believe a copyist brought that teaching over into the 1 Corinthians passage.[38] They also see apparent conflict with 11:5, women praying and prophesying. How can Paul exhort women to be silent here if he allows them to worship in 11:5? How could both be Paul's writing? Their conclusion, then, is that Paul did not write 14:34–35 as his own view.[39]

---

remain in the situation where God calls one; that long hair is a covering for women in worship; by setting aside a weekly, affordable sum a significant collection can ultimately be made, in this case, for the Jerusalem church. He is sensitively consistent in his teaching so no one can accuse him of playing politics on any major issue.

[37]Markus Barth, *Ephesians: Translation and Commentary on Chapters 4–6*, vol. 34A, The Anchor Bible Series (Garden City, N.Y.: Doubleday and Company, Inc., 1974), 656, describes the women's liberation movements of the first century in Greece, Rome, Egypt, and Sparta.

[38]See Arnold Bittlinger, *Gifts and Graces: A Commentary of First Corinthians 12 to 14* (Grand Rapids: William B. Eerdmans, 1967), 110; Fee, *First Corinthians*, 699–705; E. Schweizer, "The Service of Worship: An Exposition of 1 Corinthians 14" *Interpretation* 13 (1959) 402; and Hans Conzelmann, *First Corinthians*, vol. 43, trans. James W. Leitch, Hermeneia Series (Philadelphia: Fortress Press, 1975). W. Ward Gasque and Laurel Gasque, "F. F. Bruce: A Mind for What Matters," *Christianity Today* 33 (April 7, 1989): 25, say of these verses, "But even if they are part of the original text of Paul's letter, they have relevance only to the uttering of prophecies in church, where women are advised not to question publicly and vocally the interpretation of prophetic utterances."

[39]First Timothy 2:11,15 are seen by these same scholars as relating to a very specific situation of women who were false teachers. This situation was very different from the Corinthian situation. For example, see Gordon D. Fee and Douglas Stuart, *How to Read the Bible for All Its Worth* (Grand Rapids: Zondervan Publishing House, 1982), 57–71.

Although this option looks attractive for answering some of the difficulties of the passage, the manuscript evidence weighs strongly against it.[40] It seems better to assume these verses are inspired and look at their possible interpretations.

These perspectives reflect pastoral issues. What was the situation at Corinth and how does it affect our understanding of Paul's advice? Does that advice apply to the church today? In referring to "the Law," was Paul referring to a specific Scripture or merely a generally accepted principle? In what way does the reference to "Law" support his argument? There are two major categories of interpretations of this passage and three views within each category:

The first category has to do with cultural, or localized, application. The first view within this category construes Paul as bound to Judaism and the culture of his day. He was not free to understand what God intended in terms of Joel's "Spirit on all flesh" prophecy.[41] So this is simply Paul's statement of how he would handle the situation, given the pressures of his day. He is not saying that every age should have to do it this way. The presuppositions on the inspiration of Scripture related to this view are not acceptable to most evangelicals.

The second view states that although the problem did have to do with culture, Paul was not bound to it. He was showing the Corinthians how to be effective within it. Uneducated women, some saved from pagan temple prostitution and newly liberated in Christ, were flaunting their freedom in a way that brought shame to the Christian cause. Through Calvary, Christ had set the status and dignity of women on the same level as men. Paul's great emancipation proc-

---

[40]Most major manuscripts include these verses in the present position (P46, Aleph, A, B, K). Other manuscripts place 14:34–35 after 14:40 (D, F, G).

[41]Paul K. Jewett, *Man as Male and Female* (Grand Rapids: William B. Eerdmans, 1975), 113, calls 1 Corinthians 11 the "first expression of an uneasy conscience on the part of a Christian theologian who argues for the subordination of the female to the male by virtue of her derivation from the male." Also Paul K. Jewett, *The Ordination of Woman* (Grand Rapids: William B. Eerdmans, 1980), 67–68, where he believes 14:33–35 is genuinely Pauline, but Paul is caught in the tension between where he is culturally and the coming Kingdom. See also Kittel, *Theological Dictionary*, 776–789; and William Barclay, *The Letters to the Corinthians* (Philadelphia: The Westminster Press, 1975), 136.

lamation was, "There is neither Jew nor Greek, slave nor free, male nor female, for you are all one in Christ Jesus" (Galatians 3:28). According to F. F. Bruce, it is Paul's teaching that "so far as religious status and function are concerned, there is no difference between man and woman."[42]

But wickedness was rampant at Corinth. So-called liberated women of the world were living in immorality, defying authority and disregarding the family structure. Whether the problem was usurping authority, women chattering and dominating a service or simply asking distracting questions, unbelievers would readily associate these activities with sinful Corinthian life-styles.[43]

Communication must be seen within the cultural setting. In Paul's day, women were considered inferior to men in both Greek and Jewish cultures. Even the golden age of Socrates, Plato, and Aristotle put women in subordinate roles. Pharisees thanked God regularly that they were not women. Rabbis saw little place for women in the synagogue. What was the Christian woman to do in this setting? She was to be aware of how her actions would be interpreted by her culture and seek ways of acceptable communication. The dignity and honor of woman must be seen in the Christian woman.[44]

---

[42]Gasque, "F. F. Bruce," 25.

[43]The wickedness of Corinth is well-known. Every major commentary describes at length the vanity fair which was Corinth and the idea of "Corinthianizing."

Perhaps less known was the liberation movement among women in Greece and other parts of the ancient world. Barth, *Ephesians 4–6*, 655–661, describes this. Plato promoted civil service exams for both men and women and spoke of both men and women of gold and silver, bronze and iron, to describe their abilities. Although he thought of men as superior to women in general, he laid the foundation for a democratic state (see Eugene Freeman and David Appel, "Equal Rights for Men and Women," in *The Wisdom and Ideas of Plato* [New York: Fawcett World Library, 1952], 127–33).

Add to this the urban sins of this great seaport city (e.g., prostitution), the Greek philosophies, the Roman mystery religions, the interactions with open-minded concepts from around the world, and one can see how a women's liberation movement could flourish here. Add the great equalizing effect of the cross (where there is "neither Jew nor Greek, slave nor free, male nor female, for you are all one in Christ Jesus" [Galatians 3:28]) and the free worship style of the Corinthian church, and one can also see how some of the problems could arise.

[44]James G. Sigountos and Myron Shank, "Public Roles for Women in the Pauline Church: A Reappraisal of the Evidence," *Journal of the Evangelical Theological*

At least part of the problem may have been the asking of questions in services (14:35).[45] In the freedom of an extemporaneous worship service women felt free to ask questions. Others saw these questions as distracting, foolish, and revealing a lack of self-control. First Corinthians 14:34–35 either focuses on learning[46] or is Paul's way of sternly reprimanding the women prophets at Corinth.[47] In either case, however, women's ministering of spiritual gifts is not being denied. Whether the issue is learning or disruptive women speakers, Paul tells these women to learn at home. Their behavior did not contribute to the worship service.

A third view holds that the women were a specific group of Gnostically-inclined teachers who were boasting of angelic languages, revelations, and such spiritual attainment in the present age that a future resurrection was not needed.[48]

A second category of interpretations has to do with biblical authority. And if Paul bases his points about women in the church on universal biblical principles, what are those principles and how are they to be obeyed? Furthermore, they obviously must be binding upon all of us. Is Paul referring to Genesis 3:16, part of the curse God declared upon mankind? It seems strange to make a curse into a command and to apply it in the way 1 Corinthians 14:34–35 does.[49]

Society 26 (September 1983): 283–295, believe that how a culture viewed the role of women determined whether her ministerial actions and responses were considered insubordinant. This was Paul's accommodation to reach different cultures. "His position is coherent when understood as an attempt to provide as full a range as possible of ministries for women, without hindering the spread of the gospel" (p. 295).

[45]The idea that the Early Church met in the synagogue pattern, seated separately and having a special order of service, at this stage is speculative, being undocumented by the early fathers. See Fee, *First Corinthians*, 703.

[46]K. Stendahl, *The Bible and the Role of Women* (Philadelphia: Fortress Press, 1966), 30.

[47]For this argument, see Barrett, *First Corinthians*, 332.

[48]Martin, *Spirit and Congregation*, 86–88; Ervin, *Not Drunken*, 187–193; and Fee, *First Corinthians*, 573 (though Fee does not see Gnostic influence at this stage, the other points are valid).

[49]If "law" refers to Genesis 3:16, it seems strange because both the Massoretic Text and the Septuagint indicate the verse speaks of the woman's instinctive inclination or desire toward her husband. Thus, the husband applies this to his

The first interpretation appealing to biblical authority teaches that from creation God ordained male and female roles to be different. How much may women participate in public ministries? Those who hold this position do not believe congregational teaching positions and positions of ruling authority should be held by women.[50] Clark Pinnock, disagreeing with those who believe that women are free to carry on any ministry role without limitation, believes the only valid biblical view is a modified hierarchicalism that places men in the dominant positions of leadership.[51] Archibald Robertson wonders why so many Sunday school teachers are women if all teachers should be men.[52] James Hurley answers by saying women are authorized as such by the elders, or are in teaching functions that have no formal authority or church discipline behind it. Regular, systematic, authoritative instruction of the congregation must be the elders' responsibilities.[53] F. W. Grosheide says women may share gifts of the Spirit in private meetings.[54] Grudem allows for women to be

---

advantage to dominate her in a worship setting. The reference likely is to the creation narratives of Genesis 1 and 2 because other appeals to the law in relation to female roles (1 Corinthians 11:8,9 and 1 Timothy 2:13) refer to this. Man is created first and woman comes from his side. The emancipated women at Corinth were causing problems in the life and witness of the church. They needed to learn how to speak graciously and minister effectively. Otherwise, Paul is giving his own commandment as the Lord's.

[50]H. Wayne House, "The Ministry of Women in the Apostolic and Postapostolic Periods" Bibliotheca Sacra 145 (October/December 1988): 387–399, points out women did not have the position of teacher in mainstream Christianity, even into the second and third centuries A.D. I have not considered in this writing the position that denies women the right to preach or teach at all. For this view, see Susan T. Foh, "Women Preachers: Why Not?" Fundamentalist Journal 4 (January 1985): 17–19.

[51]Clark H. Pinnock, "Biblical Authority and the Issues in Question," ed. Berkeley and Alvera Mickelsen, Women, Authority and the Bible (Downers Grove: InterVarsity Press, 1986), 57.

[52]Archibald T.Robertson, Word Pictures in the New Testament, vol. 4 (Nashville, Broadman Press, 1931), 185. He does not think the conditions of this passage and 1 Timothy 2:12 wholly apply today.

[53]James B. Hurley, Man and Woman in Biblical Perspective (Grand Rapids: Zondervan, 1981), 246–252.

[54]Grosheide, First Corinthians, 251, 341.

involved in gift ministries, but not teaching positions or those of ruling leadership.[55]

In answering, we must note the context of 1 Corinthians 14: that all may minister all the gifts, in proper order and discipline. Paul's argument would be self-defeating if he were to say that women (over half the church!) were not allowed to minister the gifts. Some of the suggestions about why women may teach but not be authoritative or exercise discipline, or why women may exercise gifts but not in public worship services, seem to be begging the question.

Hurley reveals tremendous insights when he shows that the issue is not an either/or situation.[56] At what point does private become public? How large a group is a private meeting? If women may teach on the basis of delegated authority, is it not possible that the authority to discipline and take charge of a group also be delegated? Cannot a church send a woman to pioneer churches, disciple new Christians, and begin a central sending point, all under the jurisdiction of elders?[57] If this can be done at all, the issue of role becomes relative.

The point is, the woman's attitude and methodology must reflect a style that will not hinder the proclamation of the gospel and the witness of the church.

A second appeal to biblical authority maintains the differences between male and female roles but suggests that the issue is not women in gift ministry but women in relation to the oral evaluation of the gift. Grudem sees 1 Corinthians 14:29–36 as one distinct unit discussing the *evaluation* of prophecies. The evaluative aspect is tied together in parallel form by the verb "be silent" *(sigato)* in verses 28, 30, and 34. Before a person gives an utterance in tongues, he must determine if an interpreter is present, maintaining silence if one is not (14:28); while a person is giving a prophecy, he must be able to recognize another who is equally inspired and become

---

[55]Grudem, *Gift of Prophecy*, 255; Carson, *Showing the Spirit*, 130; and Douglas J. Moo, "1 Timothy 2:11–15: Meaning and Significance," *Trinity Journal* 1 (1980): 62–83.

[56]Hurley, 246–252.

[57]A point Hurley agrees with.

silent so he may speak (14:30); and women, although they may prophesy (11:5), are to remain silent during the oral evaluation of prophecies(14:34).[58]

To better illustrate my understanding of Grudem's position, I offer the following diagram:

Gift	Evaluative Situation	Guideline	Option
TONGUES (v. 28)	If no interpreter	Tongues speaker keeps silent	Speak quietly to God
PROPHECY (v. 30)	If another prophesies	First one keeps silent	Share at another time (implied)
PROPHECY (v. 34)	[Evaluation]	Women keep silent	Discuss at home with husbands

Figure 4. Evaluation of Prophecy—Grudem's Position

His point is silence in the final evaluation of gifts. Women were able to participate in singing, praying, and prophesying. But to assume they were able to judge others put them in an authoritative role.

Is the issue that of male and female roles in the church? Those who understand women to be in a submissive role will take this passage as an affirmation of that understanding. Those who believe every believer is a minister may take this passage as a first-century problem and not a present problem if a woman shows maturity,

---

[58]Grudem, *Gift of Prophecy*, 271.

discipline, and wisdom. Grudem's suggestion is attractive in that it seeks to combine both positions: allowing women to minister the gifts, while at the same time accepting a submissive role when it comes to evaluative processes. This appears theologically consistent with biblical teaching on male-female roles and responsibilities and seems to apply to "all the churches" as a general principle of methodology.

If one assumes Grudem's position, however, several questions remain: Is this more than a first-century principle? Can't women who are in modern society, better educated, and familiar with charismatic worship evaluate prophecies?

One must define what is meant by "evaluate." Is it some official, public proclamation of the validity of a prophecy? Could part of the evaluation process be in the form of a confirmation through another utterance? Could it be a positive response to the ministry through worship? And if the meeting is a women's gathering—does this eliminate the exercise of prophetic gifts, since no man is there to evaluate them? What of some lonely outpost of ministry where only a woman dare preach the gospel?

Women practice evaluation every day. They make judgments about business decisions, education questions, moral issues, family matters, and politics. Evaluation obviously takes place in the church, and women participate in the process. The issue is not whether they can or cannot—ultimately it is the method they use.

A third scriptural approach sees the word "head," in 11:3–16, as referring to source, not to dominance or a chain of command.[59] In that man was first created, then woman, the woman sees the man as her source. Just so, Christ is the source of all creation. Full Christian womanhood would mean full expression of ministries and gifts.

Some think that in 14:34–35 Paul quotes the views of a Judaistic

---

[59]A. Berkeley Mickelsen and Alvera Micklesen, *Women, Authority, and the Bible* (Downers Grove, Ill.: InterVarsity Press, 1986), 106–7. Also, Philip Barton Payne in the same book contributes a response to the above article substantiating the Greek basis for "source" (pp. 118–120). The appeal is to the usage of the word "head" as "source" in classical Greek. However, Kittel, *Theological Dictionary*, 430, and Bauer, *Greek-English Lexicon*, 431, make no mention of this usage in the first century.

group who were teaching minimal participation of women, just as the Jewish oral law said.[60] That Paul quotes from their letter several times in this epistle is obvious.[61] He counters their statement with 14:36–37, that what he writes is a command of the Lord.[62] The word of God did not come to the men only. The problem with this view, however, is that nothing in the context itself hints at a quotation of the Corinthians and presupposes some were forbidding the women a right to speak.

The literature on this topic is vast. Every position presupposes a given understanding of the problems at Corinth. We do know that Jews and Greeks alike had strong cultural views about the woman's place. Women with extreme views on freedom and spiritual matters were posing a problem to the ongoing witness of the church to the families and community at Corinth. Paul was not trying to hinder women's ministry, but rather wanted to free women to fulfill God's calling. Each view has its strengths and weaknesses. In love we need to try to understand each position. The unique problems of Corinth may not recur in this century, but the principles of discipline, order, and spiritual edification are always important.

The question of women in ministry, from a Pentecostal point of

---

[60]S. Aalen, "A Rabbinic Formula in 1 Corinthians 14:34," *Studia Evangelica* 2 (Texte und Untersuchungen 87: Berlin, 1964), 513–25. See also, Adam Clarke, *Clarke's Commentary*, vol. 4 (Nashville: Abingdon Press, n.d.), 278–279, who believes this is a Jewish injunction that changed after Pentecost. The only limitations were that women could not participate in discussion on doctrinal matters. The words were given to correct the disorderly and disobedient, not the rest. See also Jessie Penn-Lewis, *The Magna Charta of Woman* (Minneapolis: Bethany Fellowship, 1975), 21–34. Among other authors raising this possibility: Walter C. Kaiser Jr., "Paul, Women, and the Church," *Worldwide Challenge* 3 (1976): 9–12. Neil M. Flanagan and E. H. Snyder, "Did Paul Put Down Women in 1 Cor. 14:24–36?" *Biblical Theology Bulletin* 11 (1981): 10–12; J. Murphy O'Conner, "Interpolations in 1 Corinthians," *Catholic Biblical Quarterly* 48 (1986): 90–92, D. W. Odell-Scott, "Let the Women Speak in Church, An Egalitarian Interpretation of 1 Cor 14:33b–36," *Biblical Theology Bulletin* 13 (1983): 90–93; and Charles H. Talbert, "Paul's Understanding of the Holy Spirit: The Evidence of 1 Corinthians 12–14," in *Perspectives in Religious Studies* 11 (Winter 1984): 95–108.

[61]See 1 Corinthians 7:1; 8:1; 12:1. There are other possibilities as well, such as 12:31.

[62]Mary J. Evans, *Woman in the Bible* (Downers Grove, Ill.: InterVarsity Press, 1983), 99–100.

view, must be answered with several presuppositions in mind. First, the Holy Spirit has been poured out on everyone for ministry. Regardless of age, sex, or ability, every believer is a priest to God and to his fellowman. The Holy Spirit has ordained all to their respective work. The ordination of one to ministry by a church or denomination is but a recognition of what God has already done. We separate for service those God has already called (Acts 13:2).

Second, the Holy Spirit distributes the ministry gifts "just as He determines" (1 Corinthians 12:11). The question of what ministries are available for women is answered by those ministries God gives each woman.[63] Anna the prophetess, Deborah the judge, Dorcas the women's group leader, Phoebe the deaconess, Priscilla who (along with Aquila) taught Apollos, Philip's daughters who were prophetesses, and the women at Corinth who prayed or prophesied (11:5) are examples of women in diverse forms of ministry.

Third, according to 1 Corinthians 14:34–35 and 1 Timothy 2:11, women were not to be disruptive (as the women at Corinth and Ephesus, for whatever reason, had been). An untimely action or question could disrupt or change the whole atmosphere of the service. Such questions were best answered at home or in a small group Bible study.

Fourth, at the heart of the issue of women in ministry is not which ministries, but how they are manifested. The woman must concentrate on the *methodology* by which she communicates her God-given ministries. If she does it in a humble manner, consults with and respects the thinking of other people (both men and women), does not assume a position for her own prestige and power or covet a position that should be released to others, then God opens the doors. A woman's way of ministry can be a unique contribution to God's work. She seeks to draw out the best in others without seeking personal glory. At the same time she knows that submission does not mean suppression. It is a willingness to share all God has given

[63]Colin Brown, ed., *The New International Dictionary of New Testament Theology,* vol. 3 (Grand Rapids: Zondervan Publishing House, 1975), 1067.

her. A wise, godly woman knows to communicate in such a way as to be well received.

At least part of the problem at Corinth was the asking of questions in services. Whether this was due simply to an ignorance of proper procedure, wrong doctrine, a desire for authority, or the evaluating of prophecies, such questions disrupted the service.[64] The manner of approach was in question. There must be submission to authority in the church.

Fifth, a woman has a primary responsibility to her husband and family. She is the heart and he is the head of the home. Great honor is placed upon the woman's role in the home because of the potential benefits to home and society. One's attitudes of reverence and responsibility to the Lord can make the home a haven and the closest thing to heaven on earth.

1 Corinthians 14:36–40
Everything in Its Proper Place

[36]Did the word of God originate with you? Or are you the only people it has reached? [37]If anybody thinks he is a prophet or spiritually gifted, let him acknowledge that what I am writing to you is the Lord's command. [38]If he ignores this, he himself will be ignored. [39]Therefore, my brothers, be eager to prophesy, and do not forbid speaking in tongues. [40]But everything should be done in a fitting and orderly way.

Commentators and Bible translators disagree as to whether verse 36 goes with the previous verses on women or with the whole problem of 1 Corinthians 14.[65] Is the issue an indictment on women

---

[64]Bruce, *First and Second Corinthians*, 135, thinks it is women interrupting proceedings by asking questions they could well ask at home. Barrett, *First Corinthians*, 332, sees the problem as frivolous chattering disturbing the services. Martin, *Spirit and Congregation*, 86–88, sees a problem of liberated women teachers who embraced Gnostic views that brought revelations contrary to biblical teaching.

[65]*Jerusalem Bible, Good News Bible,* and the *New English Bible* begin a new paragraph with 14:36. Against this NASB, NIV, RSV, and ASV follow the latest Greek text of the United Bible Society by leaving it in the same paragraph as 14:34–35 on women and the gifts.

at Corinth who thought they were the beginning and end of truth? Nowhere does 14:34-35 hint that women made that claim of originating truth, unless the problem is that of Gnostically-inclined women teachers. It is not inherent in the text itself.[66] This verse sounds like the pride of any group who thought they were more spiritual and more knowledgeable than others.

The NIV brings out the meaning of the Greek verbs in 14:36 well. The verb *exelthen* is an inceptive aorist emphasizing the beginning of an action, thus the translation of "originated." The verb *katentesen* is a culminative aorist, "has reached," emphasizing the final point of an action. God's truth was not to begin and end with a select few at Corinth. They did not represent the sum total of knowledge on spiritual matters. Paul's questions are rhetorical, which made their pride seem ridiculous. At the same time, Paul does not say they are false teachers or imply truth did not reach them. It seems likely that they were believers.

The gospel originated with Jesus Christ. It had already touched much of the world. Paul emphasized "you" in 14:36 to contrast their worldly, carnal wisdom with his clear, authoritative, apostolic witness. In 14:37 he asserted his authority without hesitation.

The phrase "prophet or spiritually gifted" (14:37) clearly refers to persons, not gifts.[67] Some prophets thought they were the ones with special revelations and a giftedness transcending that of ordinary Christians. The words for "prophet" and "spiritual" are singular, so he may be confronting specific persons.

The word "command" (14:37) is singular, not plural as in the King James Version. But what command is Paul referring to? The chapter contains many imperatives (although none of them is a quote of the Lord from the Gospels). Some suggest the command is love as applied to the exercise of the gifts: Make love your aim; desire

---

[66]Also, the masculine *monous*, "only," eliminates it as a reference to women. It could be to men, or more likely, the whole church to which Paul writes these words.

[67]Paul uses *pneumatikon* (12:1), *pneumatika* (14:1), and *pneumaton* (14:12) to refer to the gifts as a whole. Grosheide, *1 Corinthians*, 344, thinks the term "spiritually gifted" (*pneumatikos*) probably refers to one who speaks in tongues in the context of 1 Corinthians 14.

spiritual gifts for the good of others. Then you will do all things in a fitting manner. Do not despise love, the gifts, or one another.[68] If so, then this command is reflective of 1 Corinthians 13. This could well be Paul speaking with the authority of an apostle, giving his own command to this divided church. They must not take his instructions lightly, but as the command of the Lord.

Note how Paul in 14:36–40 focused on the key issues of 1 Corinthians 12 to 14 (see the chart on the next page).

Paul began his discussion on gifts by saying he does not want the Corinthian believers ignorant (see also 1 Corinthians 10:1). Genuine spiritual knowledge leads to humility and mutual respect. Human knowledge can produce undue pride (1 Corinthians 8:1). Now, in 14:38, Paul finalizes his argument, resigned to the fact that some will harden their hearts to the truth. The NIV rendering translates the idea of the Greek verb best: "If he ignores this, he himself will be ignored." How ironic! The one who claims a special knowledge (*gnosis*) should be heard, if indeed he has the knowledge he claims. But rather than knowing truth, this person was ignoring and not recognizing the truth.

Paul also began this discourse on gifts with the confession of the lordship of Jesus (12:3). Now in closing the argument, he warns them not to deny this lordship by ignoring his instructions. ("Lord" is in the emphatic position in the sentence.)

Clear communication is at issue. That is why the church is to be eager for the prophetic gifts, spoken in the known language. At the same time, Paul cautions those who were despising tongues and forbidding others to speak in tongues.[69] They needed to put the gifts in their proper perspective (14:40). In emphasizing certain gifts they forgot the Giver and the ultimate purpose of gifts. When attention is centered on Christ, then all blends into the pattern without confusion, pride, carnality, or divisiveness. Indeed, others will see that

---

[68]Nils Johansson, "First Corinthians 13 and First Corinthians 14," *New Testament Studies* 10 (1963–1964): 383–392. So, also, I see love as the theme in chapters 12 to 14.

[69]*Me* with the present imperative: "Stop forbidding."

Comparison of Key Issues

14:36–40	12 to 14	
14:36 Special revelations to certain ones?	12:6,11	God works all gifts in all men
	12:12	We are parts of the Body
	13:9	We share gifts "in part."
14:37 Spiritually gifted ones	12:4–11,28–30; 13:1–3 Gift lists	
14:37–38 Knowledge and ignorance on gifts contrasted and submitted to lordship of Jesus in actual exercise	12:1	*Ignorance* concerning gifts is not desirable
	12:3	Paul makes *known* to them spiritual gifts must be exercised under the lordship of Jesus.[70]
14:37 Lord's command (*if* this is a reference to love the comparison with 1 Corinthians 13 applies)	13:1–13	Issue is love in the exercise of gifts
14:39 Commands concerning prophecy and tongues	14:1–33a	Prophecy and tongues compared as to function
14:40 Proper order	14:33	God is a God of order and peace

---

[70]Note even the words: 12:1 *agnoein*—ignorant, cf. 14:38 *agnoei, agnoeitai;* 12:3 *gnoridzo,* cf.14:37 *epignosketo.*

God is present. The word "fitting" (NIV), or "decently" (KJV), refers to the comely and the beautiful, making a pleasing impression on all. The word "orderly" contrasts with the disorder of an unruly mob or mutiny pictured in 14:33. It pictures a well-ordered army. Christian soldiers march in full and glorious array.

5

The Living Church

Romans 12, 1 Corinthians 12 through 14, and Ephesians 4 contain some of Paul's finest thinking about the Church. The first-century church was charismatic from the time of Pentecost. Based on the background of the Book of Acts and the terminology and teachings in Pauline literature, it is clear that the churches Paul established were begun through a mighty breakthrough of the Spirit of God in difficult situations.

Paul taught these churches to continue in the power and manifestation of the Spirit of God. Who else would have taught them, and how would they know how to operate in spiritual gifts? Integral to Pauline theology on the church is full understanding of the gifts. Careful study reveals that virtually all his epistles bring out, in varying degrees, some aspect of this. Thus, the Corinthian church was not unique in its operation of the gifts of the Spirit, but in its major abuse of them. Although Romans, 1 Corinthians, and Ephesians are addressed to three churches of different cultures, problems, and histories, the aforementioned chapters of these books contain one message, relevant to the Church universal. The three passages contain a common outline; similarities abound. Although many verses represent teaching unique to the epistle that contains them, other verses of the three passages are integrally related though differently expressed. And some are almost verbatim that of the other passages.

Romans 1 through 11 establishes a full doctrinal statement on salvation and sanctification. Then, Romans 12 begins the practical application, moving from doctrine to right relationships and ministries.

In 1 Corinthians 12 to 14, Paul confronts Corinthian assertions and attitudes about gifts, giving positive principles for the exercise

183

of them. He had taught the church about gifts from its founding.

Whereas in other epistles, doctrine leads to life-style, in Ephesians, worship (chapters 1 to 3) leads to life-style (chapters 4 to 6). Both doctrine and worship are necessary. A believer's life-style is the expression of his doctrine and worship. In Ephesians 4 and 5 Paul discusses principles of mutual ministry through gifts.

Commentators have noticed points of correlation in these chapters in the analogy of the body and the gift lists. Their emphasis, however, has been to let Romans 12 proceed as the developing argument on practical sanctification and ethical behavior. The gifts then seem to be incidentally thrown in at Romans 12:6–8. Ephesians 4:1–16 was not related to 4:17–32, nor was a connection made with Romans and Corinthians except to mention gifts. Current scholarship brings to light a new dimension of interpretation, showing how closely interconnected all three passages are.

These passages reveal what the Church is through the expressions of gifts. They teach the context, the preconditions, and understandings that can set a church free to exercise gifts. Rather than emphasize only the spectacular gifts, the essential nature of all gifts and their regular exercise must be seen.

These passages are written in an ethical context to show how Christians must live their lives. Believers live in the Kingdom that has come and yet await the final day of redemption. This day is spoken of as "God's wrath" (Romans 12:19); "When that which is perfect is come. . . . When I shall know as I am fully known" (1 Corinthians 13:10,12); "When we all reach unity of the faith . . . attaining to the whole measure of the fulness of Christ" and "the day of redemption" (Ephesians 5:13,30). The interrelationships of ecclesiology (the study of the church), ethics (our conduct), and eschatology (the coming of Christ) are clear and inseparable.

Ernst Käsemann thinks all of Romans 12 is related to the charismatic community. He outlines it as follows:

Romans 12:1–2	Worship in the world
:3–8	Advice for charismatics who stand out
:9–21	The charismatic community[1]

---

[1]Ernst Käsemann, *Commentary on Romans* (Grand Rapids: Eerdmans, 1980), 325–50.

Markus Barth understands Ephesians 4 as related to the charismatic people of God anticipating the eschatological judgment of God. Although the word "church" is not used here, through imperative, confessional, exegetical, narrative, eschatological, and polemical statements the context of the Church at worship and in action is clearly in focus.[2] Speaking of the relationship of Ephesians 4:1–16 and 4:17–32, he says:

> While the first half puts more stress on the order, purpose, and life of the church as a whole, the second part emphasizes above all those things that constitute the conduct and motivation of each single saint. But the two sections are not exclusive: Ecclesiology is ethics, and ethics is ecclesiology. . . . both are founded upon the coming and the proclamation of Christ.[3]

Max Turner sees four reasons for correlating Romans 12 and 1 Corinthians 12:

1. "Paul grounds *charisma* [(gifts)] in *charis* [(grace)]" (Romans 12:3,6; 15:15; 1 Corinthians 1:4–7).

2. *Charismata* is discussed within an ethical structure (Romans 12:1–3,9ff).

3. "Unity and diversity in the one body is the main illustration."

4. "Paul stresses the need . . . to understand the role of each as contributing to the whole . . . to know the limits and functions of one's *charisma(ta)* and to use them fully in the light of the fact that they are individual expressions of God's *charis* " (grace).[4]

The outline on the next pages will guide us through the discussion of the points of parallel.

---

[2]Markus Barth, *Ephesians: Translation and Commentary on Chapters 4–6*, vol. 34A, The Anchor Bible Series (Garden City, N.Y.: Doubleday and Company, Inc., 1974), 451.

[3]*Ibid.*, 525.

[4]Max M. B. Turner, "Spiritual Gifts Then and Now," *Vox Evangelica* 15 (1985): 28–29.

Parallel Passages

Main Points	Romans	1 Corinthians	Ephesians
Incarnational Nature	**12:1**	**12:1–2**	**4:1–3**
Exhortation	12:1	12:1	4:1
The body	12:1	12:2	
The renewed mind	12:2	12:3; 13:1	14:2–3,17–24
Humility	12:3	13:4–5	4:2
Meekness or loss of control?	12:1–2	12:2–3; 13:4–7	4:2,14–15
Unity and Diversity in the Trinity		**12:4–6**	**4:4–6**
Spirit		12:4	4:4
Lord		12:5	4:5
Father		12:6	4:6
The Lists of Gifts—The Diversities of Ministries (see also 1 Peter 4:9–11)	**12:6–8**	**12:7– 11,28–31** 13:1–3	**4:7–12**
Functional nature	12:6–8	12:11,29–30	4:7,11
Guidelines	12:6–8	12:7,12,19, 24–25; 13:1–31	4:11–12
One Body, Many Members	**12:4–5**	**12:12–27**	**4 :15–16,25–29**
Edification	12:6–16	12:7; 14:3–6,12, 16–17,26	4:12–13,15– 16,25–32
Empathy	12:10,15	12:25–26	4:16

Main Points	Romans	1 Corinthians	Ephesians
Sincere Love	**12:9–21**	**13:1–13**	**4:25–5:2**
Hate evil, cling to good	12:9	13:6	4:25
Gentleness	12:10	13:4–5	4:32
Zeal	12:11	13:6	4:1,23–24
Rejoicing, steadfastness, prayer	12:12	13:7–8	
Fellowship with those in need	12:8,13	13:3	4:28
No unwhole-some talk	12:14	13:11	4:26–29
Humble mindset	12:16	12:25; 13:4	4:2,23
No revenge	12:17	13:5	4:31
Be at peace	12:18		4:3
Handling anger	12:17	13:5–6	4:26,31
Final Judgment	**12:19–21**	**13:10,12**	**4:13,15,30**

The Incarnational Nature of the Gifts

EXHORTATION

> **I urge you, brothers, in view of God's mercy, to offer your bodies as living sacrifices, holy and pleasing to God—this is your spiritual act of worship (Romans 12:1).**
>
> **About spiritual gifts, brothers, I do not want you to be ignorant (1 Corinthians 12:1).**
>
> **As a prisoner for the Lord . . . I urge you to live a life worthy of the calling you have received (Ephesians 4:1).**

Because gifts are incarnational, human responsibility comes into play. Paul earnestly exhorts, "I urge you" (Romans 12:1; Ephesians 4:1); "I do not want you to be ignorant" (1 Corinthians 12:1). The call is to every believer to live his full potential with the coming of the Lord in view. God's commands and call to us are not burdensome, but liberate us to be a pure reflection of the gospel. We live out who we are in Christ.

The usage of imperatives reflects the character, diction, and content of the admonitions of wisdom teachers of Israel. Markus Barth feels Paul spoke of the church as a Messianic school where we are discipled to become like Jesus and learn to minister in His power.[5] School was not only a place to learn head knowledge about Christ, but to learn to take on His life, power, and vision. Paul did not train his coworkers *about* missions, he trained them *in* missions. Life as a member of the healthy body of Christ should naturally lead to discipleship. That Paul's focus was practical and ethically-oriented is clear. Paul's rich heritage within Judaism would not allow him to be "so heavenly minded as to be no earthly good." In fact, every statement of theological truth in Paul is followed by a prophetic command as to how to live today.[6] That he was influenced by the Old Testament wisdom movement in his ministry and writings is obvious.

THE BODY

> **I urge you, brothers, in view of God's mercy, to offer your bodies as living sacrifices, holy and pleasing to God—this is your spiritual act of worship (Romans 12:1).**

> **You know that when you were pagans, somehow or other you were influenced and led astray to mute idols (1 Corinthians 12:2).**

The first three verses of each passage (Romans 12, 1 Corinthians 12, and Ephesians 4) show how Christians must submit body, mind, conduct, and attitudes to the Lord. The human body is not, as the Greeks say, "a receptacle for the soul," but is the extension of one's personality and life. We cannot know someone apart from his being in the body. The body is not evil, but integral to a true sacrifice to God. Paul used analogies related to sacrifice and offerings to picture the totality of life as a worship to God. The NIV appropriately

---

[5]Barth, *Ephesians*, *4–6*, 529–536. See especially p. 536 on the influence of the wisdom tradition on Paul.

[6]Grammatically expressed, for Paul the indicative is followed by the prophetic imperative.

translates *latreia* as "spiritual worship." We are to settle it in our minds and offer our bodies as living sacrifices.

THE RENEWED MIND

> Do not conform any longer to the pattern of this world, but be transformed by the renewing of your mind. Then you will be able to test and approve what God's will is—his good, pleasing and perfect will (Romans 12:2).

> I tell you that no one who is speaking by the Spirit of God says, "Jesus be cursed," and no one can say, "Jesus is Lord," except by the Holy Spirit (1 Corinthians 12:3).

> When I was a child, I talked like a child, I thought like a child, I reasoned like a child. When I became a man, I put childish ways behind me (1 Corinthians 13:11).

> Brothers, stop thinking like children. In regard to evil be infants, but in your thinking be adults (1 Corinthians 14:20).

> Be completely humble and gentle; be patient, bearing with one another in love. Make every effort to keep the unity of the Spirit through the bond of peace (Ephesians 4:2–3).

> So I tell you this, and insist on it in the Lord, that you must no longer live as the Gentiles do, in the futility of their thinking. They are darkened in their understanding and separated from the life of God because of the ignorance that is in them due to the hardening of their hearts. Having lost all sensitivity, they have given themselves over to sensuality so as to indulge in every kind of impurity, with a continual lust for more. You, however, did not come to know Christ that way. Surely you heard of him and were taught in him in accordance with the truth that is in Jesus. You were taught, with regard to your former way of life, to put off your old self, which is being corrupted by its deceitful desires; to be made new in the attitude of your minds; and to put on the new self, created to be like God in true righteousness and holiness (Ephesians 4:17–24).

Paul warns the Roman Christians about a wrong, arrogant attitude they might have toward others. He wants them to be content to minister the gifts God has given. Although we know of no major problems at Rome at the time of Paul's writing, the situation at Corinth was drastically in need of healing. In spite of such contrasting contexts, the principles for resolving the situation were the same.

The mind must be transformed and renewed. Even now God is transforming us from glory to glory (2 Corinthians 3:18). So, Christians must think like mature people, renewed in spirit. A new perspective and quality of thinking is called for. The sanctified mind discerns wrong doctrine ("No one who is speaking by the Spirit of God says, 'Jesus be cursed' ") and submits to the lordship of Jesus Christ ("No one can say 'Jesus is Lord,' except by the Holy Spirit," 1 Corinthians 12:3). Paul joyfully says "I am a prisoner of the Lord" (Ephesians 4:1). There is no greater calling than to be a love-slave of Jesus Christ.

Two words for "new" are *neos* (new in point of time, as a newly-made garment) and *kainos* (new in quality and character, as a born-again Christian).[7] The Christian is new in both ways. There is B.C., before Christ, and A.C., after Christ. There is a point in time that new life is given. It is eternal and different in character from anything before. Because the earthly mind seeks security in its own perspective and worldview, it cannot comprehend this new mind-set.

The Christian life is not merely a better life, but a radically different, superior life-style that the grace of God alone makes possible. Once they were pagans (1 Corinthians 12:2, Ephesians 4:17–19), but they must not "conform any longer to the pattern of this world" (Romans 12:2). The Ephesians passage is specific about this pattern: stealing, lying, brawling, slander, anger, bitterness (Ephesians 4:17–32).

---

[7]Colin Brown, ed., *The New International Dictionary of New Testament Theology*, vol. 2 (Grand Rapids: Zondervan, 1976), s.v. "New," by H. Haarbeck, H. G. Link, and C. Brown, 669, 670. This distinction is not absolute. For example, the verb form *ananeoomai* (Ephesians 4:23) speaks of the inner nature being renewed, but Colossians 3:10 uses *anakainoomai* to say the same thing. Richardson says, "But the word 'new' acquires its distinctively biblical meaning whenever it takes on an eschatological significance and implies the passing away of the old order—this present world-age—and the breaking in of the new, 'the world to come.' " Alan Richardson, ed., *A Theological Word Book of the Bible* (New York: Macmillan Company, 1950), s.v. "New, Old, Renew, Refresh," 159.

HUMILITY

By the grace given me I say to every one of you: Do not think of yourself more highly than you ought, but rather think of yourself with sober judgment, in accordance with the measure of faith God has given you (Romans 12:3).

Love is patient, love is kind. It does not envy, it does not boast, it is not proud. It is not rude, it is not self-seeking, it is not easily angered, it keeps no record of wrongs (1 Corinthians 13:4–5).

Be completely humble and gentle; be patient, bearing with one another in love (Ephesians 4:2).

For Paul, every blessing is based on the grace of God. Salvation, election, God's call, ministry, the church, the gifts of the Spirit— all are given out of God's generosity, His grace.[8] As someone has observed, "For Paul, theology is grace, and ethics is gratitude." The Christian's ministry, life, and ethics are but a grateful response to God. No one should be conceited but, instead, modest in making a personal estimate (Romans 12:3).

God's mercies motivated our redemption: "Whereas the heathen are prone to sacrifice in order to obtain mercy, biblical faith teaches that the divine mercy provides the basis for sacrifice as the fitting response."[9]

Just as the Israelites needed daily manna, so we are daily dependent on God. The gifts we receive are partial, incomplete (e.g., a "measure" of faith, Romans 12:3; prophesying "in part," 1 Corinthians 13:9; "different kinds" of gifts, 1 Corinthians 12:4; grace as Christ "apportioned," Ephesians 4:7). God places the members of the Body where He will, and then distributes gifts according to His grace.[10] This is God's work and God will receive all the glory.

---

[8]See Romans 1:11; 5:15; 6:23; 11:29; 12:6.

[9]Everett F. Harrison, *Romans*, vol. 10, The Expositor's Bible Commentary Series (Grand Rapids: Zondervan, 1976), 127.

[10]There is no substantiated use of *charisma* before the Christian era. Paul was the first to use it technically. Sixteen of the seventeen occurrences of the word in the New Testament are found in Paul's epistles.

Because of this grace, Paul gladly suffered criticism, mistreatment, unfairness, gossip, slander, and persecution. He used terms like "prisoner of the Lord," "walk worthy of your calling," and "with all humility" to describe this mind-set. One look at God's infinite grace, His holy calling, His plan for our lives, and His love in reconciling lost humanity should help us recognize just how unmerited His favor is.

Jesus himself became the perfect example of humility by leaving heaven's palaces for death at Calvary. This is to be our mind-set. Our feelings are not the issue. Equality and rights are not the issue. Christ's glory is the only issue. If we desire a continued flow of the Spirit, a servant attitude is indispensable.

The Greeks did not consider humility a virtue, but Christians valued it highly. We must come to God poor in spirit, knowing we are sinners who need the grace of God. Then God can pour His blessings upon us. Ephesians 4:1–3 reflects on three beatitudes: be poor in spirit, be meek, and be peacemakers (Matthew 5:3,5,9). Real humility knows that God is in charge. He fights our battles for us.

MEEKNESS OR LOSS OF CONTROL?

I urge you, brothers, in view of God's mercy, to offer your bodies as living sacrifices, holy and pleasing to God—this is your spiritual act of worship. Do not conform any longer to the pattern of this world, but be transformed by the renewing of your mind. Then you will be able to test and approve what God's will is—his good, pleasing and perfect will (Romans 12:1–2).

You know that when you were pagans, somehow or other you were influenced and led astray to mute idols. Therefore I tell you that no one who is speaking by the Spirit of God says, "Jesus be cursed," and no one can say, "Jesus is Lord," except by the Holy Spirit (1 Corinthians 12:2–3).

Love is patient, love is kind. It does not envy, it does not boast, it is not proud. It is not rude, it is not self-seeking, it is not easily angered, it keeps no record of wrongs. Love does not delight in evil but rejoices with the truth. It always protects, always trusts, always hopes, always perseveres (1 Corinthians 13:4–7).

> Be completely humble and gentle; be patient, bearing with one another in love (Ephesians 4:2).

> Then we will no longer be infants, tossed back and forth by the waves, and blown here and there by every wind of teaching and by the cunning and craftiness of men in their deceitful scheming. Instead, speaking the truth in love, we will in all things grow up into him who is the Head, that is, Christ (Ephesians 4:14–15).

Spiritual gifts do not cause a person to lose control of his faculties. Rather, as the person yields himself fully to the control of the Holy Spirit, he finds he can most effectively exercise spiritual gifts as well as the full range of his natural abilities. True control comes when the Spirit leads, guides, counsels, and shapes our thought and actions, and when Jesus is Lord.

Meekness and long-suffering are part of the Christian life-style. "Meekness" speaks of a wild animal that has been disciplined and tamed, the temperament in control. The animal has potential for evil or good, and uses it for good. Moses and Jesus are spoken of as meek. Jesus said, "Blessed are the meek" (Matthew 5:5). With meekness we exercise gifts according to the measure of faith. Rather than lose control, "the spirits of the prophets are subject to the control of prophets" (1 Corinthians 14:32). If we have proper knowledge and attitudes the Spirit can work most effectively in our areas of ministry. God gives us not just saving faith, but effective faith to discharge our responsibilities (Romans 12:3).

A part of meekness is long-suffering. Ephesians 4:2 relates the word *makrothumia* to patience with our fellowman. This is first. Patience during events and trials is of no use if we are not patient with people. In 1 Corinthians 13:4–7, Paul begins with *makrothumia,* patience with people, and ends with *hupomones,* patience with circumstances. In Romans 12:12–21, Paul focuses on both types of patience (verse 12 *hupomones* and verses 17 to 21, *makrothumia*). When we see others as God sees them, then we will trust God to take care of the circumstances and work out everything for good. Godly patience is not fatalistic. It is an active, positive attitude about the person and/or situation and God.

Ephesians 4 extends the discussion of meekness from personal to corporate dimensions. Not only must individuals develop self-control, but the whole body of Christ must set aside biases, hurts, and narrow perspectives to see the greater good in serving the kingdom of God. Meekness (Ephesians 4:1–2) will lead to unity (vv. 3–6), so that the church will become mature, attaining to the whole measure of the fullness of Christ (Ephesians 4:13).

Paul appeals for unity (vv. 1–3), describing its biblical basis as the way God himself works (vv. 4–6), its diversity in gifts (vv. 7–12), and how it can be perfected to reflect the unity of God (vv. 13–32). In the context of this unity, the church can be most effective. A study of the priesthood in Palestine in the interbiblical era will reveal corruption, greed, and a grasping for political power at the expense of others. The common people suffered as a result. They longed for a teacher of righteousness who would show them the way to true religion. That priesthood is a classic example of the lack of spiritual power. Power hungry men destroyed unity. However, when the Early Church was threatened by a dispute concerning Hellenistic widows (Acts 6), the leadership sought God for wisdom and settled the situation peacefully. Jesus' prayer in John 17 was for unity that would cause his disciples to see His glory and that the world would understand the Father's love for mankind. A glimpse of God's glory will enable us to transcend human differences.

Paul builds upon the active sense of patience and urges believers to "make every effort to keep the unity of the Spirit through the bond of peace" (Ephesians 4:3). We are to expect positive results. Positionally we have peace in Christ, but practically we must guard and preserve it in relation to one another. The word peace in Greek, *eirene,* means to bring together what has been separated. Paul's use of peace also includes the Hebrew sense of *shalom,* meaning wholeness or well-being. The purpose of the Cross is reconciliation to God first, then to one another. This produces the sense of wholeness and togetherness.

Biblical peace is not forcing a settlement between two parties but seeking to restore relationships. There are genuine differences among people. Personalities, perspectives, and understandings differ. Paul is realistic: "If it is possible, as far as it depends on you, live at peace with everyone" (Romans 12:18). We must do our part. We cannot force others to respond in a certain way.[11]

In operating the gifts, in organizing the church, in blending a multicultural congregation, in addressing personal disputes, we must seek peace. This is not peace at any price or blind allegiance to a leader. It is not peace because we have the same cultural or theological perspective. It is biblical peace, based upon the grace of God revealed at Calvary.

We must not surrender control. The following verbs are passive, indicating action done to a person: to be *conformed* to the pattern of this world (Romans 12:2), to be *led astray* to dumb idols (1 Corinthians 12:2), or to be *blown here and there by every wind of teaching* (Ephesians 4:14). In the phrase "blown here and there," Paul uses the imagery of a storm to picture how false teachers manipulated the believers' immature understandings and shook their sense of stability.[12] Note the parallels in these three chapters.

Romans: Present your bodies and your minds for spiritual worship. Prove what is the good, acceptable, and perfect will of God.

1 Corinthians: Don't lose control of your bodies. Don't accept false doctrine but let Christ be Lord.

Ephesians: Live worthy of God's calling. Have the right attitude. Be renewed in the spirit of your mind.

These first verses of each passage show the importance of our role in the exercise of gifts. The focus is on who we are rather than on what we do. God desires character in those who do His will. We can see how comprehensive this truth is by looking at five foundational New Testament words of ministry: fellowship, worship, teaching, proclamation, and service. These words can be grouped in two categories: under "doing": teaching, proclamation, service; under "being": fellowship, worship (see figure 5). All

---

[11]Alford, in John Peter Lange and F. R. Fay, *The Epistle of Paul to the Romans,* trans. J. F. Hurst, vol. 10, Lange's Commentary on the Holy Scriptures (Grand Rapids: Zondervan Publishing House, 1960), 393.

[12]Barth, *Ephesians, 4–6,* 441–443.

ministries should be balanced in these two categories. Most Christians have focused on "doing" for God and settled for some distorted version of "being"—or simply neglected that aspect of their lives altogether. In order to "do" with integrity, we must "be." For example, the Holy Spirit endues us with power so we can "become" witnesses (Acts 1:8).

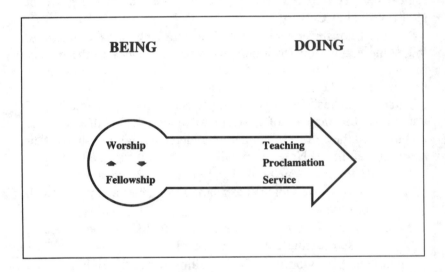

BEING

DOING

Worship

Fellowship

Teaching

Proclamation

Service

Figure 5. Ministry in Balance

The church at Antioch is an excellent example. Its leadership came from a variety of places, including Africa, Cyrene, Cyprus, Palestine, and Tarsus. "While they were *worshiping* the Lord and fasting" (Acts 13:2), the Spirit confirmed God's leading for Barnabas and Saul. This church's missions movement was birthed in worship and multicultural fellowship (Acts 13:1–3).

Worship liberates us from a fixation on adverse circumstances. It reflects our desire to live daily for God's glory. True worship leads to deeper fellowship. We cannot claim to love God and hate our brother (1 John 4:19–21). He is God's gift to us, a member of the Body, one for whom Christ died, and one who may be used of God to minister gifts to us. Thus, true worship must lead to insight, interaction, and love in the family of God. We march to Zion together. In turn, that deeper fellowship leads us to love God more. As others minister gifts of the Spirit we thank God for the gift and for the person sharing it. We value each other as persons, seeking to guard each one's dignity and save each one's pride.

By focusing on the "do" category first, we put goals ahead of people, we challenge rather than nurture, and we experience burnout and fatigue rather than strength and inspiration. The secret of the Pentecostal movement has been on the "be" category.[13] In worship we see God as our source of strength. We evangelize out of the overflow of His blessings. It is this fervency of love, witness, and friendship that attracts others.

The "be" category is in the context of the church gathered. Here we learn to exercise the gifts and minister to one another. We learn about God's ways. We accept differences, we learn from our mistakes, we laugh and cry together. We learn to be the people of God.

The "do" category is in the context of the Church scattered into the world, to be salt and light, to minister in the power of the Spirit. But how can we truly go into the world as the people of God unless we come from gathering in an atmosphere of acceptance, commitment, love, peace, and an encouragement to learn about the gifts? That is why humility, meekness, patience, and making every effort to keep unity are so important. We learn together. We gain confidence in the exercise of gifts. We find our identity and strength in the body of Christ.

The "be" category without the "do" category becomes an absorbing preoccupation with self. The "do" category without the

---

[13]Edith L. Blumhofer, *Pentecost in My Soul: Explorations in the Meaning of Pentecostal Experience in the Early Assemblies of God* (Springfield, Mo.: Gospel Publishing House, 1989), 21, observes two emphases early in the twentieth-century Pentecostal movement: one on "being" and one on evangelism, or "doing." The emphasis on being "has been obscured over the years by an ever-expanding commitment to world evangelism" and a focus on signs and wonders. John Wright Follette (whose influence on me is not small) placed a major emphasis on being when he said, "I am *more concerned* over what we *are* than what we *do*" (quoted in Blumhofer, p. 22, emphasis original). Although we must not neglect the doing, we must realize the source of strength and character is in the being.

"be" category becomes an exhausting preoccupation with task. Exercising gifts only in the church setting misses the point. Here we are "instructed," discipled (1 Corinthians 14:31; *manthano* is the verb form related to the noun *mathetes* for disciple). According to the New Testament understanding of what disciples are and do, it is clear that these disciples are in turn to go and disciple the nations in the power of God (Matthew 28:18–20 and the whole of Acts). We mistake Paul's intention in 1 Corinthians 12 to 14 by inferring the gifts belong primarily within the church. Because he confronts problem issues, he focuses on resolving the issues within the church. In Romans, proper doctrine (chapters 1 to 11) leads to practical living (chapters 12 to 16). In Ephesians, worship (chapters 1 to 3) leads to witness and conduct (chapters 4 to 6). All this must be placed in the context of Paul's vision to reach the unreached (Romans 15:18–24; 16:26; Ephesians 6:19–20). Note especially 1 Corinthians 14:21–25 and Paul's focus on the evangelistic opportunities of the worship service.

Paul has not spoken of standards of holiness, deeper spiritual life, and great revelations, but of the basic responsibilities of Christians in the incarnational exercise of gifts. The issues are different for each church, but the principles are the same throughout these parallel chapters: We must be biblical, loving, humble, mutually submissive, accepting the lordship of Christ and bearing responsibility for the way the gifts are exercised so that they will build the church; in short, we take on the mind of Christ.

Unity and Diversity in the Trinity

The Trinity is a diversity in unity. "Because God is three persons in one, he is united. A God of one person could never be united. Unless God were three in one, no great feat would be accomplished in calling him 'one.' "[14] This thought forms the theological foundation for what follows. The church functions to reflect the nature of God. Ephesians 1 through 3 teaches that Christians are to be to His glorious praise and to show forth the riches of His grace. In

---

[14]Gaugler, in Barth, *Ephesians, 4–6,* 467.

Ephesians 4 the church, by the way it acts, reveals how God works. The first three verses teach our part in the gifts.

This matter of divine unity and diversity is also the pivot point for the Corinthians and Ephesians passages. Both Epistles bring out Father, Son, and Holy Spirit as vitally involved in the redemption plan, working for the same ministry and goal. Romans 12 does not include the passage on the Trinity but, both stylistically and content-wise, teaches unity and diversity in the body of Christ.

Ephesians 4:4–6 may have been a hymn or creedal statement of the Early Church. The similarities between 1 Corinthians 12:4–6 and this passage are remarkable. The order is the same: Spirit, Lord, God.[15] In 1 Corinthians Paul identifies the Trinity with

---

[15]A parallel to this listing is found in Ephesians 1:3–14. The order is reversed, Father (1:3), Son (1:5), and Spirit (1:13), but similar descriptions are given. The Father superintends the salvation plan from eternity past to its effectual results. The Son's role is to provide salvation and its attendant blessings of predestination, redemption, forgiveness, and adoption. In Him, Jews and Gentiles are one new creation, anticipating the ultimate fulfillment of His plan. The Holy Spirit seals us, guaranteeing our inheritance until the day of redemption.

Most scholars have understood this seal as the sign of God's ownership in salvation. They see here a genitive of apposition: "The seal which is the Spirit." Everyone must have the Spirit in order to be a Christian. Recently, scholars have proposed that "seal" has a significance that pertains to witness and empowerment, a significance greater than its significance as a sign of God's ownership.

Paul used the word "seal" to refer to many things. The fruit of his labor was the seal of his genuine apostleship—it did not make him an apostle (1 Corinthians 9:2). Circumcision was an outward sign, a seal of the righteousness that he had by faith—it did not make him a Jew (Romans 4:11). The missionary task was in process of completion, not commencement (Romans 15:28; lit., "sealing to them this fruit"). The seal is a sign of ownership and a deposit of blessings to come through the Spirit (2 Corinthians 1:22). The seal looks forward to the day of redemption (Ephesians 4:30).

Markus Barth, *Ephesians: Translation and Commentary on Chapters 1–3*, vol. 34, The Anchor Bible Series (Garden City, N.Y.: Doubleday and Company, Inc., 1974), 135–43, sees the seal as a public witness by a third party and a full reflection of the Spirit-empowered life until the coming of the Lord. David Martin Lloyd-Jones, *God's Ultimate Purpose: Ephesians 1:1–23* (Edinburgh: Banner of Truth Trust, 1978), 264, relates the seal to Pentecost and the gifts of the Spirit. Walter Bauer, *A Greek-English Lexicon of the New Testament and Other Early Christian Literature*, 2nd ed., trans. F. Wilbur Gingrich and Fredrick W. Danker (Chicago: University of Chicago Press, 1979), s.v. *"sphragizo,"* 804–805, says "Rather it = endue with power from heaven . . . ." See Howard M. Ervin, *Conversion-Initiation and the Baptism of the Holy Spirit* (Peabody, Mass.: Hendrickson Pub-

"same Spirit," "same Lord," "same God." In Ephesians 4:4–6 he describes a perfect sevenfold unity through seven uses of "one." There is one Spirit, one Lord, one God and Father.

By comparing these passages we see what activities are attributed to Spirit, Lord, and Father in the matter of the *charismata* and God's whole redemptive plan.

SPIRIT

> **There are different kinds of gifts, but the same Spirit (1 Corinthians 12:4).**
>
> **There is one body and one Spirit—just as you were called to one hope when you were called (Ephesians 4:4).**

The Holy Spirit, convicting and calling us to salvation, places us in the body of Christ (1 Corinthians 12:13), enabling us to live in the hope of His calling (Ephesians 4:4). The Spirit distributes the gifts according to His own will (1 Corinthians 12:4,11). The gifts are manifestations of the Spirit (1 Corinthians 12:7). Ministered properly, the gifts beautifully reveal the coordination, mosaic, creative unity in diversity, and wisdom and power the Spirit blends together. The gifts are expressions of the personality of the Holy Spirit. At the same time the gifts have a future aspect to them, for the gifts manifested now are only a partial fulfillment.

The Holy Spirit is spoken of as the promised Holy Spirit (Luke 24:49; Ephesians 1:13). He is the fulfillment of the promises of the Old Testament and of Christ concerning the enduement of power. But grammatically Ephesians 1:13 can also read "Holy Spirit of promise." Not only does the coming of the Spirit fulfill prophecy, the Spirit brings with Him promises of God's power, protection,

---

lishers, Inc., 1984), 124, who equates the seal with "Spirit-baptism for power in mission." Also Stanley M. Horton, *What the Bible Says About the Holy Spirit* (Springfield, Mo.: Gospel Publishing House, 1976), 236–239, while agreeing that the seal and deposit is the Spirit himself, believes the seal is a witness to salvation that includes all the gifts and blessings of the Spirit as well. Thus, Ephesians 1:13–14 parallels the discussion on the Spirit in Ephesians 4:4 and 1 Corinthians 12:4 by referring to gifts and the church.

guidance, and blessing until the day of redemption. Through the Spirit, the believer is strengthened, the Church is built, and the world is changed.

LORD

> **There are different kinds of service, but the same Lord (1 Corinthians 12:5).**
>
> **. . . one Lord, one faith, one baptism . . . (Ephesians 4:5).**

Jesus is central to both the Corinthians and Ephesians lists of gifts. He is the Lord and master of our lives. We come to Him in faith to receive our salvation, to become part of the body of Christ, and to identify with Him in His suffering, death, and resurrection. Further, it is He who gives gifts to the Church.

Baptism refers to incorporation into the body of Christ (Ephesians 4:5; 1 Corinthians 12:13). Rituals do not unite the body of Christ. As a matter of fact, they sometimes occasion disagreements—to the point of division. Many baptisms are spoken of in Scripture, but the context here is that of the joining the body of Christ.[16]

Most commentators relate this baptism to water baptism. The Early Church knew nothing of long intervals between salvation and water baptism. Baptism was an early public declaration that someone had become a believer and was renouncing his former life. Upon becoming a Christian, he was baptized and joined the church.[17]

Christ gives gifts and ministries; He calls us for service (Ephesians

---

[16]Seven baptisms referred to in Scripture: cloud and sea (1 Corinthians 10:2), suffering (Mark 10:38; Luke 12:50), John's baptism before Calvary (Matthew 3:11), Christian water baptism (Matthew 28:19), Holy Spirit baptism (Matthew 3:11), incorporation into the body of Christ (1 Corinthians 12:13), and identification with Christ's death (Romans 6:4).

[17]Archibald T. Robertson, *Word Pictures in the New Testament*, vol. 4 (Nashville: Broadman Press, 1931), 535, identifies *baptisma* in Ephesians 4:4 as the "result" of baptizing and *baptismos* as the act itself. E. K. Simpson, *Commentary on the Epistle to the Ephesians*, vol. 10, The New International Commentary on the New Testament (Grand Rapids: William B. Eerdmans, 1957), 90, understands *baptisma* is symbolic of all ordinances of worship, including the Lord's Supper, preaching, and praise. One hardly sees the latter position as integral to the argument.

4:8,12).[18] The diversity of functions of members of the Body reveals His creativity in fulfilling its needs (1 Corinthians 12:12ff.). We reflect His image.

The quotation in Ephesians 4:8 is from Psalm 68, an enthronement Psalm. This passage could have referred to a triumphant king or leader, returning to Jerusalem after having defeated Israel's enemies and receiving gifts from both his enemies and the admiring crowds. Or in speaking of the crowning of an earthly king, this psalm may be prophetic of a righteous and saving Messiah.[19] The Early Church saw it fulfilled in Christ the heavenly hero. Rather than receive gifts, He gives them. He died and rose again, ascending above all principalities and powers, for the Church, not for himself.[20]

---

[18]The fact that the Spirit gives gifts also (1 Corinthians 12:11) should cause us to be cautious in making clear-cut distinctions in these roles. Overlap occurs. Paul is more interested in the creativity of the Godhead than in distinctions in the Trinity. (See Fee, *First Corinthians*, 588.)

[19]The debate on the origin and function of this psalm goes on. H. Bunkel, in *Die Psalmen*, 5th ed. (Goettingen: Vandenhoeck, 1933), 79–80, interpreted it as political and eschatological, as does Claus Westerman, *Praise and Lament in the Psalms* (Atlanta: John Knox Press, 1981), 91–93. Sigmund Mowinckel, in *Psalmenstudien*, vol. 2 (Amsterdam: Schippers, 1961), 14–15; Sigmund Mowinckel, *He that Cometh*, trans. G. W. Anderson (New York: Abingdon, 1956), 95, construed its use as more for worship ceremonies praising the heavenly King. Derek Kidner, *Psalms 1–72*, vol. 14A, The Tyndale Old Testament Commentaries (Downers Grove, Ill.: InterVarsity Press, 1973), 238, suggests the psalm "may have been composed for David's procession with the ark from the house of Obed-Edom to the city of David (2 Samuel 6:12)." Mitchell Dahood, *Psalms II, 51–100*, vol. 17, The Anchor Bible Series (Garden City, N.Y.: Doubleday and Co., Inc., 1968), 143, is convinced the historical occasion is Israel's deliverance from Egypt and God's meeting them at Sinai. Whether the psalm was based on an actual enthronement of a historical king of Israel is not certain.

[20]Calvin inferred a deliberate change by Paul from "receive" to "give." If true, then Paul does not quote the psalm to show fulfillment of prophecy, but to show that the Messiah exceeds the generosity of human victors. However, orthodox Jewry in the first century A.D. believed the psalm said, "You have given gifts among men." An early Targum found in the Peshitta is translated by Archer, "You did take gifts among men." Archer Gleason, *Encyclopedia of Bible Difficulties* (Grand Rapids: Zondervan, 1982), 404–05. If this option is correct, the idea is that this servant-conqueror receives gifts in order to bestow them on others.

Interestingly, Psalm 68:18 was associated with Pentecost in the synagogue lectionary.[21] How appropriate that the risen Lord pours out the Spirit at Pentecost. Surely He deserves and will receive gifts from men, but He is first concerned for the Church. Jesus continued to be servant, even after His Resurrection and Ascension. He is the Victor already. He has been exalted to the right hand of the Father, and thus has poured out the Spirit (Acts 2:33). This victory means that one day every knee will bow and every tongue confess that Jesus is Lord. But before that day, and in preparation for it, He instituted the Church and equipped His people with gifts of the Spirit.

FATHER

> There are different kinds of working, but the same God works all of them in all men (1 Corinthians 12:6).
>
> . . . one God and Father of all, who is over all and through all and in all (Ephesians 4:6).

God is "over all"; He is sovereign, overseeing the whole creation. We do not come to a God limited in power. He transcends all circumstances, needs, and prejudices. His goals and plans are beyond anything we can imagine.

Yet in spite of His sovereignty, among His people He acts as a father with his children: He works "through all and in you all." "Through all" could mean utilizing every person's background, talents, personality, and life situation. God beautifully superintends, weaving the flow of the gifts to accomplish His purposes. "In you all" emphasizes the Father's personal selection of each person. Our personalities are not submerged but enhanced and placed in a position of dignity.

God alone is transcendent and absolute. Yet He is immanent in each believer. Anyone exercising a gift must be humbled by this.

---

[21]Kidner, *Psalms*, 238. This psalm was read at the Jewish Feast of Weeks, or Pentecost.

What a privilege and awesome responsibility that the sovereign Father calls us to glorify Him!

The Father chose us from before the foundation of the world (Ephesians 1:4–5). He sets us in the Body according to His sovereign, unquestioned will (1 Corinthians 12:18). He works all gifts in all men (1 Corinthians 12:6). He is over all, through all, and in all (Ephesians 4:6). The conclusion is that He watches over our ministries from the beginning to the final results.

The Lists of Gifts—The Diversities of Ministries

There is much interrelationship of the gifts in the various gift lists. In 1 Corinthians 14, prophecy is used as a representative of all the oral gifts ministered in the understood language. Identifying specific gifts of utterance is not always instantaneous. What appears as a prophetic utterance may initially be seen as one of the other gifts, or a combination of several. The gift of giving may reveal itself in showing mercy, helps, exhorting, or even martyrdom. Faith, healings, and miracles are interrelated. It is easy to see a possible correlation of the teaching gift in Romans 12 and a word of wisdom and a word of knowledge in Corinthians. Indeed, it is not hard to see how gifts on one list complement gifts on another list.[22]

The whole range of gifts can be applied to individual ministries. In that the gifts in 1 Corinthians and Ephesians have already been discussed in Chapter 1, let us take as an example the list of gifts in Romans 12:6–8 and apply it to the ministry of counseling. At some stage of the counseling process, an anointed word confronting sin may be necessary; at another stage, encouragement may come through serving, straightforward biblical teaching, exhortation, giving of material possessions, or simply through a manifestation of God's grace and mercy. Yet most of these gifts in this context could be identified as exhortation, mercy, or teaching. More specific identification can come only after evaluating the effects of the ministry on the body of Christ and on lost souls. Christians cannot wait until

---

[22]In these gift lists, Paul uses the following terms interchangeably: *charismata, dorean, charitos, charis, dotheises.* By doing so, he shows he refers to the same thing. Peter uses the word *charisma* in the gift context.

they know exactly what gifts they have before the gift is exercised. They must be ready to minister to needs as they arise. Later, in a proper setting of learning, the pastor can help the congregation evaluate how to exercise the gift effectively and sharpen the focus in the manifestation of the gift.

The New Testament writings on spiritual gifts give insight into their functional nature as well as guidelines for their operation.

FUNCTIONAL NATURE

> **We have different gifts, according to the grace given us. If a man's gift is prophesying, let him use it in proportion to his faith. If it is serving, let him serve; if it is teaching, let him teach; if it is encouraging, let him encourage; if it is contributing to the needs of others, let him give generously; if it is leadership, let him govern diligently; if it is is showing mercy, let him do it cheerfully (Romans 12:6–8).**

> **All these are the work of one and the same Spirit, and he gives them to each one, just as he determines (1 Corinthians 12:11).**

> **Are all apostles? Are all prophets? Are all teachers? Do all work miracles? Do all have gifts of healing? Do all speak in tongues? Do all interpret? (1 Corinthians 12:29–30).**

> **To each one of us grace has been given as Christ apportioned it (Ephesians 4:7).**

> **It was he who gave some to be apostles, some to be prophets, some to be evangelists, and some to be pastors and teachers (Ephesians 4:11).**

The Ephesians list speaks of Christ's gifts to the Church: people who have a special leadership ministry and have the appropriate gifts to fulfill their calling. Such people may have a combination of those gifts that appear on the Romans and Corinthians lists. Peter Wagner discusses "gift mixes" that lead to church growth; leaders manifesting certain combinations of gifts tend to help a church, at various stages of its history, reach its potential.[23]

---

[23]Peter Wagner, *Your Spiritual Gifts Can Help Your Church Grow* (Glendale, Calif.: Regal Books, 1979), 137ff.

Some have seen three categories of gifts: motivational gifts (Romans 12:6–8), power gifts (more supernatural than the others only in appearance, not in fact; 1 Corinthians 12:7–11), and leadership gifts (Ephesians 4:11–13). Because of the lack of decisive biblical support for these categories and because of overlap in functions within each gift list, it is difficult to be dogmatic here. Every effort to bring the gifts into practical operation is commendable. Any categorization of gifts ought to be concerned with their function.[24] But perhaps more important than having an eye for categorization is a sensitivity for how the Holy Spirit uses individuals. The question is not so much one of biblical theology as of church dynamics. What is God uniquely doing at this point of the church's history and in individual lives?

Romans 12:6–7 describes the ministries of prophesying and teaching. The New Testament seems to clearly distinguish between teaching and prophetic ministries: The prophet was more spontaneous, giving an immediate word from God. The teacher built his teaching upon the Old Testament Scriptures, Jesus' teachings, and the material available to the Christian community at that time.[25]

The gift of serving (diakonian Romans 12:7) is exalted in the New Testament. It at once pictures the right attitude toward general ministry as well as specific service. Although the word is used to apply to all types of ministries, the focus here is on ministering to material needs. Indeed, the last three functions in Romans 12:8 may also be related to practical helping: contributing to the needs of others, administrative leadership, and showing mercy. The term diakonia may apply to deacons (for it well describes the deacons of Acts 6) but should not be limited to that. The gift of encouraging (parakalon 12:8) can mean a number of different things. The Greek word literally means "to call alongside." The expression of this gift exhorts us to claim the victory and blessings of God's Word for our specific situations.

---

[24]My understanding of the division of gifts appears in my commentary on 1 Corinthians 12:7–11, in chapter 1, p. 63ff. For lack of better terms Ephesians 4 gifts are called enabling gifts; all others are called ministry gifts.

[25]C. B. Cranfield, *The Epistle to the Romans* (Edinburgh: T & T Clark, Ltd., 1981), 623.

The Early Church accepted the responsibility of ministering to the needs of the poor, the widows, the sick, and the abandoned. This ministry undoubtedly reached beyond the Christian fellowship. In fact, the New Testament word usually translated "hospitality," *philoxenoi,* literally means "love for strangers [or guests]." In observing Christians, those outside the church likely saw a love that went beyond their comprehension.

The practice of hospitality was especially important in the first century, for churches owned no buildings, and inns were disreputable places. Itinerate Christians depended on the graciousness of fellow believers everywhere. Although believers need not practice hospitality indiscriminately, they should remember their alien status in this world and make every effort to express love to one another.

GUIDELINES

We have different gifts, according to the grace given us. If a man's gift is prophesying, let him use it in proportion to his faith. If it is serving, let him serve; if it is teaching, let him teach; if it is encouraging, let him encourage; if it is contributing to the needs of others, let him give generously; if it is leadership, let him govern diligently; if it is showing mercy, let him do it cheerfully (Romans 12:6–8).

To each one the manifestation of the Spirit is given for the common good (1 Corinthians 12:7).

The body is a unit, though it is made up of many parts; and though all its parts are many, they form one body. So it is with Christ. . . . If they were all one part, where would the body be? (1 Corinthians 12:12,19).

But God has combined the members of the body and has given greater honor to the parts that lacked it, so that there should be no division in the body, but that its parts should have equal concern for each other (1 Corinthians 12:24–25).

If I speak in the tongues of men and of angels, but have not love, I am only a resounding gong or a clanging cymbal. If I have the gift of prophecy and can fathom all mysteries and all

knowledge, and if I have a faith that can move mountains, but
have not love, I am nothing. If I give all I possess to the poor
and surrender my body to the flames, but have not love, I gain
nothing (1 Corinthians 13:1–3).

It was he who gave some to be apostles, some to be prophets,
some to be evangelists, and some to be pastors and teachers, to
prepare God's people for works of service, so that the body of
Christ may be built up (Ephesians 4:11–12).

Offer hospitality to one another without grumbling. Each one
should use whatever gift he has received to serve others, faithfully
administering God's grace in its various forms. If anyone speaks,
he should do it as one speaking the very words of God. If anyone
serves, he should do it with the strength God provides, so that
in all things God may be praised through Jesus Christ. To him
be the glory and the power for ever and ever. Amen (1 Peter
4:9–11).

Although Romans 12, 1 Corinthians 12 to 13, Ephesians 4, and
1 Peter 4 seem to have a different emphasis, at least thirteen guidelines apply to the gifts.

Romans 12:

1. We should exercise our ministry in proportion to our faith.[26]
2. We should concentrate on our known ministries and develop
   them.
3. We must maintain the right attitudes: give generously, lead
   diligently, show mercy cheerfully.

---

[26]There are many different views on what the faith to prophesy is: our grasping
hold of the gift and exercising it, spiritual power given each Christian, the spiritual
capacities given to each of us, the gifts we receive as a result of our faith, the
standard of grace by which we are to exercise our gift, or simply, faithfulness.
All these definitions have biblical foundation. The best definition is incarnational,
involving both God and man:

"Faith is the *pneuma* given to the individual and received by him. It is objective
to the degree that none can establish or take it for himself and subjective because
each must receive it for himself without being represented." Käsemann, *Romans,*
335.

1 Corinthians 12:

4. We all have different functions in the body of Christ and must understand our connection and relationship to the whole Body.
5. Gifts must be manifested for the edification of all, not just for self.
6. One must have no sense of superiority or inferiority since every member is equally important. Paul further affirms in 1 Corinthians 12:28–31 that we should concentrate on the known ministries God has given us.
7. The gifts are given to us; we do not earn them. God's will and sovereignty determine distribution. His specific action of placing these gifts in the church is shown by the following verbs: "given" (Romans 12:6), "appointed" (1 Corinthians 12:28), "gave" (Ephesians 4:11).
8. At the same time, these are God-given manifestations, not human talents. God may grant gifts as He will. We should be open to them all. We can know what part of the body we are and what our ministries are and in this way bring the gifts into the realm of practical and effective use.

1 Corinthians 13:

9. Though we may manifest a gift perfectly, done without love our presentation is hollow. Even done with love, the gifts are only a partial disclosure; we still perceive heavenly things indirectly. At the same time, gifts are continually available (rather than once for all) according to one's measure of faith. But they must be tested, for they are humanly expressed. They fall under the commands of our Lord. Paul's implied point is maturity of its exercise not greatness of the gift. Such truths should lead us to a humility, an appreciation for God and others, and an eagerness to obey Him.

Ephesians 4:

10. Public enabling ministries have the special function of setting others free for their personal ministries and developing ma-

turity in them. Apostles, prophets, evangelists, and pastor-teachers (appearing to have a historical order here, similar to 1 Corinthians 12:28) are such enabling gifts to the church.

1 Peter 4:

11. First Peter 1:6 suggests the Christians Peter was writing to may have been suffering grief from "various trials." Whatever the case, he reassures them that God has a special grace to minister to each trial with its attendant grief. That grace, however, flows through people to people. Consequently, the believer needs to be alert to the best time, place, and approach for ministering God's grace in its "various forms" to those "various trials."[27]

12. We must be neither timid about our ministry nor confident in our own strength. Rather, we must minister confidently in the strength of the Lord. This is similar to Romans 12:6, where we are to minister "according to the grace given us," "in proportion to [our] faith." For example, "If anyone speaks," says Peter, he should be as one speaking the "very words of God" (1 Peter 4:11), not the words of the world (cf. Acts 7:38 and Romans 3:2).

13. Finally, the glory must go to God: The gifts/ministries are all graces with which God has blessed His Church.

One Body, Many Members

Just as each of us has one body with many members, and these members do not all have the same function, so in Christ we who are many form one body, and each member belongs to all the others (Romans 12:4–5).

---

[27]*Poikilois* is used both in 1 Peter 1:6 and 4:10. Ephesians 3:10 describes the boundless variety of the wisdom of God that will be revealed to the rulers and authorities in the heavenlies through the Church (the stronger form, *polypoikilos* is used). Barth, *Ephesians 1–3*, 345, says the adjective "manifold," or "various," "probably denoted originally the character of an intricately embroidered pattern, e.g., of a cloth or flowers." What a picture of God's sovereign design! We may see the intricate pattern of trials. God sees His overall design.

The body is a unit, though it is made up of many parts; and though all its parts are many, they form one body. So it is with Christ. For we were all baptized by one Spirit into one body—whether Jews or Greeks, slave or free—and we were all given the one Spirit to drink. Now the body is not made up of one part but of many. If the foot should say, "Because I am not a hand, I do not belong to the body," it would not for that reason cease to be part of the body. And if the ear should say, "Because I am not an eye, I do not belong to the body," it would not for that reason cease to be part of the body. If the whole body were an eye, where would the sense of hearing be? If the whole body were an ear, where would the sense of smell be? But in fact God has arranged the parts in the body, every one of them, just as he wanted them to be. If they were all one part, where would the body be? As it is, there are many parts, but one body. The eye cannot say to the hand, "I don't need you!" And the head cannot say to the feet, "I don't need you!" On the contrary, those parts of the body that seem to be weaker are indispensable, and the parts that we think are less honorable we treat with special honor. And the parts that are unpresentable are treated with special modesty, while our presentable parts need no special treatment. But God has combined the members of the body and has given greater honor to the parts that lacked it, so that there should be no division in the body, but that its parts should have equal concern for each other. If one part suffers, every part suffers with it; if one part is honored, every part rejoices with it. Now you are the body of Christ, and each one of you is a part of it (1 Corinthians 12:12–27).

Speaking the truth in love, we will in all things grow up into him who is the Head, that is, Christ. From him the whole body, joined and held together by every supporting ligament, grows and builds itself up in love, as each part does its work (Ephesians 4:15–16).

Each of you must put off falsehood and speak truthfully to his neighbor, for we are all members of one body. "In your anger do not sin": Do not let the sun go down while you are still angry, and do not give the devil a foothold. He who has been stealing must steal no longer, but must work, doing something useful with his own hands, that he may have something to share with those in need. Do not let any unwholesome talk come out of your mouths, but only what is helpful for building others up according to their needs, that it may benefit those who listen (Ephesians 4:25–29).

We are one body because we all have had the same experience of salvation. Paul's analogy of the Church to the physical body may have been too earthly for some of the more spiritually-minded Corinthians. Yet no better picture of the Church's interaction and interdependence has been developed. We have an obligation to build one another up. Every member is to help every other member function. We seek the good of all through clear communication, by willingness to minister gifts, through commitment to one another, in love sharing with others at their point of need, and by setting others free for their ministries (Romans 12:6,10,13; 1 Corinthians 12:7; Ephesians 4:12,15–16,29).

EDIFICATION

We have different gifts, according to the grace given us. If a man's gift is prophesying, let him use it in proportion to his faith. If it is serving, let him serve; if it is teaching, let him teach; if it is encouraging, let him encourage; if it is contributing to the needs of others, let him give generously; if it is showing mercy, let him do it cheerfully. Love must be sincere. Hate what is evil; cling to what is good. Be devoted to one another in brotherly love. Honor one another above yourselves. Never be lacking in zeal but keep your spiritual fervor, serving the Lord. Be joyful in hope, patient in affliction, faithful in prayer. Share with God's people who are in need. Practice hospitality. Bless those who persecute you; bless and do not curse. Rejoice with those who rejoice; mourn with those who mourn. Live in harmony with one another. Do not be proud, but be willing to associate with people of low position. Do not be conceited (Romans 12:6–16).

To each one the manifestation of the Spirit is given for the common good (1 Corinthians 12:7).

Everyone who prophesies speaks to men for their strengthening, encouragement and comfort. He who speaks in a tongue edifies himself, but he who prophesies edifies the church. I would like every one of you to speak in tongues, but I would rather have you prophesy. He who prophesies is greater than one who speaks in tongues, unless he interprets, so that the church may be edified. Now, brothers, if I come to you and speak in tongues, what good will I be to you, unless I bring you some revelation or knowledge or prophecy or word of instruction? (1 Corinthians 14:3–6,12).

. . . to prepare God's people for works of service, so that the body of Christ may be built up until we all reach unity in the faith and in the knowledge of the Son of God and become mature, attaining to the whole measure of the fullness of Christ (Ephesians 4:12–13).

Instead, speaking the truth in love, we will in all things grow up into him who is the Head, that is, Christ. From him the whole body, joined and held together by every supporting ligament, grows and builds itself up in love, as each part does its work (Ephesians 4:15–16).

Each of you must put off falsehood and speak truthfully to his neighbor, for we are all members of one body. In your anger do not sin. Do not let the sun go down while you are still angry, and do not give the devil a foothold. He who has been stealing must steal no longer, but must work, doing something useful with his own hands, that he may have something to share with those in need. Do not let any unwholesome talk come out of your mouths, but only what is helpful for building others up according to their needs, that it may benefit those who listen. And do not grieve the Holy Spirit of God, with whom you were sealed for the day of redemption. Get rid of all bitterness, rage and anger, brawling and slander, along with every form of malice. Be kind and compassionate to one another, forgiving each other, just as in Christ God forgave you (Ephesians 4:25–32).

Christians must first build themselves up, so that they can edify others. The major part of the use of tongues should be in one's devotional life in preparation for ministry. Jude says, "Build yourselves up in your most holy faith and pray in the Holy Spirit" (Jude 20). Paul says, "He who speaks in a tongue edifies himself"

(1 Corinthians 14:4), and "If I pray in a tongue, my spirit prays" (1 Corinthians 14:14).

The issue is not personal edification versus church edification. It is personal edification with the goal of church edification. Those who seek only personal blessing can become spiritual sponges. And though they may feel more spiritual, they also become more susceptible to criticizing others as not being spiritual enough. On the other hand, those who seek only to edify the church can become susceptible to spiritual and emotional burnout.

The point is clear: Christians are not to tear people down but to build them up. "Do not let any unwholesome talk come out of your mouths, but only what is helpful for building others up" (Ephesians 4:29). A healthy body builds itself up, being able to heal its own injuries.

This sinful world groans and labors in pain. People need encouragement. Edification should be a church's highest goal. Love builds up. The purpose of gifts is to build up. A congregation should be supportive, open, forgiving, reaching out. What an example such a church can be to families and to the world!

EMPATHY

> Be devoted to one another in brotherly love. Honor one another above yourselves. . . . Rejoice with those who rejoice; mourn with those who mourn (Romans 12:10,15).
>
> . . . so that there should be no division in the body, but that its parts should have equal concern for each other. If one part suffers, every part suffers with it; if one part is honored, every part rejoices with it (1 Corinthians 12:25–26).
>
> From him the whole body, joined and held together by every supporting ligament, grows and builds itself up in love, as each part does its work (Ephesians 4:16).

True fellowship is built on genuine empathy. Humanly speaking, it is easier to see the misfortunes of others as God's judgment rather than to weep with them. Rather, we need to reach beyond judgmental attitudes to understand the perspectives and needs of others. Romans

12:5 describes a body where each member interacts with and is interdependent on every other member so that it seems as one unit. That is why he can say "members one of another"! (KJV)[28]

The parallel in 1 Corinthians 12:26 tells us that the suffering of one member is the suffering of all. The rejoicing of the one is the rejoicing of all, too. When a Christian matures, develops his ministries, lives victoriously for the Lord, and touches others for Christ, the whole Church receives encouragement and strength. Outstanding examples that readily come to mind are Lillian Trasher and her orphanage work in Egypt, David du Plessis and his building of bridges across denominational boundaries to share the Pentecostal message, Mark Buntain and his great ministry in Calcutta, and David Wilkerson and his pioneering of Teen Challenge.

On the other hand, if one falls victim to the devil's wiles, becomes defeated, develops bitterness, or commits immorality, the whole Church suffers as a result. We do not live lives independently of each other. Anything we do or become will affect the rest of the body of Christ for good or ill.

The Ephesians parallel pictures the culminating point of empathy. The body builds itself up. Each supporting ligament does its nurturing work. The word for "supporting" is *epichoregeias*. It is used in Greek literature of a choir leader bearing responsibility for his group's needs, of a leader supplying his army's needs, or of a husband caring for his wife. If each one fulfills his responsibility, health and vitality will result. What release of power can happen in this kind of fellowship! Miracles and healings can readily take place in such an atmosphere. The ability to empathize and to be supportive and open to one another can set Christians free to reach out for God's solutions.

---

[28]Scholars disagree about how far to take Paul's analogy of the body. There are three options: First, some say it has the Semitic idea of corporate personality. Thus, what happens in Adam's fall happens to the whole human race. What God covenants with Abraham is also promised to all the people of God. This option does not focus on personal interaction. Second, others suggest that we are actually the body of the resurrected Lord. We not only represent Him, we are to be Christ to others. This option should not be pushed too far. Third, Paul is merely using an analogy that fits the nature and purpose of the Church. This seems to be his only meaning.

Furthermore, empathy provides the needed respect for persons among us whose personalities, temperaments, and ministries are different. It begins with a commitment to serve each other. Christians should not only come to church to worship God, but also to learn to understand the needs of others and to draw out their gifts.[29] This takes time. As we learn about others we begin to appreciate them, grow with them in fellowship, and honor them above ourselves (Romans 12:10).

Empathy by itself, however, does not guarantee spiritual power. We do our part; the Holy Spirit does His part; the gifts will flow. The world will see that Christ is truly among us.

Sincere Love

Following his expositions on gifts in Romans 12:1–8, 1 Corinthians 12, and Ephesians 4:1–16, Paul beautifully crafts three messages from one outline on love. The similarity is not exact at every point; the Spirit through Paul was creative. Yet the tenor, the flow, and the essential points of the passages on Christian love are similar and unmistakable. Nygren says of Romans 12, "One needs only to make 'love' the subject throughout 12:9–21 to see how close the contents of this section are to 1 Corinthians 13."[30] The context of ministry is the same.

In style and content Romans 12:1–8 and 9–21 are a unit; these passages do not refer to two unrelated topics (i.e., gifts and ethics). Interpreted as a unit, Paul's implication is that Christians must take seriously their responsibilities to exercise gifts and to validate those gifts in practical living.[31] The context of Romans 12 is the urgency of the hour and living in the light of Christ's return. The people of God must live in right relationships.

---

[29]Believers need to "consider, notice in a spiritual sense, fix the eyes of the spirit upon someone" (katanoomen in Hebrews 10:24). Bauer, Greek-English Lexicon, s.v. "katanoeo," 416.

[30]Anders Nygren, Commentary on Romans (Philadelphia: Fortress Press, 1949), 425. Also, Matthew Black, Romans, The New Century Bible Series (Grand Rapids: William B. Eerdmans, 1973), 154.

[31]Käsemann, Romans, 344.

In 1 Corinthians 13 love is the subject and active verbs follow. Godly love is not passive but takes the initiative. Gifts must be exercised in love. The gifts are only temporary tools, but love endures throughout eternity. One day all will be seen in light of His perfect knowledge. Until then, love must be patient with people and with circumstances *(makrothumia* and *hupomones)*. Even though no one manifests all the gifts, all may love. Its hymnic elements have led some to call 1 Corinthians 13 a song of love.[32]

In the Ephesians passage, truth and love have an amazing interrelationship. Telling the truth alone may be legalistic, deadly, and inadequate. Truth in love seeks to communicate in a way that it can be well-received. It appeals to our highest motivations. It is practical. Grace and truth are two sides of the same coin (see John 1:14). So also are truth and love. Paul applies this principle in his contrast between the present and former lives of the believers. Formerly they were ignorant and tossed about (1 Corinthians 12:1–2), conformed to this world (Romans 12:2), and intellectually blacked out by their refusal to know God and by hardening their hearts (Ephesians 4:18). One sees similar thinking on the depraved state of humanity in Romans 1:18–32.

The three passages develop separate themes. Yet, good over evil,

---

[32]See chapter 3, footnote 1. There are many grammatical comparisons. Although perhaps none of these passages is strictly hymnic, all three contain hymnic elements. Barth, *Ephesians, 4–6,* 429, 435, 473, 557, sees 4:4–6,8–10. and 5:2 as hymnic and 4:11,13 as containing hymnic material. Ephesians 4:22ff. contain a series of triplets that could well have been a hymn or creed. Parallel lines and thoughts are characteristic of Hebrew poetry. Romans 12:9–21 uses six triplets (12:9–12,18–20) and seven doublets (12:13–17,21). Love is the subject, but only four main verbs occur—12:9, "be" is understood; 12:14, "bless . . . bless . . . curse not"; 12:16b, "be not conceited"; 12:15, "to rejoice" and "to weep." Aside from these, Paul uses a long list of participles in 12:9–13 and 12:15–18, all of an exhortational nature: rejoicing, fellowshipping, not rendering evil, living in peace. The cadence is set by the participles. The participles may reflect a rabbinic way of expressing not direct commands but rules and codes. Romans 12:12 contains a series of datives in rhetorical parallelism: in hope rejoicing, in tribulations steadfast, in prayer persevering. See David Daube, "Appended Note: Participle and Imperative in 1 Peter," in Edward Gordon Selwyn, *The Epistle of St. Peter,* 2nd ed. (London: MacMillan, 1947), 480, and Charles Kingsley Barrett, *Romans,* vol. 6, Harper's New Testament Commentaries (New York: Harper & Row, Publishers, Inc., 1957), 240.

love in the exercise of gifts, and truth in love are three dynamic expressions of love. Messiah's army marches with a different methodology.

Romans 12:9–21 gives twelve additional thoughts about love. (Romans 12:15 was discussed in the previous section on empathy and is not again considered here, and Romans 12:20–21 is discussed in the following section on final judgment.) Note now their similarities to their parallels in 1 Corinthians and Ephesians.

HATE EVIL; CLING TO GOOD

Love must be sincere. Hate what is evil; cling to what is good (Romans 12:9).

Love does not delight in evil but rejoices with the truth (1 Corinthians 13:6).

Therefore each of you must put off falsehood and speak truthfully to his neighbor, for we are all members of one body (Ephesians 4:25).

Love unfeigned is the topic. It is without hypocrisy. (Is this a reflection on the state of Pharisaic religion in Paul's day?) First John 3:1 describes this love as foreign to this world. It literally is an "out of this world" kind of love. It starts with hating evil (repelling it utterly), and moves to loving the saints and blessing our enemies. It is built on the premise that God is in charge. That is why we can love and not curse. God will mete out justice on our behalf.

In Romans, evil is spoken of. Whatever it is, Christians must hate it with deepest intensity. William Barclay says, "Our one security against sin lies in our being shocked by it."[33] The "good" *agatho* is instrumental case, both in 12:9 and 12:21. The way to conquer evil is through the instrument of the good. To use evil to fight evil is the human way. The Christian's trust is in the good. The ultimate good is God. Resist the devil in Christ's power and he will flee. "Love does not delight in evil but rejoices with the

---

[33]William Barclay, *The Letter to the Romans*, Daily Study Bible Series (Philadelphia: The Westminister Press, 1975), 177.

truth" (1 Corinthians 13:6). The parallel in Ephesians 4:25 is "put off falsehood."

The great lie is the devil's deception of mankind. Paul gives two reasons for telling the truth: This counters that deception and builds the body of Christ (Ephesians 4:17–25). Paul's ethics do not simply revolve around what is right or wrong or convenient. We are not honest simply because it is the best policy, because one day it may not seem to be the best policy. Nor is honesty simply obedience to a command. It is not simply a pursuit of truth. It is living out the life of Christ.

GENTLENESS

> Be devoted to one another in brotherly love. Honor one another above yourselves (Romans 12:10).
>
> Love is patient, love is kind. It does not envy, it does not boast, it is not proud. It is not rude, it is not self-seeking, it is not easily angered, it keeps no record of wrongs (1 Corinthians 13:4–5).
>
> Be kind and compassionate to one another, forgiving each other, just as in Christ God forgave you (Ephesians 4:32).

God's love is revealed through His people. They are to be exhibiters of gentleness, kindness, and compassion. The Romans passage uses the words for brotherly love *(philadelphia)* and family affection *(storge)* to discuss relationships. In Ephesians Paul uses an unusual word for forgiveness *(charizomenoi)*, a present participle from the root verb meaning "to give freely or graciously as a favor."[34] One may literally translate this "gracing." Paul says we are to be "gracing each other [continuously], just as in Christ God graced you [at the point of Calvary, once for all]" (Ephesians 4:32). It is not an occasional manifesting, but a life-style. What a foundation and context of ministry! We do not forgive because we are

---

[34] In Galatians 3:18 *(kecharistai)*, 1 Corinthians 2:12 *(charisthenta)*, and Romans 8:32 *(charisetai)*, Paul has used a form of this verb to talk about God's free gift. The grace of God is obviously the root idea of the verb. True pardon is the gracing action of God. Although *charizomai* is not the normal word for forgiveness, it is an excellent word for it.

noble or others are deserving. We forgive because Christ forgave us. This is good news! This love seeks the best for others. Normal defense mechanisms to protect the ego will be set aside to meet the needs and develop the potential of others. It is a necessary, healing, motivating, unifying force.

The Corinthians parallel focuses on the nature of agape love and the Christian's personal attitudes and actions in manifesting love. The graciousness of love will not turn people away. It will communicate in such humility and sensitivity that one can concentrate on the other and not on self.

ZEAL

> Never be lacking in zeal, but keep your spiritual fervor, serving the Lord[35] (Romans 12:11).
>
> Love . . . rejoices with the truth (1 Corinthians 13:6).
>
> Live a life worthy of the calling you have received. . . . Put on the new self, created to be like God in true righteousness and holiness (Ephesians 4:1,24).

Sincere love is active. We are to be diligent, not halfhearted. "Spiritual fervor" pictures the boiling of a hot spring. What a contrast this is to the lukewarmness of the church at Laodicea! If we are new creatures in Christ, have received His calling, and have put on the new self, then our disposition is to have God glorified. We will pursue righteousness and holiness. We will rejoice with truth and not evil.

Whereas many Eastern philosophies reflect a passive, protective "Do not do unto others what you don't want them to do to you," Christianity challenges one to follow the Lord in aggressive, re-

---

[35]One variant in inferior manuscripts (D, F, G) changes the phrase "serving the Lord" to "serving the opportunity" (*kairos* instead of *kurios*). Some copyist may have seen the devotional significance that every moment of time can be an opportunity to serve the Lord and may be God's special time for someone. Paul does say "Redeem the time." (Ephesians 5:16 may be translated, "Buy up every opportunity from the marketplace of life!") We are to make use of every God-given moment.

demptive ministry. Such a posture is not automatic; we need to let God renew our allegiance.

Zeal can be quenched by distraction, self-pity, sin, quarreling, lost vision, or laziness. Paul says, "Live a life worthy . . ." His attitude alone was a powerful example: He was glad to be the Lord's prisoner. His zeal was not based on emotion but upon the grace of God in salvation and calling. The joy of the Lord was his strength; Paul's response to God's grace was gratitude.

REJOICING, STEADFASTNESS, PRAYER

> **Be joyful in hope, patient in affliction, faithful in prayer (Romans 12:12).**

> **It [love] always protects, always trusts, always hopes, always perseveres (1 Corinthians 13:7).**

Romans 12:12 presents a triad—joyfulness, patience, prayerfulness—that has some parallels in 1 Corinthians 13. This triad is a theology of hope based on Jesus' work at Calvary. Because He died and rose again we have present blessing and future hope. Joy comes in the hope that we shall see face to face and will know fully as we are known (1 Corinthians 13:11–12).

A key word for "patience" is *hupomones,* bearing up under circumstances. It is the same word used in Romans 12:12, "patience in tribulation," and 1 Corinthians 13:7, "always perseveres." In these two verses Paul speaks of rejoicing in hope and being patient in tribulation at the same time. Tribulation can be a useful tool to build character. But tribulation without hope makes us of all men most miserable. At this point, the thought of the two verses diverges: Instead of faithfulness in prayer as emphasized in Romans, 1 Corinthians teaches about love that never fails.

Just as faith, hope, and love are interrelated, so also are joy (literally, "rejoicing"), steadfastness, and prayer. (Note the formulas.) If we rejoice (R) in hope and are steadfast (S) in tribulation, yet are not faithful in prayer (P), then we cannot utilize God's power to defeat the enemy. We depend only on a mental attitude of joy and try to succeed in our strength. Many Christians neglect the refuge afforded by prayer. Yet it is the lifeline to God's grace and resolution of what we face. Prayer is important to maintaining steadfastness and joy.

$$R + S - P = \text{Powerlessness}$$

If we rejoice in hope and persevere in prayer, yet are not steadfast in tribulation, we give up too easily and become frustrated. Our prayers become wishful thinking for a kind of victorious life that does not have to pay its price. Christians should thank God for every circumstance because God will use it for good.

$$R + P - S = \text{Faintheartedness}$$

Persevering in prayer and steadfastness in tribulation without rejoicing in hope results in a fatalistic "grit your teeth and bear it" attitude. Then the focus is on suffering for Jesus instead of the joy of the Lord. We lose our growing edge to press forward in faith. We take a defensive posture and become examples of gloom, while trying to look spiritual.

$$P + S - R = \text{Martyr mentality}$$

FELLOWSHIP WITH THOSE IN NEED

... If it is encouraging, let him encourage; if it is contributing to the needs of others, let him give generously; if it is leadership, let him govern diligently; if it is showing mercy, let him do it cheerfully. . . . Share with God's people who are in need. Practice hospitality (Romans 12:8,13).

If I give all I possess to the poor and surrender my body to the flames, but have not love, I gain nothing (1 Corinthians 13:3).

He who has been stealing must steal no longer, . . . that he may have something to share with those in need (Ephesians 4:28).

Biblically, "fellowship" can refer to our common salvation, sufferings, interaction with other believers, partnership in the gospel, offerings, and caring for the needs of the saints. It is not despising others because of their needs, but taking special joy in ministering in love to their needs. The ministry is in the method and motivation as well as in the action. Love unfeigned means fellowshipping *(koinonountes)* with the needs of the saints and practicing hospitality (Romans 12:13).

The thief who becomes a Christian is given a unique reason to work (Ephesians 4:28). It is not to justify himself, to gain a decent reputation, to pay back those he stole from, or simply to support himself. Although these motives may be appropriate, Paul lifts the former thief beyond selfishness to the higher motivation of service: Work to help those in need.

Hospitality and generosity were earmarks of the Early Church.[36] It was especially important in times of persecution.

No Unwholesome Talk

> **Bless those who persecute you; bless and do not curse (Romans 12:14).**

> **When I was a child, I talked like a child, I thought like a child, I reasoned like a child. When I became a man, I put childish ways behind me (1 Corinthians 13:11).**

> **"In your anger, do not sin": Do not let the sun go down while you are still angry. . . . Do not let any unwholesome talk come out of your mouths, but only what is helpful for building others up according to their needs, that it may benefit those who listen (Ephesians 4:26,29).**

Romans 12:13–16 speaks of reaching out unselfishly not just to saints, not just to the lowly of this world, but to our enemies. We are to bless and to stop cursing others. Some manuscripts read "bless

---

[36]See Luke 6:38; Galatians 6:10; 1 Timothy 3:2; Titus 1:8; Hebrews 13:2; 1 Peter 4:9; 2 John; and 3 John for the major emphases on hospitality. However, this graciousness was abused by many in the Early Church era. Guidelines had to be set up to test life, doctrine, motives, and length of stay. For more on this, see the Didache in *Early Christian Fathers,* ed. Cyril Richardson, vol. 1, The Library of Christian Classics (Philadelphia: Westminster Press, 1953), 161–179. In the Didache 11:5-6 the warning was that if an apostle stayed more then three days, he was a false prophet (p. 176).

those who persecute you," and others read simply "bless those who persecute." Whether we are the actual victims of persecution or not, we are to reach out to bless our enemies. The radical demands of Jesus as expressed in the Sermon on the Mount (Matthew 5:11) are reflected here. Christians must be different. Someone has said, "It is better to light a candle than to curse the darkness." Christians are the light of the world.

Those who persecute us are revealing their own ignorance, hurts, and insecurities. No matter how difficult it may be, our role is to share good news with them, not in order to demonstrate our wisdom, but to minister to their needs. We need not fight back; God is our defender. The human tendency is to tell the other person what he deserves, but out of the mouth can come deadly poison. Paul says that "unwholesome talk" is not to come out of our mouths.

Childish thinking and reactions (1 Corinthians 13:11; 14:20) may cause us to seek revenge. Maturity helps us to see God in control of our lives. We do not need to react to every comment or action of others. Rather, we can respond to God's justice and provision for our lives.

The proper motivation is necessary to achieve full effectiveness of the gifts. First Corinthians 13 focuses on love as the appropriate motivation. Ephesians 4:28 refines our motivation, focusing not on self-fulfillment but on the other's fulfillment. That is, it is not enough to merely be loving, to feel loving. Love that is general and lofty may not meet specific needs of people. It must be directed. This is where the fruit and gifts of the Spirit work together. The fruit develops the character and sensitivities of the believer to be used by God to meet the real needs of others. Fruit in Galatians 5:22–23 refers not just to a personal, internal state of contentment, but to a manifestation of Christlikeness by which others will be drawn to God. Thus, in Ephesians 4:28 the character, motivation, and fruit are emphasized. Fruit reflects who we *are*. Gifts reflect what we *do* in the power of the Spirit. Yet, one can readily see the overlap of the two.

HUMBLE MINDSET

Live in harmony with one another. Do not be proud, but be

willing to associate with people of low position. Do not be conceited (Romans 12:16).

. . . there should be no division in the body, . . . its parts should have equal concern for each other (1 Corinthians 12:25).

Love is patient, love is kind. It does not envy, it does not boast, it is not proud (1 Corinthians 13:4).

Be completely humble and gentle; be patient, bearing with one another in love (Ephesians 4:2).

. . . be made new in the attitude of your minds (Ephesians 4:23).

Humility is a major theme for Paul. In Philippians 2:2,5, Paul exhorted coworkers to be of the same mind and to take on the mind of Christ. Christ willingly laid aside personal glory for the greater glory of God's plan. His mind was one of humility and servanthood. Euodia and Syntyche had been contenders together with Paul for the sake of the gospel (Philippians 4:2–3 *synethlesan*—lit., "coathletes"). They were not weak, unopinionated believers. They helped Paul in the tough, early days of developing the church at Philippi. It should not surprise us that strong personalities could have major disagreements, yet all in the name of glorifying God. Paul does not speak negatively of them, but compliments their great contribution to the work of God. For these women to be of one mind would require humility and a servant spirit.

Envy, pride, and boastfulness are no part of humility or love (1 Corinthians 13:4). God desires a mind-set committed to a complete expression of humility (Ephesians 4:2,23); this should be our motivation and goal. Humility provides an excellent context for the exercise of gifts. If everyone exercised gifts humbly, everyone could learn together, less criticism would occur, God would be exalted. Christianity does not just make us better, it makes us different.

Romans 12 speaks of a transformed mind. Paul prays that Christians may be of the same mind (Romans 15:5). The spiritual battleground is in the mind. It is in the thought life that we win or lose the battle. It is here that God uses heavy artillery to demolish strongholds (2 Corinthians 10:4–5).

But the key to power is unity. Christians have too many different perspectives to be united on every issue. Humility causes believers not to exaggerate their own importance but to see the strengths of others and to help them develop their ministries. Personal ambitions must be set aside for the greater good of all.

A popular Chinese story tells of a dying father who had ten quarreling sons. He wanted to teach them about unity before he died. Gathering the sons around his bedside, he asked each one, in turn, to break a stick. Each son, eager to show his prowess, broke his stick with ease. Then, the father brought out ten sticks bound together. Try as they might, the sons could not break the bundle of sticks. The father said to the sons, "If you go out into the world one by one, the circumstances will break you. But if you go out united as one, nothing can come against you!"

What power in unity! God had promised Israel, "Five of you will chase a hundred, and a hundred of you will chase ten thousand, and your enemies will fall by the sword before you" (Leviticus 26:8). How we need to know this lesson. On most issues, rightness is not as important as unity.

No Revenge

> **Do not repay anyone evil for evil. Be careful to do what is right in the eyes of everybody (Romans 12:17).**

> **It [love] is not rude, it is not self-seeking, it is not easily angered, it keeps no record of wrongs (1 Corinthians 13:5).**

> **Get rid of all bitterness, rage and anger, brawling and slander, along with every form of malice (Ephesians 4:31).**

Romans 12:17–21 lays down basic principles of relationships, especially with those who may hurt us. We are to do right consistently before all men. We are not situation ethicists. We are not to keep a record of wrongs or to repay evil for evil. Moses' guideline of "eye for eye, tooth for tooth"—contrary to the popular misconception that it endorses revenge—sought to limit retribution, offering an objective measure of justice. For example, rather than allowing an offended party to give vent to rage, exacting retribution far out of proportion to the offense, God set down guidelines through Moses that reflected the dignity and worth of all individuals.[37] But Christian grace goes further than the Law. It adds mercy to justice. It seeks to bless others.

Doing right and showing compassion, however, are hindered by the sins within us: bitterness, rage, anger, brawling, slander, and malice. Brawling, slander, and malice come from selfish and evil motives. These belong to the old nature. Bitterness comes from a lack of forgiveness.

We fail to forgive for many reasons. Foremost is that we do not grasp God's forgiveness of us. We forgive not because we feel generous and loving but because it is God's nature to forgive. If we do not forgive men their sins, neither will our Father forgive us (Matthew 6:14–15).

Second, we fail to forgive because we forget Joseph's perspective on evil: "You meant evil against me, but God meant it for good" (Genesis 50:20, NASB). God redeems the harsh events of our lives.

Third, the old nature feels a need for self-justification—to prove itself right and the other person wrong. But God is the righteous judge and vindicator.

Fourth, we do not believe others deserve justification. Yet Christ came to redeem them and make them part of the body of Christ. Our unforgiving spirit may even cause others to stumble over the gospel and be hurt spiritually. A bitter root can cause trouble and defile many (Hebrews 12:15). Then we seek revenge.

Fifth, we fail to forgive because we don't realize how much not forgiving hurts us. Paul is concerned lest we diminish our potential. Life's hurts can make us small people on the inside. We must not give the devil any territory.

A Chinese proverb says, "It is preferable to sin against a big

---

[37]For further discussion of this, see the Code of Hammurabi (ca. 1726 B.C. in Babylon) and the Laws of Eshunna (ca. 1726 B.C. in Akkadia). Stuart, in Gordon D. Fee and Douglas Stuart, *How to Read the Bible for All Its Worth* (Grand Rapids: Zondervan Publishing House, 1982), 143–144. William Barclay, *The Gospel of Matthew: Chapters 1–10*, vol. 1, rev. ed., The Daily Study Bible Series (Philadelphia: Westminster Press, 1975), 162–165, gives further descriptions of the contrast between the Law of Moses and the laws of surrounding countries.

man rather than a small man.'' People of small character will be easily hurt and bear grudges a long time. People who are big will be magnanimous, generous. Let us be big. With a forgiving, gracing life-style, rage and anger become defused, less violent. We see from another perspective; we develop a God-sized heart.

BE AT PEACE

If it is possible, as far as it depends on you, live at peace with everyone (Romans 12:18).

Make every effort to keep the unity of the Spirit through the bond of peace (Ephesians 4:3).

Peace is not just a state of mind. It is a methodology (Ephesians 4:3). It seeks to bring together what has been separated until a sense of wholeness and well-being has been achieved. (The bond is peace itself [genitive of apposition].) We are literally to be "peacing it with all men" (Romans 12:18). However, love is realistic: A person cannot make others love or be at peace with him. But we don't have to be the stumbling blocks. We are to seek reconciliation and develop bridge-building skills. If the other party rebuffs our continued attempts at reconciliation, then we have done our part.

HANDLING ANGER

Do not take revenge, my friends, but leave room for God's wrath, for it is written: "It is mine to avenge; I will repay," says the Lord (Romans 12:19).

. . . [Love] is not easily angered, it keeps no record of wrongs. Love does not delight in evil (1 Corinthians 13:5–6).

"In your anger, do not sin": Do not let the sun go down while you are still angry. . . . Get rid of . . . every form of malice (Ephesians 4:26,31).

Anger is not evil in itself. For example, it is good to be angry at sin and injustice. God's anger is expressed in ultimate judgment. But anger in humans can become the devil's opportunity. So Paul cautions, "In your anger, do not sin" (Ephesians 4:26). Anger must be settled quickly, before permanent damage is done. God's solution is not found in suppression, but in control of anger. By viewing life through the lens of His grace, peace, and forgiveness, we learn to trust Him to take care of our concerns.

Anger and depression both may reflect a mishandling of emotions. Anger turns the emotion outward, often to hurt our fellowman. Depression turns the emotion inward, hurting ourselves. But anger hurts us too. To keep a record of wrongs and to rejoice when another suffers misfortune (1 Corinthians 13:5–6) demeans us and makes us less than we could be. Worse yet, such behavior affects our relationship with God. The temptation of anger is that temporarily we feel the immediate gain: We believe the anger justifies us and proves the other wrong. But we are only dealing with the problem at an emotional level, not at the issue level. The problem that caused the anger does not go away, but usually intensifies. Love, on the other hand, controls the anger so that an adequate solution may be found.

On the sensitive issue of loving enemies, Paul addresses the Romans affectionately and gently. He calls them, "My friends" (Romans 12:19). This quote about God's wrath is from Deuteronomy 32:35. The Law spoke against revenge because of God's ultimate justice. The reason we can love our enemies is that God is just. We don't tell God how to resolve a matter, or try to resolve those problems for Him. We simply submit to Him who does all things well. We can go the second mile and reach out to love our enemies.

Final Judgment

... Leave room for God's wrath, for it is written: "It is mine to avenge; I will repay," says the Lord. On the contrary: "If your enemy is hungry, feed him; if he is thirsty, give him something to drink. In doing this you will heap burning coals on his head." Do not be overcome by evil, but overcome evil with good (Romans 12:19–21).

> **When perfection comes, the imperfect disappears. . . . Now**
> **we see but a poor reflection; then we shall see face to face. Now**
> **I know in part; then I shall know fully, even as I am fully known**
> **(1 Corinthians 13:10,12).**

> **. . . Reach unity in the faith, . . . become mature, attaining**
> **the whole measure of the fullness of Christ. . . . in all things**
> **grow up into him who is the Head, that is, Christ. . . . And do**
> **not grieve the Holy Spirit of God, with whom you were sealed**
> **for the day of redemption (Ephesians 4:13,15,30).**

All three passages on love are written in the context of Christian conduct in light of the Lord's coming. Theologians call it kingdom life-style, or eschatological conduct.[38] We do not build our ethics around philosophy, culture, or convenience, but around the righteousness of God and in view of His final judgment. I have given

---

[38]Most evangelical theologians believe that these principles are valid for the whole Church Age, that we live in the tension between the "now and the not yet," thus the term "eschatological conduct." See Käsemann, *Romans,* 349 ("When a person burns in the Spirit and simultaneously associates with the lowly, this involves eschatological conduct, and the other requirements [of Romans 12] are also seen against this background"). Barth, *Ephesians 1–3* and *Ephesians 4–6,* gives extensive discussion of the realized eschatology of Paul in Ephesians and the implication for present conduct. See especially p. 143 (*Ephesians 1–3*) where he discusses the seal of the Spirit in its "ministerial, missionary, evangelistic character," p. 155 where he distinguishes the past age of evil and the present age of "peace, sanctification, revelation, light," and his discussion "Ecclesiology of Hope," pp. 322–325. George Eldon Ladd, *A Theology of the New Testament* (Grand Rapids: William B. Eerdmans, 1974), and Fee, *How to Read the Bible,* and others use the term "kingdom life-style" synonymously with "eschatological conduct." The Church lives in light of Christ's first coming and the inbreaking of the kingdom of God now. It faithfully witnesses, whether Christ will come in two days or one hundred years. God is judge, His righteousness will be vindicated, the Church will be victorious, and Satan will be vanquished. Our lives, empowered by the Spirit, should express that.

In the early 1900s, men like Albert Schweitzer spoke of Paul's theology as "interim ethics." They said both Jesus and Paul had been mistaken about the timing of the Second Coming. Therefore, Paul and others wrote about a radically demanding life-style, an interim ethic, just until the Lord's soon return. Supposedly this explained some of their strong statements on holiness, marriage, loving enemies, and doing good to those who hurt us. But Schweitzer (et al.) based his teaching on mistaken assumptions about the nature of the authority and inspiration of the Word.

this topic a separate heading rather than include it in the section on "Sincere Love" because of its significance in these passages.

The quote in Romans 12:20 is from the wisdom literature of the Old Testament (Proverbs 25:21–22). In these passages on love, Paul has quoted Jesus, the Law, the wisdom literature, and shared a prophetic concern for the poor and needy. This is God's wisdom.

The burning coals may picture an Egyptian practice that indicated penitence, when a person put a pan of burning charcoal on his head. If so, Paul is saying that through love we may lead the person to repentance (see also 1 Peter 3:1–2). Whatever the meaning of this reference, we still have the command to give our enemy food and drink: Let the enemy realize it is God he is fighting, not us. We do not want to defeat our enemies. Rather, we wish to win them to the Lord. We do not have to succumb to the devil's pressures. The warfare is between evil and good. We can conquer evil only with good.

First Corinthians points to a time of total clarity, when we shall see face to face and know fully as we are fully known. It is the day of the coming of the Lord. It is judgment day. All our actions will be judged by His standards.

In Ephesians, eschatological references are plentiful. Paul speaks of the future point of full maturity and the day of redemption. We are sealed by the Spirit until that day (Ephesians 4:13,15,30). The gifts are at work until Jesus comes. The times will reach their fulfillment (Ephesians 1:10). The deposit guarantees our inheritance until the redemption of those who are God's possession (Ephesians 1:14). The commands throughout Ephesians indicate radical, dramatic, urgent change is required. Redeem the time (Ephesians 5:16). Christ seeks to present to himself a radiant church (Ephesians 5:27). Slaves and masters have a Master in heaven to answer to (Ephesians 6:9). And "finally" may be a reference to the final days when the day of evil comes (Ephesians 6:13).

In recent years, evangelicals have focused on either one of two perspectives. The first is that of a salvation wherein all has been accomplished, including being sealed by the Spirit. Its focus is on positional justification, sanctification, redemption, and eternal security. Unfortunately, this view misses Paul's mission-oriented theology. It does not adequately elaborate the present practical implications of these passages for personal victory, empowerment by the Spirit, gifts for building the church, and evangelization of the world.[39]

The second perspective has focused on the future. When is Christ returning? Is it before, during, or after the Great Tribulation? What are the signs of his coming? How do *I* prepare for it?

Paul's questions transcend both perspectives. What is the Church? Who are the people of God? What are its purpose and calling? How should the body of believers live now in light of God's ultimate judgment?

Let us claim our empowering, rise above our petty quarrels and insecurities, live up to our inheritance as children of God, and get the job done. It is in light of His coming that the gifts are to operate to edify the believer and penetrate the darkness. Everything Christians do should be in view of His kingdom, both present and future. That is why we must be fervent in Spirit, care for the poor, love our enemies, strive for unity, and live up to our calling.[40] We are witnesses to the nature and power of His kingdom in an evil world.

---

[39]See Harry R. Boer, *Pentecost and Missions* (Grand Rapids: Zondervan Publishing House, 1961), for a fuller treatment of this issue.

[40]Barth, *Ephesians 4–6*, 526. Markus Barth summarizes the practical opportunities and obligations of Kingdom life-style in Ephesians 4:17–32—"[t]he relationship of the saints as members of one body, the exclusion of any legal claim of the devil upon the saints, the right of the needy to receive support, the opportunity to help one's fellowman by good works, to address him with true and constructive words, and to meet him with goodness (vv. 25,27,28,29,32)."

PART TWO

Exhortation

Introduction

To encourage a life-style of worship as a medium for gift ministry, I have included summaries of three sermons. The first message lays down foundational principles from Romans for a life-style of worship and ministry. The second message discusses how to begin ministering utterance gifts. The third message is a walk through Ephesians, showing how worship leads to mission.

6

Exercising the Gifts

The gifts must become part of our life-style, not merely an occasional incident. Romans 12 reveals seven principles for an ongoing exercise of gifts.

Life Is Worship

The first eleven chapters of Romans detail the rich grace of God in the Christian's calling, salvation, sanctification, and victorious living. In 12:1, the word "therefore" refers to all of those privileges. Privilege implies responsibility. Our responsibility is to be a living sacrifice of worship to God. When we have this perspective, we can readily see how God may manifest a gift through us at any time and in any situation. To exercise gifts only in the setting of the church service misses the wider possibilities. The Church is to be a living worship to God, reflecting His love and glory to the world.

This emphasis on worship is not only in Romans, but in Thessalonians, Corinthians, Philippians, Colossians, and Ephesians as well.

Paul's prayer for the Thessalonians was, "May God himself, the God of peace, *sanctify* you through and through. May your whole spirit, soul and body be kept *blameless* at the coming of our Lord Jesus Christ" (1 Thessalonians 5:23, emphasis added). The words "sanctify" and "blameless" are used in offering sacrifices. The Corinthians' generosity in a love offering caused Paul to point out both the horizontal and vertical dimensions of worship: "This service that you perform is not only supplying the needs of God's people but is also overflowing in many expressions of thanks to God" (2 Corinthians 9:12). Paul told the Philippians, "He who *began* a good work in you will *carry it on to completion* until the day of Christ Jesus'' (Philippians 1:6, emphasis added). The italicized words are from Greek words picturing the beginning and ending of a perfect sacrifice. Paul's prayer for the Colossians was that they might ''live a life worthy of the Lord and please him in every way'' (Colossians 1:10).

Paul's epistles normally begin with doctrine and move to the practical aspects of the believer's life. Life-style is built upon the solid foundation of eternal truth. The Book of Ephesians, however, shows how genuine worship leads to a powerful practice of eternal truths and a dynamic Christian life-style.

Transformed thinking enables us to recognize and accept the good, pleasing, and perfect will of God. God's will is that we become more like Christ and that we proclaim the good news to all. And only Christ's righteousness in our lives will meet the test of ''the good.'' In the Old Testament, offerings were either acceptable or unacceptable. They were not just passable. Either the offerings were unblemished and presented from a proper spirit, pleasing God, or they were an abomination. God's will is perfect. He desires that our lives from beginning to end be offered as worship to Him.

Paul exhorts us to have sober judgment about ourselves, to divest ourselves of pride. I believe most Spirit-filled Christians strongly desire to exercise such judgment on all teachings as well. I appreciate the prophetic element and the challenge to move ahead in faith. Some prophecies and teachings, however, contain a self-destructive element. For example, blind faith and presumptuous actions may devastate fellow Christians. Extremes in doctrine lead to the neglect of the rest of Scripture, ignoring the possible consequences of such action.

We cannot minister gifts based on emotions, dogmatism, or wild claims. Some may say, ''But God told me to do this,'' or ''The church has to do this now or it will be out of the will of God.'' We must test and approve what God's will is. In the 1960s it was not unusual to hear some say, ''Mortgage your properties and let the devil have the debt, because the Lord is coming soon!'' Leaders have a great responsibility to think through what they wish to teach and say it clearly so that they will not be misunderstood.

Esteem in Christ Liberates

In Romans 12:3 Paul says, "Do not think of yourself more highly than you ought, but rather think of yourself with sober judgment, in accordance with the measure of faith God has given you." How we see ourselves determines how we project our personal ministries.

Pride distorts our ministries. It is the basic sin of all mankind. The serpent tempted Adam and Eve with the possibility of being like God. Mankind tries to make its own way. Even the plague of inferiority that has infected people worldwide is basically a manifestation of pride in reverse, a result of the Fall. People, in trying to be like God, discover they cannot even be the people they want to be. Jesus came to set us free from our sin, carnality, pride, and low self-esteem. Human identity, health, and wholeness are in Christ.

John describes our problem as "the cravings of sinful man, the lust of his eyes and the boasting of what he has and does" (1 John 2:16). There is a parallel to this in Genesis 3:6. Adam and Eve, though not yet fallen, saw that the fruit was good for food ("cravings"), pleasing to the eye ("the lust of [the] eyes"), and desirable for gaining wisdom ("boasting"). In a similar way Jesus was tempted to turn stones into bread ("cravings"), to see and claim the kingdoms of the world ("lust of [the] eyes"), and to jump from the highest point of the temple ("boastings"). But He refused Satan's options so that He could reveal God's plan of redemption.

Figure 6 clarifies differences between a healthy, biblical view of self and either pride or low self-esteem. Both pride and low self-esteem are destructive of and unproductive in eternal values and the exercise of gifts. Pride limits us to our abilities. Low esteem limits us to our perceived inabilities. Faith in God's sufficiency liberates us to pursue our potential. Both pride and perfectionism are hindrances to fulfilling the Great Commission. Only Spirit-enabled believers can fulfill that task.

Mature Christians are free. Paul was such a Christian. He rose above opinions of others, legalism, self-righteousness, fear, and a need for personal ego fulfillment. He had died to self and was alive in the Spirit. F. F. Bruce, commenting on 2 Corinthians 3:17, calls Paul the "apostle of the free spirit."[1]

Pride Promotes:	Bible Promotes:	Low Self-esteem Promotes:
Self-sufficiency	Dependence on God	Self-condemnation
Self-confidence	Spirit-led living	Overcautiousness
Striving for fulfillment	Contentment	False guilt
Justification by works	Justification by grace through faith	Justification by works
Personal abilities and successes	Sober thinking of self	Inferiority
Glorification of self	Glorification of God	Inadequacy in light of perfectionist standards
Legalism or license	Freedom in Christ	Legalism or license

Figure 6. Views of Self

True mental health and humility are not found in self-abasement. Although prideful boasts do not honor God, neither do derogatory statements about oneself. In the context of Romans 12, sober judgment relates to ultimate judgment and the day of God's wrath. Before the judgment seat of Christ many of our statements about ourselves will seem so foolish. The question is not, Who am I? It is, What is Christ doing in my life? Our identity is found in Christ, not in our achievements. It is not found in self-fulfillment but in fulfillment in God through service to Him and others. It is not found in self-justification but in Christ's justification of us: "Nought of good that I have done / Nothing but the blood of Jesus." A proper view of ourselves will lead to real freedom of ministry. We are not here to impress ourselves or others. God must be glorified.

---

[1]F. F. Bruce, *The Apostle of the Heart Set Free* (Grand Rapids: William B. Eerdmans, 1977), 18–21.

Different Functions Develop Diverse Ministries

No one can, or should, do all the functions in the church. Everyone has strengths and weaknesses. To be able to recognize where we fit in the body of Christ, to be content in our place of ministry, is of singular importance. This allows each believer to concentrate on his ministry (or ministries), grow in the exercise of it, and become open to what the Spirit may do through him. Finding and accepting one's place in the Body frees one to recognize and encourage the ministries of others. The Spirit creatively touches believers in delightfully different ways.

The Early Church was a striking example of this principle. Mary was the devotional, meditative type. Martha was busy with her hospitality. Thomas knew how to question; he sought proof. Peter was impulsive, action-oriented, and full of leadership qualities. Barnabas was a reconciler, seeking to develop the ministries of others, even when they were considered rejects. Paul was emotional, goal-oriented, intelligent, a highly motivated overachiever. And Aquila and Priscilla were a standout teaching team to all the churches of the Gentiles.

The churches in the first century were often pastored by more than one person. A team of leaders modeled unity in diversity. A difficulty of present approaches to solo leadership is that pastors often do not build on diversity but on sameness. Management experts show that an organization built on sameness has limited potential for growth. When Christians basically try to help the pastor fulfill his ministry, the biblical order is reversed. The pastor must seek to help people fulfill their ministries. This allows for a telescoping of growth, both spiritually and numerically. We must appreciate and utilize differences in personality and ability.

Some fear diversity because they anticipate conflict. Diversity means there will be different viewpoints. A Book of Acts perspective on conflict sees proper handling of conflict as one of the key methods of growth in the Church. The Early Church faced problems that might have torn it apart. But God's hand was in the midst of each situation.

Our Identity Is Individual, Yet Integral to the Body

Romans 12:5 says, "So in Christ we who are many form one body, and each member belongs to all the others." Secular humanism says man is central. Some authoritarian forms of government say the state is central. Biblically, we are individuals, yet we are part of the Church. We belong to each other. Identity is found in knowing who we are in Christ and in relationship with other members of the Body. In ministering gifts we must consider the good of all. Even when we are personally hurt by others or our ideas seem to be rejected, we must not lose sight of the importance of edifying the Church to fulfill His plan for this world. We must strive to do nothing to hurt the cause of Christ.

The question is not, What are my gifts? The question is, How will my gifts and ministries relate to the purpose, direction, and edification of the Church? Let us dream together for the church of Jesus Christ. When we exercise gifts and ministries we begin to grow and discover who we are in the body of Christ. As we encourage others to minister their gifts, they too find they are valued and anointed members of the body of Christ. We have not arrived at our destination yet. We are a pilgrim people marching together to the heavenly city.

Personal Inadequacy Leads to Interdependence

Romans 12:6 says, "We have different gifts, according to the grace given us. If a man's gift is prophesying, let him use it in proportion to his faith." Everything that Christians have is by the grace of God. Human talent will never change the world for Christ. We feel utterly inadequate when we realize the task before us. Jesus "has saved us and called us to a holy life—not because of anything we have done but because of his own purpose and grace" (2 Timothy 1:9).

If God gives gifts to others, then you cannot claim exclusive rights to hear from God. If you are one member of the body of Christ, it means you are not the whole body. Paul pictures the absurdity of an eye or an ear saying, "I am the body of Christ" (1 Corinthians 12:17). We need each other. You have an emphasis and ability that I do not have. You minister gifts that I do not minister. Even when you minister the same gift, you do so in a different manner. I am made complete by all the other believers.

Our sharing of gifts is partial, imperfect. Romans 12:6–8 emphasizes growth. We tend to prophesy in *proportion* to our faith. We concentrate on the areas we know God can use us in. If gifts were received full and complete, no exhortation on their use would be necessary. But Peter has to counsel, "If anyone speaks, he should do it as one speaking the very words of God" (1 Peter 4:11). And Paul must urge Timothy, "Fan into flame the gift of God, which is in you through the laying on of my hands" (2 Timothy 1:6).

Furthermore, the gifts need to be tested. Their exercise has the potential of misuse, the liability of human weakness, the possibility of being misunderstood. Love helps us grow through these difficulties. It covers the multitude of sins. It does not hide sin, but gives room for us to grow. We will make mistakes. We are inadequate. But God is gracious. He sets us free for His royal service.

Servanthood Sets Free All Types of Gifts

Romans 12:6–8 lists seven gifts. Four seem to be less noticed gifts: serving, encouraging, giving, showing mercy. Among them are three public ministries: prophesying, teaching, leadership.

Paul does a similar thing in 1 Corinthians 12:28–31, combining enabling gifts of apostles, prophets, and teachers with ministry gifts of workings of miracles, healings, helps, administrations, tongues, and interpretations. To a limited extent, administrations may also be an enabling gift, like that of apostle, prophet, and teacher. There is much overlap in operation and interaction that is necessary for the church to function well.

God's sovereignty, personality, and creativity are reflected in the distribution of gifts. Our interdependence on each other and our dependence upon God's grace are inherent in these lists. We know who we are in Christ. Romans 1 through 11 has clarified that. Now, as our loving worship to God, we are to serve one another. In Romans 12, as in 1 Corinthians 12 and 13, everything said about this spiritual worship relates to edifying our fellowman. Let us seek to be all we can be for God. Let us allow the gifts of the Spirit to flow through us.

Gifts Reach Out beyond the Church

Romans 12:14–21 pictures a life-style of ministry that will even bless our enemies with God's grace. The Church should be a "go" structure. Many churches have become "come" structures. The pastor sets up the program and if people are faithful and spiritual, they will come to the program. If only a few come, frustration sets in and a gap develops between those who come (the "spiritual" ones) and those who do not. The work of God is narrowed to church programming, usually within the confines of the facilities, and its support.

Biblically, we gather in order to go to fulfill our mission. The enabling pastor seeks to develop people for their ministries. He is person-centered rather than program-centered. He shows his members how to do their ministries and provides opportunities for ministry suited to them, so they may be uniquely used by God. Elton Trueblood calls the pastor the coach of a team.[2] His glory is showing the team how to win the game. They carry the ball.

The purpose of the Body is to be God's agency of reconciliation for a lost world. According to this passage, we are not to seek to be victorious over human enemies. We have good news for them. They can be liberated through the grace of God. They have been fighting in vain for goals and projects they themselves have not understood. Now they can find fulfillment in Christ. Now we can reach out to them, empowered by the Spirit, secure in our identity, confident of our victory, and sure of God's ultimate judgment. Kingdom living is to reach out in love to the lowly, the mourner,

---

[2]Elton Trueblood, *The Incendiary Fellowship* (New York: Harper & Row, Publishers, Inc., 1967), 43.

the persecutor, the enemy, overwhelming them with blessing and goodness and peace.

These seven principles of exercising the gifts tie together key elements about the purposes and perspectives we must have concerning gifts. From this basis, let us build.

7

Begin to Minister the Gifts

When Israel was in Sinai, God anointed seventy elders to prophesy. Two of them, Eldad and Medad, had remained in the camp and did not go out to the tent where the others were. They also began to prophesy. Joshua feared they might form a rival authority to Moses, but Moses was not threatened. He said, " 'Are you jealous for my sake? I wish that all the Lord's people were prophets and that the Lord would put his Spirit on them' " (Numbers 11:29).

This prayer was not fulfilled in Old Testament times. Prophetic anointing and empowering for ministry came only upon a few people. Israel believed that when the Messiah came the Spirit would be poured out on all people (Joel 2:28–29). When prophetic utterances came forth from Mary, Elizabeth, Zechariah, Simeon, and Anna (Luke 1 through 4), God made very clear that the Messianic Age had come. All of God's people could be endued with power. They would be a prophetic people. Moses' prayer would be fulfilled.

Biblical prophecy implies a sovereign God who is above all and knows all. He is greater than His creation. He commands and it shall be accomplished (e.g., Isaiah 45:18–25). Prediction and its fulfillment reveal His omniscience and omnipotence. He shapes the course of the universe, the destiny of nations, and the direction of individual lives. Yet, because He does speak to human beings through prophecy about their sin and need for repentance, about His hope in the midst of their despair, of restoration, encouragement, and blessing, we see God as very near and very involved in our lives. He is both transcendent and immanent. Some say that God speaks to us only from the written Word. Although prophecy must be subject to the teaching and authority of Scripture, God has never stopped speaking to His people. He can break into the midst of any situation with His special word at anytime.

All believers make up the prophetic people of God (Acts 2:17–18). The elderly are not the church of yesterday and the youth are not the church of tomorrow. We must all function as the people of God now. The people of God when gathered for worship should be in microcosm what they are when scattered in a sinful world. True worship will be reflected in one's attitudes and actions. Life is not to be compartmentalized into the sacred and the secular. We come together to worship and renew our strength so we may touch others. We come to learn to flow in the Spirit. We interact and are accountable to each other. Then we go forth in confidence that God ministers through us supernaturally.

Some believe gifts are primarily manifested in the church service. But one cannot separate the gifts in the church service from the gifts in missions/evangelism. The context of gifts in 1 Corinthians is obviously in the church, but Acts takes us out into the lost world: The Holy Spirit may work through us at any time. Evangelism is based upon Jesus' redemptive sacrifice and the Great Commission, but the impetus of evangelism dramatically comes to life through the empowering of the Spirit.

In the context of 1 Corinthians 14 the gift of prophecy is representative of all anointed speech gifts using the language understood by the congregation. These gifts can be readily tested, encouraged, and confirmed. Paul says, "For you can all prophesy in turn so that everyone may be instructed and encouraged. . . . Be eager to prophesy" (1 Corinthians 14:31,39). By understanding Paul's principles for sharing the gift of prophecy we can better understand the whole realm of the gifts.

The Principle of Incarnation

Samuel Shoemaker makes some interesting observations about the first-century Christians, which imply the incarnational aspects of prophecy:

> What was the content of [their] prophesyings? There was then no New Testament to speak from. These ordinary believers were scarcely sufficiently schooled to offer theological instruction. The prophe-

sying must have been their own personal witness and testimony, the inspired, relevant word given. They were, I profoundly believe, sharing with others their own Spirit-given experiences.[1]

God works through people. But how significant is a person's part in the exercise of gifts? Tremendously significant. In any utterance the messenger is an inseparable part of the message. A person's background, personality, vocabulary, level of maturity, strengths and weaknesses, and relationships all become part of the message.

For example, God may impress several to give a word about the Second Coming. Each one may use different words and yet communicate the same essential message. A witnessing Christian may include an emphasis on witnessing because Jesus is coming soon. A person whose beloved friend has just died may communicate the comfort and hope we have in Jesus' imminent return. Another, who has been sensitive to the church's lack of commitment to true discipleship, might exhort to holiness. But all will share the emphasis of the one message about the coming of the Lord.

If the prophesy giver's life-style doesn't match his words, the message becomes unclear. It is inconsistent to give a message of hope if one's life portrays pessimism and despair. Nor does one have to give a message in a language and tone that is artificial and stilted. It can come forth naturally. As we give our all to God, He equips us supernaturally.

Knowing this truth about the incarnational nature of the gifts, Christians need to learn how to listen to one another. Rather than listening, we have been quick to judge, isolate, and condemn. We should listen in love, teach, encourage, and affirm one another.

The Principle of Process

In prophecy many Christians focus only on the words spoken. The process includes at least four elements: the sharer, the church, the utterance, and the results.

---

[1] Samuel M. Shoemaker, *With the Holy Spirit and With Fire* (New York: Harper and Brothers Publishers, 1960), 106.

Consider the life and background of the sharer. Is he growing in the Lord? What is he now experiencing? A Christian ministers from weakness as well as strength. Perhaps he needs others to minister to him as well. A teachable spirit is necessary. Gifts are shared imperfectly. Since all may prophesy, giving a prophecy is not a sign of deep spirituality. Paul told the charismatic Corinthians that knowledge did not begin and end with them. No matter how great we are, we can learn from the simplest saint. We mature in effectiveness as we learn to minister gifts. We must be willing to learn from leadership and fellow believers.

Understand what God is doing in the church. Unless a church has deviated from God's intended course, prophetic utterances usually are in line with what God is doing in that church, and with the congregation's level of development. Will this prophecy draw people together? The gifts are meant to build a strong, interacting fellowship.

The utterance must be evaluated. Some statements are biblical and helpful. Sometimes we must listen in love and overlook things that reflect personality quirks or hurts. Other statements must be set aside for later consideration. Immediate rejection of an utterance should be reserved for those situations that may damage the body of Christ or promote heretical doctrine.

I remember a new convert giving a prophetic utterance in a Sunday school class. He did not speak forth in the traditionally forceful Pentecostal manner. Someone asked me afterwards whether I felt it was of God. I replied that everything he said was biblical. The new convert was willing to share. No harm had been done to the body of Christ. We need to encourage manifestations, not quench them. We need not become overly critical. The gifts may be manifested during any of our worship forms: Bible readings, songs, testimonies, sermons—as well as through any of our people.

A word should be said about evaluating prophecies. In some circles, testing prophecy supposedly indicates a lack of faith. But because the "spirits of prophets are subject to the control of prophets" (1 Corinthians 14:32), whoever exercises such a gift should recognize the built-in accountability factor to the church, particularly if he does not practice such control. We should welcome proper teaching. "Thus saith the Lord . . ." can be a presumptuous assertion. Christians need the wisdom of God to discern truth; prophecy must stand under the scrutiny of Scripture. Subjective guidelines (e.g., "wasn't anointed" or "wasn't spiritual enough") are insufficient in themselves. Further, the awaiting of prophetic fulfillment has its dangers. By that time damage may have been done to the body of Christ.

Evaluation is best done in the context of a local church where each person's life is accountable to all. Notice Peter's guidelines:

1. Were the prophecies initiated by man without reference to the impulse of the Holy Spirit? (2 Peter 1:21)
2. Were heresies being taught that denied Christ's lordship? (2 Peter 2:1)
3. Was the motive greed? (2 Peter 2:3)
4. Are those prophesying bold and arrogant? Do they follow the desires of the sinful nature? (2 Peter 2:10)
5. Are their lives and messages without content? (2 Peter 2:17)
6. Do they lead others to immoral behavior? (1 Peter 2:19)

The process points to the final results. Were lives touched? Was the church edified? Are people growing in their abilities to minister? One problem in Pentecostal churches is the inability and fear of Christians to evaluate prophecy and its results. Families have been broken up, churches split, and logic cast aside because of an undiscerning, simplistic acceptance of any prophetic word as the infallible word of God. The issue is not what gift it is, or whether it is a gift, but does it edify the body of Christ? Can everyone be instructed and encouraged (1 Corinthians 14:31)? The gifts are not given for our personal glory or for others to look up to us. Even the unbeliever can respond to prophetic utterance (1 Corinthians 14:24–25). Gifts should be evaluated as to Scriptural truth, application to the immediate hearers, the flow of the service, the discernment of the leadership, and the sensitivity of others to the Spirit.

The Principle of Preparation and Confirmation

The gift of prophecy is not meant to initiate personal direction.

To illustrate this, let us examine three episodes from the Book of Acts. First, the prophet Agabus predicted a major famine. Then, in prayer for wisdom, each one determined to give according to his ability (Acts 11:27–30). No response was mandated; sharing with the Jerusalem brethren who would face deprivation was voluntary. The prophecy was preparatory.

Second, while the church at Antioch worshiped and fasted, the Holy Spirit confirmed Barnabas and Paul's mission through a prophetic word. "Set apart for me Barnabas and Saul for the work to which I have called them" (Acts 13:2). The utterance did not initiate the call. They already had been called.

A third example relates to Paul's going to Jerusalem. He knew in the Spirit that he was to go. "And now, compelled by the Spirit [literally, "in the S/spirit"] I am going to Jerusalem, not knowing what will happen to me there. I only know that in every city the Holy Spirit warns me that prison and hardships are facing me. However, I consider my life worth nothing to me, if only I may finish the race and complete the task the Lord Jesus has given me— the task of testifying to the gospel of God's grace" (Acts 20:22–24, see also Acts 19:21).

Prophecies confirmed Paul would be in bondage, and they prepared him and the church for the crisis. Paul knew God's will. Yet note a different prophetic utterance of the disciples in Caesarea: "Through the Spirit they urged Paul not to go on to Jerusalem" (Acts 21:4). Some think Paul was out of the will of God in going to Jerusalem. Let us look further and then return to this verse. When Agabus prophesied Paul would be bound, he gave no directive (Acts 21:11). The Christians at Caesarea pled with him not to go (Acts 21:12). Contrast the utterance of the experienced prophet and the desire of Paul's brethren at Caesarea. When Paul reasserted his willingness to suffer and die for Christ, they concluded, "The Lord's will be done" (Acts 21:13–14). It is safe to conclude that God's will was for Paul to go to Jerusalem. The great Apostle of the Gentiles, who founded many churches and wrote many Epistles, was not wrong here. In fact, from a Roman prison his influence affected Caesar's household, Rome, and the world. Afterwards he was released for further ministry.

How, then, do we explain the apparent contradiction of Acts 21:4? Was this utterance of the devil? Luke emphatically says the disciples urged Paul "through the Spirit." In this context the word "Spirit" could not mean human spirit. At the same time, Paul did not understand what they were saying as a command of God to him. Otherwise, he would either have to rebuke them for hearing the wrong thing from God or accept the command. He did neither.

The explanation, of course, is in the incarnational nature of the gifts. It was God speaking through people. These disciples loved Paul. They could not bear to see Paul arrested and possibly executed; they wanted to warn Paul of possible danger. God had spoken through many others that Paul would be bound. But these men felt God would not want him to go to Jerusalem. But Paul did not recognize prophecy as initiating guidance. Prophecy never initiates guidance in the New Testament. Futhermore, in the few cases it was directive in the Old Testament, it had to be tested. In fact, a prophet died for disobeying and not evaluating what was said to him (1 Kings 13)! Christians need wisdom to discern an issue and to know what practical steps to take.

A pre-Pentecost example of evaluating utterances is found in the encounter between Jesus and Peter. Peter had, in one moment, the revelation that Jesus was the Christ, the Son of the living God. This was the first time Jesus allowed a public declaration of who He was. In the next moment Peter rebuked Jesus for saying He would suffer and die. Jesus rebuked Peter harshly with almost the same words He used to rebuke Satan during the wilderness temptations (Matthew 4:10; 16:23).

Some say Peter was demon-inspired to rebuke Jesus, because they think the word *satana* (Matthew 16:23) here refers to the devil. It should be translated "opponent." Jesus said Peter's words were not of God but from a human source *(ton anthropon)*. Peter, without realizing it, had taken an adversarial role to Jesus' mission. Peter, who dearly loved Jesus, had urged Him to take the easier road. In the wilderness, Satan had urged Jesus to take the easier road to gaining the kingdoms of this world by bowing to him rather than take the way of the Cross. Jesus faced this same temptation throughout his ministry because many wanted Him to be their political messiah, not a suffering servant. This would have undone the mission for which Jesus had come into the world.

The Principle of Interdependence

Because we know and share in part, we are dependent upon others hearing from God as well. All may come to the meeting prepared to minister gifts. Listen to what the Holy Spirit says to your spirit as others are exercising gifts. You may sense a confirmation that God is indeed saying that to the body of Christ, because you felt the same thing. God doesn't reveal himself to just one or two. Revelation does not come by the prophet's own interpretation.

Paul says, "If a revelation comes to someone who is sitting down, the first speaker should stop" (1 Corinthians 14:30). The point of this verse is twofold. First, because God says something to you does not mean you must share it then. In the proper timing it will do the most good for the church. Second, allowing others opportunities to minister the gifts is important. Often the more aggressive among us dominate in this area so that the more timid back off entirely from it. Some share, and others may respond to or confirm what is being shared. One time you may share, the next time you may confirm. Everyone should have opportunity to grow through ministering (1 Corinthians 14:29–31).

Listen to the whole flow of the service. Each part of it may be part of the whole work that God is seeking to do among his people. If what you desire to share is in line with what God is doing in the service, God may want you to minister a prophetic word.

I well remember one meeting where I was asked to preach just moments before the service. Wishing to be "instant in season and out," I accepted without having any sermon notes in my Bible. I preached a message I had used before, sensing it was God's message to this congregation. I poured out my heart in full dependence upon God. Yet as I sat down, I became dejected because I had forgotten three key points in my sermon. But the Spirit was at work: Three people felt prompted to give messages, each one speaking on one of the points I had missed. God taught me something from that: It was not just my presentation that God was speaking through, He was using the whole service, the whole body of Christ, to get His message across.

You may have given a prophetic utterance in a testimony service, a word of wisdom in a board meeting, or a word of knowledge in a Sunday school class and not have been fully aware of it. Yet God's will was accomplished. You may not know until afterwards whether it was clearly a gift of the Spirit. The confirmation by others and their ministries of gifts will put your utterance in total perspective. We know and share in part. "Two or three prophets should speak, and the others should weigh carefully what is said" (1 Corinthians 14:29). Evaluation comes after several have shared. If we share in part it means we need others to share too. We cannot be on our own.

The prophetic gift is easy to initiate. If you are not sure it is a gift, you can offer it humbly to the congregation with a statement like, "I feel impressed that . . . ." You need not begin with a powerful, "Thus saith the Lord." It can be ministered quietly and conversationally, as well as loudly and dramatically. The important thing is that we come together ready to listen and to minister. The church should not need half an hour to get charged up spiritually to minister. Paul pictures God's people as prepared. Whenever "you come together, everyone has a hymn, or a word of instruction" (1 Corinthians 14:26).

The Principle of Clear Communication

Never has the need for clear communication among Christians been greater. Prophecies need not be mysterious and hard to understand. Paul used the example of a trumpet call (1 Corinthians 14:7–11) to make this point: If the sound was not distinct, others could not tell the difference between someone practicing and someone mustering the troops for battle. In spiritual warfare, the message must be clear. The Shannon-Weaver Communication Model illustrates what we mean by clear communication. Five elements of communication include the sender, the encoding, the signal, the decoding, and the receiver. I include one more element: The receiver should become another sender.

The sender is part of the message. It should be obvious to all observers that the medium (our life) is consistent with the message. Secret sin could cause the name of Jesus to be shamed and the ministry of the Spirit to be quenched or distorted.

Encoding involves the actual words of communication. Are they clear and understandable? Are they biblical? Do they build up others?

The signal is very important. In radio communication there are two frequency waves by which a message is received. The first is the carrier wave, which has the strength to project the signal. The second is the signal wave; it rides on top of the carrier wave to the radio, giving the actual programming. In normal communication the signal could include body language, gestures, or tone of voice. For the gifts, such things as anointing, love, proper timing, life commitment to Christ, an understanding and caring attitude, humility, and submission are part of a clear signal. Domineeringness, harshness, hypocrisy, and self-centeredness give a distorted signal. If the signal is clear, the Holy Spirit can act as a carrier wave to bring the message to the hearer.

Many people think communication has to do with only the first three elements: sender, encoding, and signal. But this is one-way communication. For Christians, the message is not effective unless it is accurately received.

Decoding is very important. Did the receiver hear what was really being said? So often we think we have heard, but in reality we have misunderstood. The receiver must have an open spirit and be willing to hear what the Holy Spirit is saying. He may have a role of confirming, adding to, or evaluating. The decoding must be done in a spirit of acceptance, not criticism. People who minister gifts may be discouraged by the judgmental attitudes of others.

On the other hand, most Christians do not take the ministries of the Spirit seriously enough. We need to listen. The receiver must come to the service with his total being, open and responsive to the teaching of the Bible. He must learn how to assimilate the data, apply it to his own life, and become discipled in Christ.

Most people think that communication has been clear and complete when what the sender transmits is what the receiver understands. Although this is a great feat, it falls short in Christian communication. The sender's ultimate goal is that the receiver becomes another sender. The receiver may in turn transmit the message in a different way and in the context of different ministries, but he is, nevertheless, a sender.

Three Components of Ministering Gifts

There are three vital components to effective gift ministry: worship, the sharer, and the responder.

First, someone must be willing to share. A climate of openness and love—not criticism, perfectionism, and rebuke—is necessary. A wise pastor can give direction to set each person in his most effective place of ministry. In my early ministry, without realizing it I imposed the task of speaking on many who would never become speakers. I was attempting to fit them into my mold. The Holy Spirit may rather use some in gifts of helps, administrations, or giving. When we seek to fit into our most effective role in the body of Christ, God can bestow gifts through us.

Second, there must be those who respond. Some churches seem to be transplants from the Antarctic: If a match is lit, it freezes out. If gifts are to be shared, a proper environment of openness and responsiveness must be evident. Manifesting a gift is no particular sign of holiness. The Corinthian church manifested gifts and carnality at the same time. Some desire to throw out the gifts with the carnality, but wise Christians know the difference. If we are one body, then we must allow every member to minister to us. Some minister from strength and some from weakness. Genuine strength reflects maturity, holy living, and concern with building others up. We need more of these people. Those who are weak struggle with their faith, have many spiritual ups and downs, and may not apply the Bible well. We will always have these in our congregations. Are we to reject them?

The church's task is to evoke the gift. Hebrews 10:24 says, "Let us consider how we may spur one another on toward love and good deeds." One of our greatest ministries is to set someone free to share his gift. Paul writes, "Fan into flame the gift of God" (2 Timothy 1:6). The gift must be exercised or it may be hidden. Therein lies the value of people who honestly know and share freely with one another. They can encourage one another to exercise their gifts.

Third, the church must learn how to worship God as gifts are being ministered. As part of this worship, we thank God for the person He uses to help us. Sometimes, however, we thank God for the gift and yet, at the same time, prefer that God would use someone else. God may use the most unlikely vessels if they are yielded to Him. This draws the church closer together in acceptance and interaction.

The church will never be out of date or behind the times if it emphasizes accepting people where they are and then helping them develop. Doctors, teachers, construction workers, students, businessmen, homemakers—daily they face the advances and the complexities of modern life. They speak the language of the marketplace. When the gospel and the ministries of the church touch their lives, when they feel they are vital, valued persons in the kingdom of God, and when they learn to minister in the power of the Spirit— then they can impact their world. Their ministries will be relevant, changing, even as they grow with the times and mature in Christ. Rather than a professional clergy doing all the ministries, the whole body of Christ will be involved.

The whole of 1 Corinthians 14 centers on clear communication of gifts. Paul concludes this chapter with, "Be eager to prophesy" (1 Corinthians 14:39). The Thessalonians had experienced false doctrine on the coming of the Lord through a misuse of prophetic utterance. Paul did not seek to eliminate prophecy among them, but rather exhorted them to test and hold to the good (1 Thessalonians 5:20–21). The possibility of an extreme in practice should not cause Christians to avoid the good. That quenches the Spirit. One of our securities against excess and extreme is in the multitude of people who know how to exercise gifts. A healthy, normal exercise of gifts will keep people from seeking extremes.

Too often we are distracted from the real essence of prophetic utterance. We focus on whether or not it is a hundred percent supernatural, or how deeply spiritual the sharer is. Then we tend to reject the utterance as satanic if it doesn't meet our expectations.

We are living in crisis days. We need to be alert and ready to serve God. We must exhort one another while it is called today. When we know that God can use any of us supernaturally, then the church assembles with a readiness to hear from God, with faith and expectancy that God can touch our human situation. This is the cutting edge of the church. If we are willing to share, aim to edify, and submit ourselves to testing and authority, then God will surely use us in this prophetic area. We are not only priests to one another. We are also a prophetic people, touched and empowered of God with a message for a lost and dying world.

When God speaks to us, the world will know that we have been with Jesus. We will see the sick healed, lives touched, a unity develop in the church, and people finding their ministries. Then, after we have learned about the charismata in the context of the church, we will let God use us to minister to a desperate, hurting world. W. I. Evans exhorts, "Let us wait on our ministry! I believe that God is longing to lay hold of our poor, feeble, human instrumentality and pour through it the streams of divine power for the manifestation and revelation of Himself."[2]

---

[2]W. I. Evans, *This River Must Flow* (Springfield, Mo.: Gospel Publishing House, 1954), 36.

8

Why Focus on Worship?

The apostle Paul was the most effective missionary of all time. Modern missiologists still explore the depths of his simple, yet profound principles of discipleship, church planting, and evangelism. One clear principle is inherent in the structure of most of his epistles: Solid doctrine, properly taught, leads to right practice in Christian living. Nearly two-thirds of each of his epistles reflects this emphasis on doctrine. The last third relates to proper practice. For example, Romans 1 through 11 is the doctrinal portion of the epistle, and 12 through 16 gives practical instructions.

The Book of Ephesians gives another key principle: Genuine worship leads to a vision for reaching the world for Christ. Sitting in a prison in Rome, chained to guards, caring for the needs of all the churches, sensing his own life might be nearing an end, Paul found a liberation in his ministry that placed him above his adverse circumstances. Rather than seeing problems, he saw the God who is above the problems, sovereignly working all things to the praise of His glory.

For Paul, true worship was not merely a verbal or physical expression in church, but a dynamic that led to a changed life that could affect a world. He did not preach and teach to impress others or to meet his own ego needs; he sought to please God alone. Paul's life and ministry were to be a worship to God. Despite the prison setting, the practical portion of the epistle to the Ephesians indicates that our lives are to be a living worship to God. This is liberating. Why does Paul focus on worship? Before we examine Ephesians further on this subject, let us review God's purpose in the Old Testament.

From Genesis onward, God has been seeking a people who will worship Him genuinely. The first eleven chapters of Genesis describe both the multiplication and the degeneration of humanity—and God's desire to redeem it. People are the apex of God's creation, made with a purpose and a mission. Human beings, made in the image of God, were to co-rule with God over His creation and to walk in fellowship with Him. Tragically, Adam sinned. Mercifully, God provided a way of redemption so His creation could once again serve Him.

Then Cain murdered Abel. The first murder was the result of a dispute about worship. God's redemption was once more revealed in the judgment and protection of Cain after he killed Abel. The provision of an ark in the midst of gross wickedness in Noah's day shows God's desire to save His people. They were delivered for a purpose, to "be fruitful and increase in number and fill the earth" (Genesis 9:1).

Genesis 10 and 11 provide a fitting climax to the theme of these chapters. In order, we have three topics: the table of nations, the account of Babel, and the genealogy of Abraham. Chronologically, the Babel account of Genesis 11 should precede the table of nations of Genesis 10. God's purpose in rearranging the order is to show us where the nations originated and how God dispersed His people among the nations. This dispersal was involuntary, because of the disobedience of God's people at Babel.

Then comes the climax of these chapters: the call of Abraham. From among His people, God chose Abraham to lead the faithful, to be the father of Israel and of all the people of God. Through Abraham and his descendants God would bless the world. From the beginning God has prepared a people to send them forth on a mission. As Ralph Winter has observed: "The Bible is not the basis for missions. Missions is the basis for the Bible."[1]

When Israel began to develop as a nation in the Sinai peninsula, God promised many blessings if they would be a holy people to witness to the glory of God. But Israel quickly forgot its mission. The people committed idolatry, became corrupt, and turned genuine worship into a ritual. Even surrounding nations knew the Israelites

---

[1] Ralph Winter, Class on perspectives in world missions, January 1985, William Carey University, Pasadena, Calif.

were not faithful to their God. God had to judge Israel. First, Assyria took the Northern Kingdom captive. The Southern Kingdom, however, did not think God would allow them to be judged: After all, they were the people of God; the king from David's line was upon the throne; the temple was in Jerusalem; they were in the Promised Land; they were not as wicked as their northern neighbors (or so they said). In 586 B.C. they were taken captive into Babylon.

During those critical times, the Jews went through a major identity crisis: The theology they had depended on, the traditional approaches to sacrifice, their preconceptions about being the chosen people, were shattered. They were so backslidden that they thought they could commit fornication, worship idols, treat their fellowman unjustly, and ignore the holiness of God, yet keep the externals of religion and be accepted by God.

Many prophets rose to speak to this situation. Isaiah proclaimed a new hope. The Messiah would come to form a new people of God. The Spirit of God would be poured out upon Him without measure. He would be a suffering servant, but would be ultimately successful in His mission.

Although Jeremiah did not speak of the Spirit of God, he emphasized the new covenant that would be written on the minds and hearts of God's people, when all would know God, from the least to the greatest (Jeremiah 31:31–34). He boldly prophesied that God was using the Babylonians to judge them and their external rituals of righteousness. Jerusalem, including its magnificent temple, was destroyed. Yet, during this darkest hour, Jeremiah said God still loved His people. The covenant was a new covenant, yet fully based on the eternal principles found in the Abrahamic and Mosaic covenants. Their religion needed to be internalized.

Ezekiel spoke of hope. He saw a vision of a valley of dry bones and could only comment that they looked very dry. God told him to prophesy to the bones. The bones came to life as spirit (*ruach*) entered into them. Ezekiel spoke of a day when God's people would have a heart of flesh and a new spirit from God (Ezekiel 36:26). Many in captivity longed for the day when true faith would be renewed in holiness and power.

In the interbiblical era, many efforts were made to find the true teacher of righteousness, establish a holy community of God's people, and bring in the Messiah.[2] Some Israelites believed that if the country as a whole could simply observe one Sabbath day properly, the Messiah would come. Even though these efforts centered on works, special knowledge, and personal attainments, some positive effects did result: Scripture was carefully copied; people began anticipating the Messiah (whether political or spiritual). The soil was prepared.

When Jesus began ministering He was filled with the Spirit. His followers were clothed by the same Spirit. They would be the new people of God who would witness, by worship, life-style, and proclamation, to God's glory. The New Testament church grew through the empowering of the Spirit in spite of many obstacles. The deception by Ananias and Sapphira could have shaken the innocent trust of the newborn Church. The problem with the Hellenistic widows could have split the Church. The Jewish-Gentile problem threatened to stunt the growth of the Church from its beginning. Instead, all these problems became opportunities for the people of God to reveal love, faith, and wisdom. Explosive growth resulted. They served a God who was above any crisis. The Spirit was in control.

Further, God could take Saul of Tarsus, who persecuted the Christians, and transform him into Paul the successful missionary.

Undoubtedly Paul's greatest results in church planting came in Asia Minor. Using Ephesus as a base for training and evangelism, Paul was instrumental in the whole of Asia Minor receiving a dramatic witness of Jesus Christ in a little over two years. It is to the

---

[2]The Qumran community spoke of the doctrines of the Teacher of Righteousness. The apocryphal Psalm of Solomon (17:32) applies the word "righteous" to the Messiah (see also Psalm of Solomon 17:21ff; 18:5ff). Strong expectations of a Davidic messiah, an "eschatological Jewish national ideal ruler figure," developed from the thinking of the Maccabees and Hasmoneans. Apocalyptic texts (Ethiopic Enoch, 2 Esdras) spoke of a Davidic messiah. Some texts even suggested a messianic high priest. See "Jesus Christ," and "Righteousness," in *The New International Dictionary of New Testament Theology*, ed. Colin Brown (Grand Rapids: Zondervan Publishing House, 1975; originally Coenen, Lothar, Erich Beyreuther, and Hans Bietenhard. *Theologisches Begriffslexikon zum Neuen Testament*, R. Brockhaus: Verlag, Wuppertal), 2:337, 3:358–359.

churches of Asia Minor that Ephesians was written.[3] Paul had become so overwhelmed by God's grace and sovereignty at work in the churches and in his own life that, in spite of imprisonments, hardships, and church problems, he focused on worship.

After his standard greeting, Paul breaks into a song of worship to God. It includes three stanzas. In Ephesians 1:3–6, he praises the Father for choosing us and blessing us with every blessing. In Ephesians 1:7–12, he praises Jesus Christ for the special blessings of salvation and redemption, particularly for the Jews. And in Ephesians 1:13–14 he brings the song to a climax by speaking of the Holy Spirit's work in bringing Gentiles not only to salvation, but also to the mission of serving God until the fulfillment of the plan of redemption. He is so caught up in praise that 1:3–14 actually constitutes one sentence. (The one main verb "be" at the beginning of 1:3 is understood, but not written. The language of praise may defy normal approaches to grammar.) Then, in 1:15–23 Paul breaks forth into another song. He gets back to addressing the Ephesians in 2:1. Even then, he is praising God for His blessings.

The powerful Ephesian revival likely began with a handful of synagogue converts under the persuasive ministry of Apollos. Aquila and Priscilla were there to consolidate the results. When Paul came, he did not ask the question of salvation, he asked the question of reception of the Holy Spirit. "Did you receive the Holy Spirit when you believed?" (Acts 19:2).[4] For Paul, salvation must lead to service

---

[3]The best manuscripts leave out the destination of this epistle in Ephesians 1:1. The letter was likely meant for circulation to several churches in Asia Minor. To personalize the letter, the reader for each congregation likely read in the name of their city. Most likely because of Paul's tenure and work at Ephesus, as well as the city's prominence and location, this circular epistle may have gone to Ephesus first and then become identified with it or was eventually returned to it.

[4]Donald C. Stamps, ed., *The Full Life Study Bible* (Grand Rapids, Mich.: Zondervan Publishing House, 1990), 269. "The literal translation of Paul's question is, 'Having believed, did you receive the Holy Spirit?' 'Having believed' (Greek: *pisteusantes,* from *pisteuo*) is an aorist participle, which normally indicates action prior to the action of the main verb (in this case, 'receive')." Stanley M. Horton, *The Book of Acts,* The Radiant Commentary on the New Testament (Springfield, Mo.: Gospel Publishing House, 1981), 222, points to a similar construction and meaning in Hebrews 7:27, Matthew 27:4, Acts 10:33, 1 Corinthians 15:18, and others.

empowered by the Spirit of God. It is not enough to pray a sinner's prayer and qualify to enter heaven. God calls us to a mission of reconciling a world to himself. It was important that this Church learn about Spirit-empowering and spiritual gifts from the beginning. Almost ten years later, in 62 A.D., Paul reflects on that pattern which he established from the beginning. "Having believed, you were marked in him with a seal, the promised Holy Spirit" (Ephesians 1:13–14). Markus Barth says of these verses,

> Sealing is the designation, appointment, and equipment of the saints for a public ministry—a ministry which includes the power to understand, to endure, to pray, to sing, and to live in hope.[5]

Paul expected all Christians to be filled with the Spirit. What is the purpose? Those who teach concerning a second blessing do not agree as to its purpose. The holiness movement has seen the second blessing as an experience of sanctification, cleansing the dross within us. The Keswick Movement has insisted that the second experience was an empowering for service; divine equipment was given. Then, modern day charismatic believers have focused on the worship value of tongues, sometimes to the neglect of both of the previous positions. But are these purposes mutually exclusive? Can one really separate sanctification, service, and worship?

Sanctification basically means to set apart for holy purposes. It is not a conforming to external standards, but an inner change that makes us effective for God. *Empowering* is obviously the work of the Spirit. The Great Commission must be fulfilled. Souls must be saved. Missions must move ahead on divine power. Yet, the ultimate goal is *worship*. We want all that we do to be a symphony of praise to God. When redemption's plan is complete, every knee will bow before Him and every tongue will confess that Jesus is Lord (Philippians 2:10–11). It is in worship that we see God in His glory and power. There we renew our impetus to evangelize a lost world and

---

[5]Markus Barth, *Ephesians: Translation and Commentary on Chapters 1–3*, vol. 34, The Anchor Bible Series (Garden City, N.Y.: Doubleday and Company, 1974), 143. (See also pages 135–143.)

face the challenges of our churches. All three of these words, properly understood, are interrelated and lead to mission.

Let us look at the consequences of not interrelating the three elements in our mission.

One may be empowered (E), seeing miracles happen, knowing every technique to lead in a certain worship style, indeed, sincerely desiring to worship (W) God—but apart from sanctification (S) no ongoing revival occurs. The name of Christ is brought down. People feel they can do anything they want and still serve the Lord. They forget that God is a holy God. Our whole lives are to be sanctified before Him as a living worship. Using a mathematical formula, it would look something like this:

$$E + W - S = \text{Compromised Christianity}$$

If a church worships freely, ministers the gifts to each other, teaches strongly on sanctification, but neglects to apply the empowering aspect of the Holy Spirit, it will become ingrown and proud of its spirituality and high standards. The energies expended, the gifts ministered, the praise rendered, must be harnessed for the winning of the world or the church will become a self-assuring "bless me" club. Indeed, the danger of that happening even now is great. Over half the world has yet to hear the gospel. If we do not learn what the Spirit is saying to the churches, we may be content to reach only to those who have already heard. Worse yet, we may be talking primarily to those who are already in the church.

$$W + S - E = \text{Ingrown Christianity}$$

The combination of sanctification and empowering is effective, but misses the liberation that comes in drawing strength from the Lord. Nevertheless, it is an acceptable combination to many. Some churches have been content not to exercise the gifts in corporate worship. Sanctification and empowering become ends in themselves, symbols of spiritual attainment. Because the vision is so vast, we feel overwhelmed and emotionally drained. Yet Paul saw the need for continuous self-edification, for praying and singing in the Spirit. He saw the need to allow others to edify him through ministries of gifts. This happens first of all in worship.

$$S + E - W = \text{Exhausted Christianity}$$

No two of these elements should be without the third element. Even more tragically, some churches have tried to have one element without the other two. When we realize that the infilling of the Holy Spirit properly understood and controlled means worship, sanctification, and empowering, then we see why Paul set high priorities on it for the Ephesian believers. The churches in Asia Minor continued the emphasis of the mother church in Ephesus. Even those who had not seen Paul personally would be acquainted with this pattern. The revival had touched all of Asia Minor.

Why focus on worship? Ephesians gives five reasons.

All to the Praise of His Glory:
Ephesians 1

Ephesians 1 tells us that the goal of all that the Father, Son, and Holy Spirit do in and through the Church is for the praise of His glory. Three times the phrase "unto the praise of His glory" is repeated in the first song. The issue is not how much we do for Jesus, how skillful we may be, or how many gifts are ministered. Rather, it is that God be glorified in all things. This is liberating. Our responsibility is to dedicate our beings, talents, life-styles, and intellects for expression of worship to God. His responsibility is to empower us, minister through us, and shape us into the image of Christ.

The Powerful Early Church Crosses Barriers:
Ephesians 2 and 3

Ephesians 2 describes Christians as those who receive the grace of God, becoming fellow-citizens with God's people, members of God's household, alive in Christ, united in fellowship with God and one another, heirs together with Israel, and recipients and executors of the mysteries of God. The early Christians realized who they were in Christ.

This was so precious that it broke down walls of prejudice and cultural blindness. The biggest barrier to evangelization of the world was in getting the gospel beyond Jewish perspectives and language so that Gentiles could come into the kingdom of God. That could come only through a full vision of who God is, who we are in Christ, and what He desires for the world. Somehow, when we are touched by grace, human differences are either minimized or more deeply appreciated. God fills all with the same Spirit.

There is no specific reference to the Great Commission in the Book of Acts and in the writings of Paul. However, the Early Church's acceptance of it is reflected in what they said and did. The Early Church went forth on the power of the Holy Spirit: They were given wisdom, signs and wonders, divine unity, and the leading of the Lord. Christians had their personal Pentecost, thrusting them beyond anything they could do by themselves.

The apostle Paul always recognized God's personal call on his life and his special mission to the Gentiles. He spoke of God's special revelation to him, yet sought confirmation of it with the leaders of the Jerusalem church. It was in the force of this personal commission and the power of spiritual gifts that Paul effectively planted churches thoughout the Mediterranean world. The truth of the matter is, the church can never fulfill the Great Commission by trying to obey it in human strength. Even if the spirit is willing, the flesh is weak. We need spiritual empowering and God's personal visitation on our lives.

The Church Is a School to Prepare Us:
Ephesians 4

Ephesians 4 and the parallels in 1 Corinthians 14 and Romans 12 picture the church as a school of the Messiah. All the following phrases put us in the context of a school.

Ephesians 4 uses, "He gave . . . teachers to prepare God's people for works of service, . . . reach unity in the faith and in the knowledge of the Son of God, . . . no longer be infants, . . . blown here and there by every wind of teaching, . . . you did not come to know *[mathetes:* learn, be discipled] Christ that way, . . . speak truthfully." First Corinthians 14 has phrases such as "All may be instructed

[mathetes] and encouraged, . . . I would rather . . . instruct others
. . . , prophecy is for believers, . . . weigh carefully what is said.''
Romans 12 speaks of transformation of the mind, testing and ap-
proving what is God's will, thinking with sober judgment, exercising
gifts with all diligence, and the day of His judgment.

We assemble to worship because in the assembly we learn to use
our whole lives to express worship to God. That is, the church is
not the primary place where the work of God is done; the church
is the primary place where the work of God is learned. We learn
about the exercise of spiritual gifts. Jesus is the administrator, teacher,
curriculum, and final goal of this school. The Holy Spirit disciples
us in ministry to one another. We grow as we come together to
worship and fellowship. Worship leads us to deeper fellowship. We
learn to love and accept others as they are. We seek to build them
up. We realize every member needs every other member. Deeper
fellowship, in turn, leads us to love God more. We develop a life-
style that reflects God's glory.

Changed Lives Touch the World:
Ephesians 5 and 6

The missionary implications of worship are clear. When God
truly touches us, our lives will be different. Ephesians 5:22 to 6:9
mention a series of earthly relationships that are to be built on eternal
principles. These relationships are part of our worship to God. The
relationship of Christ to the church forms the basis for personal
relationships in the church. Family behavior and employer-employee
matters are opportunities for us to glorify our Father in heaven. We
live, not for what we can get out of life, but for the love of Christ
we can share with others. For Paul, theology is grace and ethics is
gratitude. The first three chapters overwhelmed us with God's grace.
Now Paul responds with gratitude.

Husbands and wives are gifts to each other from God. Although
there are issues of marriage important for all couples to consider,
the key issue is what will be their responses to the grace of God.
Greater than the questions of submission and equality in leadership,
roles for the man and the woman, is the question, Do we act from
grace? Parent-child relationships are based on greater principles than

authority and freedom, discipline and permissiveness, environment and heredity. The ultimate question is, How does my life reflect the grace of God in my situation?

Employers must realize they are employees of their Master in heaven and must treat their earthly employees as fairly as Christ treats them. And employees can take the drudgery out of their work by working as if the Lord were their employer. They will receive due reward from Him, even if life may seem unfair here. This revolutionary new life-style represented inroads of the Kingdom into the first-century world.

Worship Leads to Effective Warfare: Ephesians 6

Ephesians 6:10–19 tells us how to fight against Satan. We cannot come against the devil with our degrees, family heritage, human ingenuity, or social position. Satan would only laugh at us. We must come with the equipment that God alone can provide. Isaiah 11:4–5 and 59:17 picture the Messiah himself clothed with this armor. Now we are privileged to wear this same armor in battle against the enemy.

Some scholars see the armor of God as fulfilled in putting on Jesus Christ himself. How else do we identify the belt of truth, the helmet of salvation, the breastplate of righteousness, the feet shod with the gospel of peace, the shield of faith, and the sword of the Spirit? These terms are fulfilled in Christ. We must be clothed with the new creation, Jesus himself (see 2 Corinthians 5:17). This can happen only by letting Jesus rule our lives. That happens when we have spent time in His presence, beholding His nature and understanding His ways. When Satan attacks, we do not come with sword or spear, but in the name and nature of Jesus Christ. We let Christ do the fighting for us. In Him we have the victory. Indeed, as Paul declares, we are more than conquerors.

9

Commencement

The Gospels do not formally conclude: Matthew records the Great Commission, which the Church must yet fulfill under the authority given to Jesus. Mark concludes abruptly, leaving the reader in silent awe and expectation of the powerful, all-sufficient Lord who could interrupt any situation, no matter how desperate. Luke-Acts is really one volume; Luke 24 is not the conclusion. The Early Church carries on the mission and work that Christ performed on earth. And Acts does not conclude. John, by including the personal post-Resurrection commission to Peter in chapter 21, clearly implies that the Church will carry on.

All of Paul's epistles were written to proclaim the Lord's death *till* He comes. The gifts of the Spirit were given as a deposit, in anticipation of the full inheritance that the Church shall receive. Hebrews encourages us to "run with perseverance the race marked out for us" (Hebrews 12:1). Revelation concludes with "Amen. Come, Lord Jesus" (Revelation 22:20).

Although there will be no new revelations to supersede or bypass the Bible, God continues to speak to and through His Spirit-empowered Church.

So, too, this book does not have a concluding chapter. My hope is that this book will serve as a beginning for many churches in gift ministry. Commencement for students is graduation, a completion of their course of study. But the word *commencement* really means "beginning." A Christian should not exult in his knowledge, but in his healthy growth, maturation. Realizing we are still students may be the mark of true learning. Biblical scholarship must lead to practice of our faith and the equipping of believers for ministry.

The church is a school. As believers gather, they learn how to operate in the gifts and be disciples of Christ; they learn how to edify one another. As they go forth, they apply God's power to life's situations. Gifts are exercised best through a life-style and mind-set that expects the leading of the Lord and the voice of the Spirit through each believer at any time. Unfortunately,

> this is exactly what is seldom understood. As long as the movement of the Spirit is thought of in terms only of something happening to an institution, or to people, as a kind of tonic, nothing significant is going to occur. Indeed, even the symbol of Pentecost can be misused so as to suggest only an external addition to faith. But—and it cannot be emphasized too strongly—the effusion of the Spirit is profoundly existential and personal. It is not mere supplement, but the movement through the whole being (community and/or individual) of a mighty power that *renews* the whole situation.[1]

Because of spiritual warfare, Christians must utilize Holy Spirit power. Spiritual logic dictates that we must speak clearly so that the Christian army may move forward together. Part of our proclamation to the world is our life together; our fellowship tells the world who we are. No gift is to be quenched, but all gifts are to be used in a proper manner and for their intended purposes. The world needs to see, hear, and know of the radically different life we have in Christ.

Over the years, however, the Church has often asked the wrong questions: Questions about God's kingdom, power, and glory have sometimes been replaced by questions about personal power, prestige, and position. But no man can receive the glory due to God. We must learn to ask the right questions.

Concerning spiritual gifts, the question is not which gifts we have, but what function those gifts perform in the body of Christ. Rather than trying to determine who is most spiritual among us, we should learn to value each other's contribution. Rather than debating whether women have a place in public ministry, we should emphsize proper methodologies of ministry. Rather than asking whether the gifts are

---

[1] J. Rodman Williams, *The Era of the Spirit* (Plainfield, N.J.: Logos International, 1971), 56.

totally supernatural (and therefore infallible), we need to realize that the gifts are incarnational, ought to be tested, and should be welcomed as a stimulus to growth as we learn how to exercise them. Rather than theologizing on the greatest gift, we need to share all God-given gifts in love. Then, rather than being a "come" structure, we will become a "go" structure. We will ask the needed questions to glorify God, build our churches, and impact the world.

Human as it is, the Church often adopts extremes. One extreme is a subjective, naive use of gifts that dismisses the rest of the Church as being unspiritual. The other extreme is to react to negative experiences by avoidance: The fire is feared because of possible wildfire, or, as the Chinese proverb puts it, we trim the toe to fit the shoe. The first position is self-destructive: Although hunger for more of God is commendable, to avoid solid biblical principles is to invite problems that will destroy the very revival that is so eagerly sought. The second position is self-defeating: A church that ignores the full flow of the gifts makes itself ineffective in the world.

God seeks a people to fulfill His task. With a world population rapidly approaching six billion, the challenge of that task is greater than ever. In reaction to dry orthodoxy comes a desire for restoration of first-century Christianity. The cry is for a power and holiness beyond the natural. God does not disappoint this hunger. The Holy Spirit has been poured out upon all people, making all believers both priests to God and prophets to the world, a world lost and dying without the gospel message. The Church must be at its finest, yielded to and refined by the Spirit of God, so it might follow through on its mission.

By some estimates, up to 352 million claim to be charismatic.[2] These numbers represent varying doctrinal and organizational perspectives, every economic and educational level, diverse cultural backgrounds, and a multitude of creative expressions of the Spirit working through human beings. For the first time, more Christian converts and missionaries are being produced in the non-Western world than in the West. In these countries Pentecostal dimensions

---

[2]David B. Barrett and Frank Kaleb Johnson, "The World in Figures" in Lausanne II Congress Notebook 13:16, July 1989.

of Christianity are assumed and applied. Proper teaching will encourage ongoing exercise of gifts without fear. With a balance of teaching, Body ministries, and worship, as well as faith, hope, and love, the Church will move from victory to victory. Faith will always lead us beyond where we are, but not beyond where we should be.

My prayer is that each church will aggressively press into the area of spiritual gifts. All believers should determine which church they will commit themselves to and follow its leadership into the use of the gifts. Leaders are the key. Although God gives persons the gift of leadership, they also need to be affirmed in their leadership by the congregation. Willing, encouraging, sensitive team members help the leader grow beyond his abilities and perspectives. Together the church learns and grows. There is no pattern and personality set for all churches. The personality and worship style of one Spirit-led church may be different from that of others. The important thing is to begin with a solid basis of teaching. Then, times for exercise of gifts should be set aside. As we become sensitive to the Spirit and to one another, Jesus becomes our teacher and leads us on to fulfilling His plans.

Everything that Christians do is their worship to God. He is the audience, and our lives are the stage of redemption on which our worship is expressed. The preacher does not labor in the Word to impress his congregation, but to present it as an offering to the Lord. We do not act Christianly toward one another or work in church to impress others with our spirituality and churchmanship. We do it all as an act of worship to God. This liberates our ministries. We are not then bound by the fear of others' opinions but seek only to be faithful to our calling in Christ. From the overflow of worship we find God's supernatural enabling. Burnout will be replaced by rest in the Lord and encouragement from other believers. Saints will come alive and get excited. The gifts will flow as part of the normal life-style of the church to edify and evangelize. H. W. Robinson points out:

> The members do not so much "join" a Church, which exists completely without them; they help to constitute it, in their own intrinsic degree, by awakening to their own share in the welfare of the body. The true aspiration of the believer is thus fitly expressed

in the well-known sentence of the *Theologica Germanica:* "I would fain be to the Eternal Goodness what his own hand is to a man." In this sense we may rightly speak of the Church as the continued Incarnation of Christ.[3]

R. B. Chapman adds,

The individuals of such an *ekklesia* will each be a powerful witness (Acts 1:8), possessed of a deep filial affection for the Lord, fearing lest they should hurt or grieve Him. The demonstration of God's power will be the normal function of their community (Acts 4:33), who will be held in favor and respect by all and to whose company will come a daily increase as souls are saved (Acts 2:47).[4]

Amen! May it be so. May the Church fulfill its potential and touch the world.

---

[3]H. Wheeler Robinson, *The Christian Experience of the Holy Spirit* (London: Collins, 1962), 132.

[4]R. B. Chapman, "The Purpose and Value of Spiritual Gifts," *Paraclete* 2:4 (Fall 1968): 28.

APPENDIX

Is Healing in the Atonement?

Is Healing in the Atonement?

Many denominations have witnessed a revival of God's healing gifts. Church growth experts declare that signs and wonders are the primary reason for the church's rapid growth worldwide. Mark dramatizes the Early Church's emphasis on this: About 18 percent of his gospel is healing narrative (121 of 677 verses). And of his first ten chapters (Jesus' ministry up to the triumphal entry into Jerusalem) more than half (220 of 425 verses) relate to the miraculous. Clearly, healing and deliverance are integral to proclaiming the Kingdom. Alan Richardson points out that one key to Christianity's conquest of heathenism in the ancient world was the power to free people from the fear of demons.[1]

Some Christians believe the gifts of healings were confined to the first century, to the period before the completion of Scripture, others believe healing is based solely on God's sovereignty, and still others believe healings are signs of the inbreaking of the kingdom of God, a foretaste of future glory. Pentecostals have insisted that healing is in the Atonement, a part of the provision of Calvary.

The Biblical Basis

At issue in this discussion is whether or not healing is in the Atonement. It is abundantly clear that Christ came to bring in the power of the Kingdom. Although we do not yet experience the total fulfillment of the blessings of the kingdom of God, we can now begin sharing those blessings. The crucial passage for interpretation

---

[1]Alan Richardson, *The Miracle Stories of the Gospels* (London: SCM Press Ltd., 1941), 68.

is Isaiah 53:4–5: "Surely he took up our infirmities and carried our sorrows, yet we considered him stricken by God, smitten by him, and afflicted. But he was pierced for our transgressions, he was crushed for our iniquities; the punishment that brought us peace was upon him, and by his wounds we are healed."

Although the primary reference of these verses is to the salvation of Israel, can these verses refer to physical healing as well as spiritual?[2] We believe that if the passage refers to substitutionary redemption then physical healing is included. Fee acknowledges that "the Isaiah passage itself is ambiguous." Nevertheless, "it is clearly a metaphor for salvation," and, furthermore, "in the prophetic tradition such salvation also included the healing of the people's wounds incurred in their judgment."[3]

Indeed, it is extremely difficult to avoid substitutionary implications in the passage. The verb *nasa* (to bear) is regularly used in Leviticus 16 to speak of the expiation of sacrifices. The contrast of pronouns, "he"/"we," "his"/"our," (53:4–6,8,11–12) brings out

---

[2]Some do not view Isaiah 52:13 to 53:12 as referring to vicarious Atonement. See H. M. Orlinsky, "The So-Called 'Servant' of the Lord and 'Suffering Servant' in Second Isaiah" in *Studies on the Second Part of the Book of Isaiah,* supplement to *Vetus Testamentum* (London: E. J. Brill, 1967), 54. He denies vicarious suffering here or anywhere in the Old Testament, believing it to be a concept developed much later. See also, George A. F. Knight, *Deutero-Isaiah: A Theological Commentary on Isaiah 40–55* (Nashville: Abingdon Press, 1955), 273; R. N. Whybray, *The Second Isaiah* (Sheffield: JSOT Press, 1983), 68; Eduard Schweitzer, *The Good News According to Matthew* (Atlanta: John Knox Press, 1975), 217; William L. Holladay, *Isaiah: Scroll of a Prophetic Heritage* (Grand Rapids: Eerdmans, 1978). They believe some prophet suffered and unjustly *because of,* not on behalf of, Israel's sins.

On the other hand, the vast majority of evangelical scholars insist on vicarious Atonement in Isaiah 53. See C. F. Keil and F. Delitzsch, eds., *Commentary of the Old Testament in Ten Volumes,* vol. 7, *Isaiah,* F. Delitzsch, trans. James Martin (Grand Rapids: William B. Eerdmans, 1969; repr., 1978), 315–317; William S. Lasor, David A. Hubbard and Frederic W. Bush, *Old Testament Survey* (Grand Rapids: Eerdmans, 1982), 394; also Westermann, Young, MacRae, Martin and Martin, Alexander, and Allis in their commentaries on Isaiah. They argue strongly that this passage prophesies of the Messiah's vicarious Atonement on behalf of His people. While the reference is primarily to spiritual healing, they would not deny that physical healing is included.

[3]Gordon D. Fee, *The Epistle to the First Corinthians,* The New International Commentary on the New Testament (Grand Rapids: William B. Eerdmans, 1987), 594n.62.

the substitionary quality of this passage; it speaks of a work the suffering servant alone could accomplish for our sins.[4]

The word "infirmities" (*choli*) is used in the Old Testament primarily for physical sicknesses and occasionally wounds (e.g., Deuteronomy 7:15, "diseases"; 28:59 "illnesses"; 28:61, "sickness"). The word *makob* (carried in Isaiah 53:4) is used for pain, usually spiritual or psychological, though occasionally physical.[5] The suffering servant is "a man of sorrows" (*makob*, Isaiah 53:3). He "carried our sorrows" (Isaiah 53:4). The word "healed" (Isaiah 53:5) is probably perfect passive and can readily be translated "were healed," anticipating prophetically the completed work of redemption. The phrase "stricken by God, smitten of him, and afflicted" is prophetic of the Cross. Thus Isaiah 53:5 pictures the healing as completed through the wounds of the servant.

> The meaning is not merely that the Servant of God entered into the fellowship of our sufferings, but that He took upon himself the sufferings which we had to bear and deserved to bear, and therefore not only took them away (as Matthew 8:17 might make it appear), but bore them in His own person, that He might deliver us from them.[6]

"Thus," according to Claus Westermann, "the healing gained for the others (v. 5) by his stripes includes as well the forgiveness of their sins and the removal of their punishment, that is to say, the suffering."[7]

The Holy Spirit inspired New Testament writers to refer to this

---

[4]F. Duane Lindsey, *The Servant Songs* (Chicago: Moody Press, 1985), 118–119. Also, David J. A. Clines, *I, He, We, and They: A Literary Approach to Isaiah 53* (Sheffield: Journal for the Study of the Old Testament Press, 1983).

[5]Julius A. Bewer, *The Book of Isaiah*, vol. 2 (New York: Harper and and Brothers Publishers, 1950), 42–43, suggests "infirmities" and "sorrows" in Isaiah 53 are better translated as "diseases" and "sicknesses," respectively. His translation does not bring out the psychological anguish of sorrows, but rather the physical side of suffering.

[6]Keil and Delitzsch, *Isaiah*, 316.

[7]Claus Westermann, *Isaiah 40–66* (Philadelphia: The Westminster Press, 1969), 263.

passage as fulfilled in the Messiah. Both Matthew 8:17 and 1 Peter 2:24 refer to Isaiah 53 in relation to salvation and vicarious suffering. Robert Gundry says concerning Matthew's references, "The quotations from Isaiah all occur in the summaries of Jesus' salvific work. (See also Matthew 27:57; cf. Isaiah 53:9.)"[8] David Hill says, "By the time of Matthew, Isaiah 53 was certainly interpreted messianically and applied to Jesus."[9] Fee, in looking at the New Testament understanding of Isaiah 53, points out that Jesus, Paul, and the Early Church regularly expected that God would heal physically, that they accepted this passage "both as a metaphor for salvation (1 Peter 2:24) and as a promise of physical healing (Matthew 8:17)."[10]

Philip's reference to Isaiah 53:7–8 in Acts (8:32–35) and Paul's reference to Isaiah 52:15 in Romans (15:21) are both in the context of Christ as the suffering servant. Indeed, Jesus' own understanding of His ministry relates greatly to the suffering servant passages. (See the close relationship between Isaiah 53 and Mark 8:31; 9:12,31; 10:45. Also, see 1 Peter 2:22,24; cf. Isaiah 53:5,9.)

Some do not accept Isaiah 53 as prophetic of the Messiah or as a teaching about vicarious Atonement. They believe Jesus conveniently applied the passage to himself, not as fulfillment of prophecy nor as the result of exegetical interpretation. This argument poses major questions about the liberty with which the New Testament writers and Jesus himself utilized the Old Testament passages. Clearly, Isaiah 52:13 through 53:12 discusses the vicarious Atonement of the suffering servant. It is affirmed by all New Testament references to the passage.

What of the Matthew 8:16–17 reference to Isaiah 53:4? Is this truly a reference to the Atonement, the bearing of sin and sickness, or only a sign confirming Jesus' messiahship? Some think that the Matthew passage does not refer to the Atonement or substitutionary suffering because the Greek verbs do not imply Atonement, but

[8]Robert H. Gundry, *Matthew, A Commentary on His Literary and Theological Art* (Grand Rapids: William B. Eerdmans, 1981), 150.

[9]David Hill, ed., *The Gospel of Matthew*, The New Century Bible Commentary (London: Butler & Tanner Ltd., 1972), 161.

[10]Fee, *First Corinthians*, 594n.62.

simply miraculous healings to remove suffering *(elaben,* "took"; *ebastasen,* "removed"). However, W. F. Albright and C. S. Mann say, "In the context of Isaiah 53, the identification of Jesus with the Servant would appear to demand far more than a mere removal of suffering."[11] The Matthew 8:17 quote of Isaiah 53:4 must refer to Christ's redemptive work, and here is applied to physical healing.

It is true that Christ is the unique man of history, the Messiah, the God-man; we cannot compare His ministry with ours in every aspect. But neither can we isolate Matthew 8:16–17 from its Early Church context. Matthew's perspective when writing was after Calvary. He sought to prove to his Jewish audience that the crucified and resurrected Christ indeed was the Messiah and that He had fulfilled all that was spoken of Him in the Old Testament. The healing the Messiah provided would ultimately include spiritual, emotional, physical, economic, and political deliverance. The Early Church believed it. They saw miracles in abundance causing the Church to grow. As MacDonald concludes,

> The objection that these verses could not refer to the Atonement, because Christ had not yet been crucified, is groundless. He was the "Lamb slain from the foundation of the world," and on this basis He also could and did forgive sin prior to the cross.[12]

Note the parallel of the Great Commission with Jesus' own ministry:

"Jesus went . . . teaching . . . preaching . . . healing" (Matthew 4:23).

"Jesus went . . . teaching . . . preaching . . . healing" (Matthew 9:35).

"As you go, preach . . . heal" (Matthew 10:7).

"All authority . . . has been given to me. Therefore go and make disciples . . . baptizing . . . teaching" (Matthew 28:19–20).

---

[11]W. F. Albright and C. S. Mann, *Matthew,* vol. 26, The Anchor Bible Series (Garden City, N.Y.: Doubleday and Co., 1968), 94.

[12]William MacDonald, Lecture notes on soteriology, 77.

In both grammatical parallel and theological content, the pattern for Jesus' ministry and His commission for His disciples are the same. In two internships, Jesus had given the disciples authority to heal the sick. And although Matthew 28 does not mention healing, it may very well be subsumed under the "all authority" that Christ received. And Jesus in turn saw His ministry and authority as being given to His followers.

Further, just as the healing miracles follow the training of the disciples in Matthew (chs. 8–9 and 5–7, respectively), so some of the same miracles are recorded by Luke in the context of discipleship training (Luke 5:27 to 6:49). In other words, these miracles were not simply public confirmation of Jesus' claims, but a deliberate training of His disciples in their ministries. Luke understood that what began in his gospel with the inauguration of Jesus' earthly ministry continued after Jesus' ascension (in the Book of Acts). The Gospel writers saw the Church as the continuing ministry of Christ on earth. The miracles were not peripheral, but integral to ministry. For as Gundry says (regarding Matthew 8:17), "Along with forgiveness of sin . . . physical well being was thought to characterize the messianic age (Isaiah 29:18; 32:3–9; 35:5–6). We therefore do well to follow Matthew's literalism."[13]

The issue of healing in the Atonement must begin with the fall of mankind in Genesis 3. The curse included the following: The image of God in us was marred, nature and creation would not be as fruitful for mankind as it once was, and everyone would face suffering and die physically. In the midst of this curse God pronounced hope that would issue forth from woman. A Messiah would come who would destroy all that the serpent represented. The hint of a redeemer begins in the Garden of Eden. What is comprehended by that redemption? Ultimately, all the effects of the curse are reversed.

The marred image of God in human beings can begin to find its full potential through growth in the image of Jesus Christ: Believers are a new creation in Christ (1 Corinthians 5:17). The universe will

---

[13]Gundry, *Matthew*, 150. One need not agree completely with Gundry's hermeneutical approach to recognize the truth of this statement.

be ultimately redeemed as well as the body (Romans 8:21,23). Christ has power over death itself (1 Corinthians 15:54–57). The prospects of a glorified body, a new heaven and a new earth, and eternal fellowship with God are available because Jesus reversed the effects of the curse by defeating Satan at Calvary. He has redeemed mankind from the curse of the Law (Galatians 3:13).

That curse included physical as well as spiritual bondage in the Old Testament. The dying Israelites were required to look at a bronze serpent to appropriate spiritual and physical healing. This was a type of Jesus' death on Calvary. If both forgiveness and healing came by looking at the type, how much more the fulfillment of the type? Indeed, every blessing we receive is either directly or indirectly a result of the atoning work of Christ. Turner sums up the discussion best when he points out that the apostolic presentation of the gospel applies to the whole person, not some platonic or aristotelian disembodied soul. Speaking of Pentecostals, he says:

> They put healing back into the spiritual agenda, and located it firmly in the atonement (cf. Matthew 8:17; Isaiah 53:4), where it rightly belongs—indeed what benefit of salvation does not derive from the atonement?[14]

On what other basis does the Church minister the gift of healing? Why does James command us to call for the elders of the church to anoint with oil and pray for one's healing? Are not the Church itself and all the gifts of the Spirit the outcome of the Atonement of Jesus Christ? How can we preach of a glorified resurrection body if the body is not included in our redemption? God by His very nature is Jehovah-Ropheke, the God who heals. He gave His name to reveal His nature when providing healing for the waters in the wilderness. The Greek word *sozo* means salvation as well as healing.[15]

---

[14]Max M. B. Turner, "Spiritual Gifts, Then and Now," *Vox Evangelica* 15 (1985): 48.

[15]References to salvation for *sozo* include Matthew 1:21; 10:22; 18:11; 19:25; 24:13; Mark 10:26; 13:13; Luke 8:12; 9:24,56; 13:23; 18:25; John 3:17; 5:34; 10:9; 12:47; Acts 2:21,47; Romans 5:9–10; 8:24.

References to physical healing for *sozo* include Matthew 9:21–22; Mark 3:4;

Jesus came to redeem the total person. His ministry and that of His disciples proved it. Jesus did not heal simply for the sake of healing people. God was glorified, His ministry was vindicated, suffering was relieved, and people were drawn to a deeper understanding of His messiahship and their responsibilities in discipleship. All that He did was based on the work He came to do at Calvary.

Biblical thought addresses the former times and the latter times. The latter times are to be when the Messiah arrives. The Spirit would be poured out on all people, miracles would abound. The signs were not to be limited to the first part of the last times, nor an interim period between the former times and the latter times. The messianic kingdom of God would be a liberating, redemptive, life-changing, healing Kingdom. At the same time, these blessings would only be a down payment of the more complete blessedness of future fullness in Christ.

An Incarnational Approach to Healing

To believe in miracles simply as the sovereign act of God is to ignore the many Scripture references that speak of God honoring the faith of those who seek Him, based on the great work He has done at Calvary. This position places no responsibility upon a person and often leads to a passive stance on faith. "If God wills" becomes a fatalistic statement to justify a lack of aggressive faith.

On the other hand, some believe healing is totally a matter of human choice, since Christ has already atoned for our sins and our sicknesses. God's covenant has become mankind's responsibility because God has already done His part. They believe sickness is a direct result of sin in one's life. Although this position encourages aggressive faith, its practitioners are often guilty of presumption and pride. Those who are not healed are made to feel guilty; sup-

---

5:23,28,34; 6:56; Luke 8:36,48,50; Acts 4:9; 14:9; James 5:15.

See also Walter Bauer, *A Greek-English Lexicon of the New Testament and Other Early Christian Literature*, 2nd ed., trans. F. Wilbur Gingrich and Fredrick W. Danker (Chicago: University of Chicago Press, 1979), 798. Bauer's first definition relates to natural dangers, afflictions, and physical healing. His second refers to salvation from eternal death.

posedly they are sick because of some sin, a lack of faith, or a lack of prayer.

But if God is offended by every lack in our lives, what does this say about the nature of God? Is He fickle, temperamental, and judgmental, or is He loving, gracious, and faithful? Neither the sovereignty nor the free will position adequately answers the questions of God's part and our part in the matter of healing.[16]

Some emphasize instantaneous, miraculous healing. They insist that the sick should not seek the help of medical doctors or counselors because doing so indicates either a lack of faith or a lesser degree of faith. From their perspective, those healed progressively are not healed by the gift of healing, but by some other means, such as laying on of hands of the elders, anointing with oil, prayer of faith, or two or three agreeing in prayer.

Although all these are different methods of healing, one is not greater or more spiritual than another. All healing comes through God's gracious provision.

In healing, God has His part, we have our part. Healing is not only an individual's responsibility, but the responsibility of the whole caring community of Christ. Some healings may be miraculous, and other healings may be progressive. The ultimate goal is maturation into the image of Christ.

Although God heals, we may have a responsibility in that healing. For every part of our person is interrelated and affects every other part (note figure 7). Much illness is related to maladjusted emotional, spiritual, or mental processes.[17]

Sin in the spirit can affect the body. Feeding the mind with negative thoughts of anger, depression, and hatred can affect our bodies, relationships, words, emotions. We can talk ourselves into

---

[16]Gordon Wright, *In Quest of Healing* (Springfield, Mo: Gospel Publishing House, 1984), presents a fairly comprehensive, balanced, overall discussion of the issue of healing. Although he firmly believes healing is in the Atonement, he has had to face a chronic illness for much of his life.

[17]Counseling therapies focus on one or more of these areas. Rational emotive therapy emphasizes thinking the right thoughts. Reality therapy and behavioral modification focus on responsible actions. Nouthetic counseling focuses on sin and guilt issues and the need to repent.

defeat and sickness. Eating the wrong things, not guarding unity in relationships, and not growing spiritually—all affect one's entire being.

Figure 7. Elements of the Total Person for Healing

Christ seeks to destroy the enemy and all that he represents. He desires only the best for us. The following steps seem to be human responsibility in receiving healing.

First, repent of sin. Sickness may or may not be the result of sin in our lives. For the paralytic man let down through the rooftop, Jesus related sickness to sin (Mark 2:5); but for the man born blind, Jesus said neither he nor his parents sinned (John 9:3). Some (like Job's comforters) insist Job became sick because of his sins, yet God had declared him righteous (Job 1:8; 2:3).[18] Our first responsibility is to examine our own lives and repent of any real sin.

---

[18]Some insist Job's sin was fear, and because of that fear calamity came to his household and sickness came to him (Job 3:25). For them, sickness is the result of fear and wrong statements. It is true that we can worry ourselves sick and talk ourselves into ill health, but this interpretation of Job ignores all consistent hermeneutical principles.

First, Satan is declared the instigator and cause of Job's illness (Job 1:6,11–12; 2:4,7). Job is declared innocent (Job 1:8,22; 2:10). The New Testament speaks not of Job's fears or sins, but of his perseverance (James 5:11). Ezekiel speaks of his righteousness (Ezekiel 14:14).

Second, God is a merciful and compassionate God (James 5:11; Job 42:12–17). To say Job's fear caused his calamity is to imply a fickle, testy God who weighs

Repentance is bidding farewell to the past and looking to Jesus for the present and the future. It is facing responsibility for our actions and submitting those actions to the all-encompassing grace of God. A great hindrance to healing is the nagging fear that we have done something wrong somewhere, or that we are unworthy. This should be taken care of at the very earliest. Be reconciled to God and settle in your heart that you are a forgiven child of God. Therein is joy, liberation, and, quite possibly, healing.

Second, examine all the interrelated areas of your life (see figure 7). Rather than concentrate on the immediate need of a miracle of healing, we have a responsibility to grow in all other areas of our lives as well.

Is our speech in line with the principles of God's Word—Do we praise or complain? Do we confront our emotions or do we bury them? Do our life-styles line up with our spirits? Are we feeding our minds edifying information? Do we take sufficient time to direct feelings toward worship and intercessory prayer rather than frustration, burden, and regret? Have we forgiven others who may have hurt us? Are we taking care of our bodies through proper food, rest, and exercise? Do we take time to commune with God in prayer and study of His Word? All these are important to growth in Christ's image and God's will.

Our responsibility is to be healthy in every area we can. Then we can intelligently focus our prayers on our areas of real need, such as the physical area. Then the resources God has given in the other areas can be called upon to encourage total healing.

Third, immerse your mind in God's Word and teaching. Remember that God's Word alone is eternal and true. All else will pass

---

every emotion on His scales of divine wrath and justice, gives a person his due, and then changes His mind at the end to give him greater blessing. If Job suffered for his fear, then we should suffer far more for our shortcomings, fears, and pride.

Third, this position agrees that the first three comforters of Job were correct, that Job suffered because he sinned. It misses the depth of teaching of the book: Will people serve God for nothing in return, or will they serve God only for what they can get out of Him?

Spiritual warfare means Satan instigates much that causes human suffering, either directly or indirectly. Suffering cannot be understood fully on earth and can only be comprehended from God's eternal perspective. God is in control.

away. We live in the overlap of the present age and the age to come. The age to come has not fully dawned upon us, so God's glory has not found its greatest manifestation. But we hope for what we don't see (Romans 8:24–25). We build on eternal foundations. This strengthens our faith so that we are not conformed to the thinking of this world. We must not accommodate fatalistic perspectives.

Fourth, realize we are in spiritual warfare. We must fight the fight of faith. To deny pain or illness in the body when it is there is self-deceiving. But to let that infirmity bring us down completely is to give up. Francis MacNutt illustrates it this way:

> I think it's something like being bombarded in a trench during a war. I can feel certain that God does not want war; I can believe firmly that He wants peace. But because I live in this confused world, I try to survive, to endure as best I can with spirit intact while the rockets and shells go over. I don't get involved in trying to say that God wants the war; rather, I say that an enemy has done this. I would rather be back home, out of danger, out of the filthy water. Yet, here I am, so I do my best to endure in the midst of this evil, until such time as it goes away. I don't have to say that the evil is God's will. In one way I accept the war, because that's the way the world is. But I also say that war is hell, and I pray for peace! So it is with sickness.[19]

The very fact that we need the gifts of healings implies that we are not exempt from emotional and physical sufferings. Great Christian leaders—mightily used in healing ministries—faced physical sufferings. A. B. Simpson, founder of the Christian and Missionary Alliance, George and Stephen Jeffreys, founders of the Elim Pentecostal Alliance, and Pastor Hsi, of the China Inland Mission, faced physical frailties. Hebrews 11 is a record of mighty servants of God suffering because of serving God. C. S. Lewis points out that pain and suffering have beneficial purposes, too. Through pain God can get our attention and teach us what we might not otherwise hear:

---

[19]Francis MacNutt, *The Power to Heal* (Notre Dame: Ave Maria Press, 1977), 140.

"God whispers to us in our pleasures, speaks in our conscience, but shouts in our pains: It is His megaphone to arouse a deaf world."[20]

Because suffering is so real, the body of Christ has the tremendous responsibility of sharing it, not condemning those who experience it. We are to bear one another's burdens, weeping with those who weep. Genuine empathy can set a brother or sister free to reach out in faith for healing. On occasion, listening can be more powerful than preaching. When someone who is weak knows another cares, he gains strength to find victory.

Satan accused God of putting a hedge around Job (Job 1:10). God protected the Israelites in the land of Goshen from certain plagues (Exodus 8:22–23, flies; 9:6–7, plague on livestock; 9:11, boils; and 9:26, hail). He offered a special health, a freedom from certain illnesses, if Israel would obey His decrees (Exodus 15:26). Ephesians 6 speaks of an armor of protection in this spiritual warfare.

In this warfare we may not know whether to pray for the Lord to heal a person or to take him home. We can pray that God will build a hedge of protection around that person from Satan's fiery darts and that the enemy can make no further gains. (Old-time Pentecostals called this "pleading the blood," referring to the blood applied on the horns of the incense altar in the Old Testament tabernacle [Leviticus 16:18–19].) Then, when we pray, "Your kingdom come, your will be done," it is not a passive, fatalistic prayer, but an aggressive eagerness for the total will of God.

In spiritual warfare it is important to hear God's special word for you. Universal principles apply in all situations at all times, but particular situations may require specific words of knowledge. Take the case of the march around Jericho. In all of Israel's conquest of Canaan, only one city was taken by a march. We err when we universalize the specifics, saying that what happens in one case must happen in all. God is not obligated to repeat the same method every time. Even though we may face an obstacle, it is unlikely that we would be called to walk around it seven times (assuming we could). When we pray thoroughly about a matter, then we know what to believe for and will grow in faith to claim it.

---

[20]C. S. Lewis, *The Problem of Pain* (Glasgow, Scotland: Collins, 1957), 81.

Fifth, positionally claim total healing, practically claim progress. Jesus accomplished healing for the total person and, ultimately, relief from suffering. We stand on Jesus' finished work at Calvary. But until we are fully healed we should praise God for the little mercies.[21] Sometimes God relieves the pain; perhaps He stops the progress of the disease. Sometimes He gives a partial healing and then the total healing. But for each situation we should give thanks to God. MacNutt speaks of "the more and the less," rather than the yes and the no, of healing.[22] His focus is on the process of healing, the time element. Any improvement can be a sign of Gods' grace at work in our bodies.

In the cases of the man who was touched twice (Mark 8:22–25), the lepers who were cleansed as they went from Jesus (Luke 17:12–14), the blind man who had mud applied to his eyes and was commanded to wash in the pool of Siloam (John 9:6–7), a passage of time was involved. This perspective enables us to grow positively through each experience. It believes for an instantaneous miracle but understands that God can also heal progressively.

While the human focus is naturally on physical healing, God's primary desire is for our salvation and conformity to the image of Christ (Romans 8:28–30). He desires that others be brought to the Kingdom through our lives. Although physical healing is important, it is not the ultimate priority. Unfortunately, for some who are sick it becomes the only priority. Our prayer should be, "Lord, use every means and every situation to bring glory to you."

Sixth, praise God and rest in Him. Some areas are a mystery. We fulfill our areas of responsibilities and leave the rest to God. When we are not yet healed we tend to hold onto our illness, emotionally and intellectually. This becomes a discouragement to our faith.

We must do what we can for our health, wholeness, and growth

---

[21]L. Thomas Holdcroft, *The Holy Spirit: A Pentecostal Interpretation* (Springfield, Mo.: Gospel Publishing House, 1979), 155, distinguishes between the miraculous sign element of healings that take place immediately and the gift of healing that may take a period of time.

[22]MacNutt, *Healing*, 33.

into the image of Christ; we can grow in the midst of our trial. Hebrews 11 speaks of some who while living by faith were stoned, sawed in two, put to the sword. We may not have answers to all our questions. We must do our part and rest in Him. Praise helps us to see the world from God's perspective. We enter His gates with thanksgiving and His courts with praise (Psalm 100:4). Praise releases the problem to God; it is a step of faith, anticipating God's best. It is an attitude of life that testifies to others of the practical grace of God.

We cannot here discuss fully the issue of suffering and sickness. Cases exist of people who meet every qualification and yet are not healed. Further, there are the innocent victims of societal sins or parental sins, and, in many instances, no sin—other than the fact that we live in a fallen world. What of the mentally handicapped and the accident victim? The church's responsibility is to confront suffering and sickness wherever possible with the redemptive power of God.

Sickness is not shameful if we do not lose the victory in our spirits and become bitter and defeated. The timing and methodology belong to God. We can be assured that ultimate wholeness awaits us in heaven.

Let us summarize this perspective. Although total healing is included in the Atonement, clearly God's first and ultimate goal is the salvation of people and their being made into the image of His Son.

When a person receives Christ by faith, he has eternal life. Yet his full reception of the blessings of that life awaits a future day. Even our salvation has a past, present, and future: We were saved, we are being saved, and we shall be saved.

Because we live in the time of the inbreaking of God's kingdom, but not in the total fulfillment of that Kingdom, the Church is engaged in spiritual warfare. Although the victory is ultimately ours through Christ, our physical healing may not be immediate. At the same time, the Christian should live up to his privilege and position as a child of God; he should not let Satan get the best of him. Rather, his faith should claim God's best. He should aggressively bear witness to the powerful and faithful God that he serves. It is in confronting Satan and proclaiming the gospel that the power of God is most readily manifested on behalf of His people.

The vastness of the issues should humble us. After all, we are imperfect vessels. No one should think he has the special truth of God that transcends every other person's understanding. If we are dogmatic on a position, we must be humbly and lovingly so. The substitute for an extreme is not another extreme, but a full preaching of the Word of God.

It is God's will to heal, unless God has a higher will for the immediate situation. That is to say, God always desires the best for us that we might glorify Him most effectively. He is not simply the head of the department of welfare to give us what we need. His gifts are purposeful, that we may build up the Church and touch lost humanity for Him. If He works through seeming tragedy, that is His prerogative. We must keep looking to Him, not the circumstances. We evaluate what is best on a temporal basis. God knows what is best on an eternal basis.

The Early Church did not try to set a dogmatic doctrine to answer all the questions about divine healing. Theirs was the goal of appropriating God's power to accomplish the task. They moved forward in mighty Pentecostal power. Yet, they realized acceptance by God and of one another is based on Christ's redemption of sinful mankind. Christians are sinners saved by grace. Maturity is not measured by revelations, but by a heart of love, a mind of wisdom, a spirit of humility, and a goal of reconciliation.

Paul's address to the Ephesian elders reflects this best (Acts 20:19–27). He had the right attitude: humility and tears. He had the right method: preaching the full gospel and all that would be helpful to them. He had the right goal: the salvation of all mankind. The Kingdom he preached was not his own; he would not see them again. He sought as much as possible to preach the whole counsel of God. "All this is from God, who reconciled us to himself through Christ and gave us a ministry of reconciliation" (2 Corinthians 5:18). Amen. Let it be so with us.

Bibliography

Books

Albright, W. F. and C. S. Mann. *Matthew*. Vol. 26. The Anchor Bible Series. Garden City, N.Y.: Doubleday and Company, Inc., 1968.

Alexander, Joseph A. *Commentary on the Prophecies of Isaiah*. Grand Rapids: Zondervan, 1977.

Allen, Roland. *The Ministry of the Spirit*. Grand Rapids: Eerdmans, 1960.

Allis, Oswald T. *The Unity of Isaiah: A Study in Prophecy*. USA: Presbyterian and Reformed Publishing, 1972.

Anderson, Hugh. *The Gospel of Mark*. The New Century Bible Commentary Series. Grand Rapids: William B. Eerdmans, 1976.

Archer, Gleason. *Encyclopedia of Bible Difficulties*. Grand Rapids: Zondervan, 1982.

Atter, Gordon F. *Rivers of Blessing*. Toronto: Full Gospel Publishing House, 1960.

Baker, John P. *Baptized in One Spirit*. Plainfield: Logos Books, 1967.

Barclay, William. *The Gospel of Matthew: Chapters 1–10*. Vol. 1. Daily Study Bible Series. Philadelphia: Westminster Press, 1975.

————. William. *The Letters to the Corinthians*. Philadelphia: The Westminister Press, 1975.

————. *The Letter to the Romans*. Daily Study Bible Series. Philadelphia: The Westminster Press, 1975.

Barker, Kenneth, ed. *The NIV Study Bible*. Grand Rapids: Zondervan Bible Publishers, 1985.

Barnette, Henlee H. *Christian Calling and Vocation*. Grand Rapids: Baker Book House, 1965.

Barrett, Charles Kingsley. *A Commentary on the First Epistle to the Corinthians*. San Francisco: Harper & Row, Publishers, Inc., 1968.

_____. *Romans*. Vol. 6. Harper's New Testament Commentaries. New York: Harper & Row, Publishers, Inc., 1957.

Barth, Karl. *Church Dogmatics*. Vol. 4. Edited by G. W. Bromiley and T. F. Torrance. Edinburgh: T & T Clark, 1957.

Barth, Markus. *Ephesians: Translation and Commentary on Chapters 1–3*, Vol. 34. and *Chapters 4–6*, Vol. 34A. The Anchor Bible Series. Garden City, N.Y.: Doubleday and Company, Inc., 1974.

Bauer, Walter. *A Greek-English Lexicon of the New Testament and Other Early Christian Literature*. 2nd Edition. Translated by F. Wilbur Gingrich and Fredrick W. Danker. Chicago: University of Chicago Press, 1979.

Baxter, Sidlow J. *Divine Healing of the Body*. Grand Rapids: Zondervan, 1979.

Bernard, J. H. *The Pastoral Epistles*. Grand Rapids: Baker Book House, 1980.

Bewer, Julius A. *The Book of Isaiah*. Vol. 2. New York: Harper & Row, Publishers, Inc., 1950.

Bittlinger, Arnold. *Gifts and Graces: A Commentary of First Corinthians 12 to 14*. Grand Rapids: William B. Eerdmans, 1967.

Black, Matthew. *Romans*. The New Century Bible Series. Grand Rapids: William B. Eerdmans, 1973.

Blass, F., A. DeBrunner, and R. W. Funk. *A Greek Grammar of the New Testament*. Chicago: University of Chicago Press, 1961.

Blumhofer, Edith L. *Pentecost in My Soul: Explorations in the Meaning of Pentecostal Experience in the Early Assemblies of God*. Springfield, Mo.: Gospel Publishing House, 1989.

Boer, Harry R. *Pentecost and Missions*. Grand Rapids: Zondervan Publishing House, 1961.

Brown, Colin, ed. *The New International Dictionary of New Testament Theology*. Grand Rapids: Zondervan Publishing House, 1975; originally Coenen, Lothar, Erich Beyreuther, and Hans

Bietenhard. *Theologisches Begriffslexikon zum Neuen Testament.* R. Brockhaus: Verlag, Wuppertal.

Bruce F. F. *The Apostle of the Heart Set Free.* Grand Rapids: William B. Eerdmans, 1977.

――――. *The Book of Acts.* The New International Commentary on the New Testament. Grand Rapids: William B. Eerdmans, 1977.

――――. *The Epistle of Paul to the Romans.* Grand Rapids: Eerdmans, 1963.

――――. *First and Second Corinthians.* The New Century Bible Commentary. Grand Rapids: William B. Eerdmans, 1971.

――――. *The Epistles to the Colossians, to Philemon, and to the Ephesians.* The New International Commentary on the New Testament. Grand Rapids: William B. Eerdmans, 1984.

Bruner, Frederick Dale. *A Theology of the Holy Spirit: The Pentecostal Experience and the New Testament Witness.* Grand Rapids: William B. Eerdmans, 1970.

Bunkel, H. *Die Psalmen.* Fifth Edition. Goettingen: Vandenhoeck, 1933.

Calvin, John. *The Epistles of Paul the Apostle to the Galatians, Ephesians, Philippians, and Colossians.* Grand Rapids: Eerdmans, 1965.

――――. *The First Epistle of Paul the Apostle to the Corinthians.* Translated by John W. Fraser. Calvin's New Testament Commentaries. Grand Rapids: William B. Eerdmans, 1960.

Carson, Donald A. *Showing the Spirit: A Theological Exposition of 1 Corinthians 12–14.* Grand Rapids: Baker Book House, 1987.

Carter, Charles W. *1 Corinthians.* The Wesleyan Bible Commentary Series. Peabody, Mass.: Hendrickson Publishers, Inc., 1986.

Carter, Howard. *Spiritual Gifts and Their Operation.* Springfield, Mo.: Gospel Publishing House, 1968.

Chadwick, Samuel. *The Way to Pentecost.* Berne, Indiana: Light and Hope Publications, 1937.

Charlesworth, James H., ed. *The Old Testament Pseudepigrapha.* Vol. 1, *Apocalyptic Literature and Testaments.* Garden City, N.Y.: Doubleday & Company, Inc., 1983.

Clark, Stephen B. *Spiritual Gifts*. Pecos, New Mexico: Dove Publications, 1969.

Clarke, Adam. *Clarke's Commentary*. Vol 4. Nashville: Abingdon, n.d.

Clines, David J. A. *I, He, We, and They: A Literary Approach to Isaiah 53*. Sheffield: Journal for the Study of the Old Testament Press, 1983.

Coneybeare, W. J. and J. S. Howson. *The Life and Epistles of St. Paul*. Grand Rapids: William B. Eerdmans, 1949.

Conner, Walter Thomas. *The Work of the Holy Spirit*. Nashville: Broadman Press, 1940.

Conzelmann, Hans. *First Corinthians*. Vol. 43. Translated by James W. Leitch. Hermeneia Series. Philadelphia: Fortress Press, 1975.

Courtney, Howard P. *The Vocal Gifts of the Spirit*. Los Angeles: B. N. Robertson Co., 1956.

Cranfield, C. B. *The Epistle to the Romans*. Edinburgh: T & T Clark, Ltd., 1981.

Criswell, W. A. *The Holy Spirit in Today's World*. Grand Rapids: Zondervan, 1966.

Cruz, Nicky. *Satan on the Loose*. New Jersey: Fleming H. Revell, 1973.

Dahood, Mitchell. *Psalms II, 51–100*. Vol. 17. The Anchor Bible Series. Garden City, N.Y.: Doubleday and Co., Inc., 1968.

Dickason, C. Fred. *Angels, Elect and Evil*. Chicago: Moody Press, 1975.

Dorrance, Edythe Guerin. *Operation Pentecost*. Los Angeles: B.N. Robertson Co., 1962.

Dunn, James D. G. *Baptism in the Holy Spirit*. Philadelphia: The Westminster Press, 1970.

_____. *Jesus and the Spirit*. Philadelphia: Westminster Press, 1975.

Ervin, Howard M. *Conversion-Initiation and the Baptism of the Holy Spirit*. Peabody, Mass.: Hendrickson Publishers, Inc., 1984.

_____. *These Are Not Drunken As Ye Suppose*. Plainfield: Logos Books, 1968.

Eusebius, *Hist. Eccl. II*. xxxix.15.

Evans, Mary J. *Woman in the Bible*. Downers Grove, Ill.: InterVarsity Press, 1983.

Evans, W. I. *This River Must Flow*. Springfield, Mo.: Gospel Publishing House, 1954.

Farmer, W. *The Last Twelve Verses of Mark*. London: Cambridge University Press, 1974.

Fee, Gordon D. *The Epistle to the First Corinthians*. The New International Commentary on the New Testament. Grand Rapids: William B. Eerdmans, 1987.

Fee, Gordon D. and Douglas Stuart. *How to Read the Bible for All Its Worth*. Grand Rapids: Zondervan Publishing House, 1982.

Findlay, George G. "St. Paul's First Epistle to the Corinthians." In *The Expositor's Greek Testament*, Edited by W. Robertson Nicoll. London: Hodder and Stoughton, Ltd., n.d.

Fisher, Fred. *First and Second Corinthians*. Waco: Word Books, 1975.

Ford, Murray J. S. *Church Vocations: A New Look*. Valley Forge: Judson Press, 1970.

Foulkes, Francis. *Ephesians*. Tyndale series. Grand Rapids: Eerdmans, 1975.

Frost, Robert. *Aglow With the Spirit*. Northridge, Ca: Voice Christian Publications, 1965.

Gee, Donald. *Concerning Spiritual Gifts*. Springfield, Mo.: Gospel Publishing House, 1949.

————. *Ministry Gifts in the Twentieth Century*. Springfield, Mo.: Gospel Publishing House, 1930.

————. *Spiritual Gifts in the Work of the Ministry Today*. Springfield, Mo.: Gospel Publishing House, 1963.

————. *Pentecost*. Springfield, Mo.: Gospel Publishing House, 1932.

Godet, Frederic L. *Commentary on First Corinthians*. Vol. 2. Edinburgh: T. & T. Clark, 1886.

Gordon, Adoniram Judson. *The Ministry of the Spirit*. Philadelphia: Judson Press, 1949.

Grosheide, F. W. *Commentary on the First Epistle to the Corinthians*. Grand Rapids: William B. Eerdmans, 1955.

Grudem, Wayne. *The Gift of Prophecy in 1 Corinthians 12–14*. Lanham, Md.: University Press of America, 1982.

Gundry, Robert H. *Matthew, A Commentary on His Literary and Theological Art*. Grand Rapids: Eerdmans, 1981.

Harper, Michael. *Power for the Body of Christ*. London: The Fountain Trust, 1969.

Harrison, Everett F. *Romans*. Vol. 10. The Expositor's Bible Commentary Series. Vol. 10, Grand Rapids: Zondervan, 1976.

Henry, Rodney L. *Filipino Spirit World*. Manila: OMF Literature, Inc., 1986.

Hill, David, ed. *The Gospel of Matthew*. The New Century Bible Commentary. London: Butler & Tanner Ltd., 1972.

Hodge, Charles. *An Exposition of the First Epistle to the Corinthians*. New York: Robert Carter and Brothers, 1857.

Hodges, Melvin L. *Spiritual Gifts*. Springfield, Mo.: Gospel Publishing House, 1964.

Holdcroft, L. Thomas. *Divine Healing: A Comparative Study*. Springfield, Mo.: Gospel Publishing House, 1967.

_____. *The Holy Spirit: A Pentecostal Interpretation*. Springfield, Mo.: Gospel Publishing House, 1979.

Holladay, William L. *Isaiah: Scroll of a Prophetic Heritage*. Grand Rapids: Eerdmans, 1978.

Hooker, Morna D. *The Message of Mark*. London: Epworth Press, 1983.

Horton, Harold. *The Gifts of the Spirit*. London: Assemblies of God Publishing House, 1962.

Horton, Stanley M. *The Book of Acts*, The Radiant Commentary on the New Testament. Springfield, Mo.: Gospel Publishing House, 1981.

_____. *Desire Spiritual Gifts Earnestly*. Springfield Mo.: Gospel Publishing House, 1966.

_____. *What the Bible Says About the Holy Spirit*. Springfield, Mo.: Gospel Publishing House, 1976.

Huffman, Jasper A. *The Holy Spirit*. Winona Lake: The Standard Press, 1944.

Hunter, Harold. *Spirit Baptism: A Pentecostal Alternative*. Lanham, Md.: University Press of America, 1983.

Hurley, James B. *Man and Woman in Biblical Perspective*. Grand Rapids: Zondervan, 1981.

Hurtado, Larry W. *Mark*. The Good News Commentary. San Francisco: Harper & Row, Publishers, Inc., 1983.

James, Maynard. *I Believe in the Holy Spirit*. Minneapolis: Bethany Fellowship, 1975.

Jewett, Paul K. *Man as Male and Female*. Grand Rapids: William B. Eerdmans, 1975.

————. *The Ordination of Woman*. Grand Rapids: William B. Eerdmans, 1980.

Käsemann, Ernst. *Commentary on Romans*. Grand Rapids: William B. Eerdmans, 1980.

Keil, C. F. and F. Delitzsch, eds. *Commentary of the Old Testament in Ten Volumes*, Vol. 7, *Isaiah*, by F. Delitzsch. Translated by James Martin. Grand Rapids: William B. Eerdmans, 1969; Repr., 1978.

Kelly, J. N. D. *A Commentary on the Pastoral Epistles*. Grand Rapids: Baker Book House, 1963.

Kent, Homer A. *The Pastoral Epistles*. Chicago: Moody Press, 1962.

Kidner, Derek. *Psalms 1–72*. Vol. 14A. The Tyndale Old Testament Commentaries. Downers Grove, Ill.: InterVarsity Press, 1973.

Kittel, Gerhard. *Theological Dictionary of the New Testament*. Translated and Edited by Geoffrey W. Bromily. Grand Rapids: William B. Eerdmans, 1964.

Knight, George A. F. *Deutero-Isaiah: A Theological Commentary on Isaiah 40–55*. Nashville: Abingdon, 1965.

Kydd, Ronald A. N. *Charismatic Gifts in the Early Church*. Peabody, Mass.: Hendrickson Publishers, Inc., 1984.

Ladd, George Eldon. *A Theology of the New Testament*. Grand Rapids: William B. Eerdmans, 1974.

Lane, William. *The Gospel According to Mark*. New International Commentary on the New Testament. Grand Rapids: William B. Eerdmans, 1974.

Lange, John Peter, and F. R. Fay. *The Epistle of Paul to the Romans*. Translated by J. F. Hurst. Vol. 10. Lange's Commentary on the Holy Scriptures. Grand Rapids: Zondervan Publishing House, 1960.

LaSor, William S., David A. Hubbard, and Frederic W. Bush. *Old Testament Survey*. Grand Rapids: Eerdmans, 1982.

Lenski, Richard Charles Henry. *The Interpretation of St. Paul's First Epistle to the Corinthians*. Columbus, Ohio: Wartburg Press, 1937.

Lewis, C. S. *The Four Loves*. Fourth Edition, Revised and Enlarged. New York: MacMillan Publishing Company, 1960.

_____. *Mere Christianity*. New York: MacMillan, 1952.

_____. *Miracles, A Preliminary Study*. New York: The MacMillan Company, 1952.

_____. *The Problem of Pain*. Glasgow, Scotland: Collins, 1957.

Lightfoot, Robert H. *The Gospel Message of St. Mark*. Oxford: Clarendon Press, 1950.

Lillie, David G. *Tongues Under Fire*. Plainfield: Logos Books, 1966.

Lindsay, Gordon. *All About the Gift of Prophecy and Interpretation of Tongues*. Dallas: The Voice of Healing Publishing Co., 1964.

Lindsey, F. Duane. *The Servant Songs*. Chicago: Moody Press, 1985.

Lloyd-Jones, David Martyn. *God's Ultimate Purpose: Ephesians 1:1–23*. Edinburgh: Banner of Truth Trust, 1978.

Kurt, Koch. *The Revival in Indonesia*. Grand Rapids: Kregel Publications, 1970.

MacDonald, William G. *Glossolalia in the New Testament*. Springfield: Gospel Publishing House, 1964.

MacNutt, Francis. *Healing*. Notre Dame: Ave Maria Press, 1974.

_____. *The Power to Heal*. Notre Dame: Ave Maria Press, 1977.

MacPherson, Ian. *Like a Dove Descending*. Minneapolis: Bethany Fellowship, 1970.

MacRae, Alan A. *The Gospel of Isaiah*. Chicago: Moody Press, 1977.

Mansfield, M. Robert. *"Spirit and Gospel" in Mark*. Peabody, Mass.: Hendrickson Publishers, Inc., 1987.

Mare, Harold. *First Corinthians*. Expositor's Bible Commentary Series. Grand Rapids: Zondervan, 1976.

Marshall, I. Howard. *The Gospel of Luke*. New International Greek Testament. Grand Rapids: Eerdmans, 1978.

————. *Luke: Historian and Theologian*. New International Greek Testament. Grand Rapids: Eerdmans, 1970.

————. *The Acts of the Apostles*. Grand Rapids: Eerdmans, 1980.

Martin, Alfred and John Martin. *Isaiah: The Glory of the Messiah*. Chicago: Moody Press, 1983.

Martin, Ralph P. *Mark: Evangelist and Theologian*. Grand Rapids: Zondervan Publishing House, 1972.

————. *The Spirit and the Congregation: Studies in 1 Corinthians 12–15*. Grand Rapids: William B. Eerdmans, 1984.

Maynard, James. *I Believe in the Holy Spirit*. Minneapolis: Bethany Fellowship, 1965.

McAlister, R. E. *The Manifestations of the Spirit*. Toronto: Gospel Publishing House, n.d.

McDonnell, Killian and Arnold Bittlinger. *The Baptism in the Holy Spirit as an Ecumenical Problem*. Notre Dame: Charismatic Renewal Services, Inc., 1972.

Metzger, Bruce M. *The Text of the New Testament*. Oxford: Clarendon Press, 1968.

Mickelsen, A. Berkeley. *Interpreting the Bible*. Grand Rapids: Eerdmans, 1963.

Mickelsen, A. Berkeley and Alvera Micklesen, *Women, Authority and the Bible*. Downers Grove, Ill.: InterVarsity Press, 1986.

Miller, Keith. *The Taste of New Wine*. Waco: Word Books, 1965.

Montgomery, John W. *Demon Possession*. Minneapolis: Bethany Fellowship, Inc., 1976.

Moody, Dale. *Spirit of the Living God*. Philadelphia: The Westminster Press, 1968.

Moulton, James Hope and George Millgan. *The Vocabulary of the Greek New Testament*. Grand Rapids: William B. Eerdmans, 1972.

Mowinckel, Sigmund. *He that Cometh*. Translated by G. W. Anderson. New York: Abingdon, 1956.

————. *Psalmenstudien*, Vol. 2. Amsterdam: Schippers, 1961.

Muhlenberg, James. *The Book of Isaiah 40–66*. Nashville: Abingdon Press, 1956.

Ness, Henry H. *Dunamis and the Church*. Springfield: Gospel Publishing House, 1968.

Nineham, Dennis E. *Saint Mark*. Philadelphia: The Westminster Press, 1963.

Nygren, Anders. *Agape and Eros*. New York: Harper & Row, Publishers, Inc., 1969.

————. *Commentary on Romans*. Philadelphia: Fortress Press, 1949.

Oepke, A. "Woman." *Theological Dictionary of the New Testament*, Vol. I. Grand Rapids: Eerdmans.

Orlinsky, H. M. "The So-Called 'Servant of the Lord' and 'Suffering Servant' in Second Isaiah." *Studies on the Second Part of the Book of Isaiah*, supplement to *Vetus Testamentum*. London: E. J. Brill, 1967.

Penn-Lewis, Jessie. *The Magna Charta of Woman*. Minneapolis: Bethany Fellowship, 1975.

Pickford, J. H. *The Charismatic Experience: A Fresh Breeze or a False Belief?* Vancouver: Northwest Baptist Theological College, n.d.

Pinnock, Clark H. "Biblical Authority and the Issues in Question," in A. Berkeley and Alvera Micklesen, ed. *Women, Authority and the Bible*. Downers Grove: InterVarsity Press, 1986.

Plumptre, E. H. *The Book of the Prophet Isaiah*, Vol. II. Grand Rapids: Zondervan. 1960.

Richards, Larry and Clyde Hoeldtke. *A Theology of Church Leadership*. Grand Rapids: Zondervan, 1980.

Richardson, Alan. *The Miracle Stories of the Gospels*. London: SCM Press Ltd., 1941.

————, ed. *A Theological Wordbook of the Bible*. New York: MacMillan, 1950.

Richardson, Cyril, ed. *Early Christian Fathers*. Vol. 1. The Library of Christian Classics. Philadelphia: Westminster Press, 1953.

Riggs, Ralph M. *The Spirit Himself*. Springfield, Mo.: Gospel Publishing House, 1962.

Robertson, Archibald T. *Word Pictures in the New Testament,* Vol. 4. Nashville: Broadman Press, 1931.

Robertson, Archibald and A. Plummer. *A Critical and Exegetical Commentary on the First Epistle of St. Paul to the Corinthians.* Edinburgh: T & T Clark, 1911.

Robinson, H. Wheeler. *The Christian Experience of the Holy Spirit.* London: Collins, 1962.

Robinson, J. A. *St. Paul's Epistle to the Ephesians.* London: Clark, 1922.

Ryrie, Charles Caldwell. *The Holy Spirit.* Chicago: Moody Press, 1965.

Sanders, J. Oswald. *The Holy Spirit and His Gifts.* Grand Rapids: Zondervan Publishing House, 1940.

Sartre, Jean-Paul. *No Exit and Three Other Plays.* New York: Vintage Books, 1946.

Schatzmann, Siegfried. *A Pauline Theology of Charismata.* Peabody, Mass.: Hendrickson Publishers, Inc., 1987.

Schweizer, Eduard. *The Good News According to Matthew.* Atlanta: John Knox Press, 1975.

Scott, Ernest F. *The Spirit in the New Testament.* London: Hodder and Stoughton, 1923.

Selwyn, Edward Gordon. *The Epistle of St. Peter.* 2nd ed. London: MacMillan, 1947.

Shoemaker, Samuel M. *With the Holy Spirit and With Fire.* New York: Harper and Brothers Publishers, 1960.

Simpson, E. K. *Commentary on the Epistle to the Ephesians.* Vol. 10. The New International Commentary on the New Testament. Grand Rapids: Eerdmans, 1957.

Smedes, Lewis B. *Love Within Limits: Realizing Selfless Love in a Selfish World.* Grand Rapids: William B. Eerdmans, 1978.

Smith, George A. *The Book of Isaiah.* London: Hodder and Stoughton, 1879.

Spicq, P. C.. *Agape in the New Testament.* Vol. 2. St. Louis: n.p., 1965.

Stahlin, G. "Comfort," in Gerhard Kittel and Gerhard Friederich, ed., abridged and translated by Geoffrey W. Bromiley. *Theological Dictionary of the New Testament.* Grand Rapids: Eerdmans, 1985.

Stamps, Donald C., ed. *The Full Life Study Bible*. Grand Rapids, Mich.: Zondervan Publishing House, 1990.

Stein, Robert H. *The Synoptic Problem: An Introduction*. Grand Rapids: Baker Book House, 1987.

Stendahl, K. *The Bible and the Role of Women*. Philadelphia: Fortress Press, 1966.

Strack, H. L. and P. Billerbeck. *Kommentar zum Neuen Testament aus Talmud und Midrasch*. Munich: C. H. Beck, 1965.

Stronstad, Roger. *The Charismatic Theology of St. Luke*. Peabody, Mass.: Hendrickson Publishers, Inc., 1984.

Swete, Henry B., ed. *Essays on the Early History of the Church and the Ministry*. London: MacMillan and Co., 1918.

Talbert, Charles H. *Literary Patterns, Theological Themes and the Genre of Luke-Acts*. Society of Biblical Literature Monograph Series, No. 20. Missoula, Mont.: Scholars Press, 1974.

The Testament of Job. Translated by R. P. Spittler. In *The Old Testament Pseudepigrapha*. Vol. 1, *Apocalyptic Literature and Testaments,* ed. James Charlesworth. Garden City, N.Y.: Doubleday & Company, Inc., 1983.

Thayer, Joseph H. *Greek-English Lexicon of the New Testament*. Grand Rapids: Baker Book House, 1977.

Trueblood, Elton. *The Incendiary Fellowship*. New York: Harper & Row, Publishers, Inc., 1967.

Underwood, B. E. *The Gifts of the Spirit—Supernatural Equipment for Christian Service*. Franklin Springs: Advocate Press, 1967.

Unger, Merrill F. *Demons in the World Today*. Wheaton: Tyndale, 1971.

————. *New Testament Teaching on Tongues*. Grand Rapids: Kregel Publishers, 1971.

Vine, W. E. *Expository Dictionary of New Testament Words*. New Jersey: Fleming H. Revell, 1940.

————. *First Corinthians*. Grand Rapids: Zondervan, 1961.

Wagner, Peter. *Your Spiritual Gifts Can Help Your Church Grow*. Glendale, Calif.: Regal Books, 1979.

Westermann, Claus. *Isaiah 40–66*. Philadelphia: The Westminster Press, 1969.

————. *Praise and Lament in the Psalms*. Atlanta: John Knox Press, 1981.

Whybray, R. N. *Isaiah 40–66*. New Century Bible series. London: Marshall, Morgan and Scott, 1975.

————. *The Second Isaiah*. Sheffield: JSOT Press, 1983.

Williams, J. Rodman. *The Era of the Spirit*. Plainfield, N.J.: Logos International, 1971.

Wright, Gordon. *In Quest of Healing*. Springfield, Mo.: Gospel Publishing House, 1984.

Young, Edward J. *The Book of Isaiah*. Grand Rapids: Eerdmans, 1969.

Periodicals

Aalen, S. "A Rabbinic Formula in 1 Corinthians 14:34." *Studia Evangelica* 2 (Texte und Untersuchungen 87: Berlin, 1964): 513–25.

Callan, Terrance. "Prophecy and Ecstacy in Greco-Roman Religion and in 1 Corinthians." *Novum Testamentum* 27:2 (April 1985): 125–140.

Carlson, G. Raymond. "Covet Earnestly." *Paraclete* 6:1 (Winter 1972): 16–19.

Chapman, R. B. "The Purpose and Value of Spiritual Gifts." *Paraclete* 2:4 (Fall 1968): 24–28.

Cosby, Gordon. "Evoking the Gift." *Baptist Faculty Paper* 16:1 (Fall 1972): 1–2.

Davies, J. G. "Pentecost and Glossolalia." *Journal of Theological Studies* 3 (October 1952): 228–231.

Derrett, J. Duncan M. "Cursing Jesus (1 Corinthians 12:3): The Jews as Religious Persecutors." *New Testament Studies* 21 (July 1975): 544–554.

Dominy, Bert. "Paul and Spiritual Gifts: Reflections on 1 Cor. 12–14." *Southern Journal of Theology* 26 (Fall 1983): 49–68.

Dresselhaus, Richard. "The Interpretation of Tongues." *Paraclete* 6 (Fall 1972): 11–12.

Fee, Gordon. "Tongues—Least of the Gifts: Some Exegetical Observations on 1 Corinthians 12–14." *Pneuma* 2 (Fall 1980): 3–14.

Flanagan, Neil M. and E. H. Snyder. "Did Paul Put Down Women in 1 Cor. 14:24–36?" *Biblical Theology Bulletin* 11 (1981): 10–12.

Flower, J. Roswell. "Speaking With Tongues—Sign or Stumbling-block?" *Paraclete* 2 (Spring 1968): 16–19.

Foh, Susan T. "Women Preachers: Why Not?" *Fundamentalist Journal* 4 (January 1985): 17–19.

Forbes, Christopher. "Early Christian Inspired Speech and Hellenistic Popular Religion." *Novum Testamentum* 28 (July 1986): 257–270.

Fung, Ronald Y. K. "Function or Office? A Survey of the New Testament Evidence." *Evangelical Review of Theology* 8 (April 1984): 16–19.

———. "Ministry, Community and Spiritual Gifts." *Evangelical Quarterly* 56 (January 20, 1984): 3–20.

Gasque, W. Ward and Laurel Gasque. "F. F. Bruce: A Mind for What Matters." *Christianity Today* 33 (April 7, 1989): 22–25.

Gee, Donald. "Spiritual Gifts." *Paraclete* 1 (Fall 1967): 23–26.

Gillespie, Thomas W. "A Pattern of Prophetic Speech in 1 Corinthians." *Journal of Biblical Literature* 97 (March 1978): 74–95.

Grudem, Wayne. "1 Corinthians 14:20–25: Prophecy and Tongues as Signs of God's Attitude." *Westminster Theological Journal* 4 (Spring 1979): 381–396.

———. "Prophecy—Yes, But Teaching—No: Paul's Consistent Advocacy of Women's Participation Without Governing Authority." *Journal of the Evangelical Theological Society* 30 (March 1987): 11–23.

———. "Why Christians Can Still Prophesy." *Christianity Today* 32 (September 16, 1988): 29–31, 34–35.

Gundry, R. H. "Ecstatic Utterance (NEB)?" *Journal of Theological Studies* 17 (1966): 299–307.

Haefner, Alfred E. "The Bridge Between Mark and Acts." *Journal of Biblical Literature* 77 (1958): 67–71.

Hinton, Keith and Linnet Hinton. "Conversion Patterns in Asia." *Evangelical Missions Quarterly* 25 (January 1989): 42–43.

Hocken, Peter. "Jesus Christ and the Gifts of the Spirit." *Pneuma* 5 (Spring 1983): 12.

Hodges, Melvin L. "Operations, Ministries and Gifts." *Paraclete* 7 (Spring 1973): 18–21.

Hodges, Zane C. "A Symposium on the Tongues Movement: The Purpose of Tongues." *Bibliotheca Sacra* 120 (1963): 223–233.

Holmes, B. T. "Luke's Description of John Mark." *Journal of Biblical Literature* 54 (June 1935): 63–72.

Horton, Stanley M. "Is Mark 16:9–20 Inspired?" *Paraclete* (Winter 1970): 7–12.

House, H. Wayne. "The Ministry of Women in the Apostolic and Postapostolic Periods." *Bibliotheca Sacra* 145 (October/December 1988): 387–399.

————. "Tongues and the Mystery Religions of Corinth." *Bibliotheca Sacra* 140 (April-June 1983): 134–150.

Iber, Gerhard. "Zum Verstaandnis von 1 Corinthians 12:31." *ZNW* 54 (1963): 43–54.

Isbell, Charles D. "Glossalalia & Propheteialalia: A Study of 1 Corinthians 14." *Wesleyan Theological Journal* 10 (Spring 1925): 15–22.

Johanson, B. C. "Tongues, A Sign for Unbelievers?" *New Testament Studies* 24 (January 1979): 180–203.

Johansson, Nils. "First Corinthians 13 and First Corinthians 14." *New Testament Studies* 10 (1963–64): 383–392.

Kaiser, Walter C., Jr. "Paul, Women, and the Church." *Worldwide Challenge* 3 (1976): 9–12.

Lincoln, A. T. "Luke's Pentecost: Theology and History." *The Expository Times* 96 (April 1985): 204–209.

MacGorman, J. W. "Glossalalic Error & Its Correction: 1 Cor. 12–14." *Review & Expositor* 80 (Summer 1983): 389–400.

Martin, Ralph. "A Suggested Exegesis of 1 Corinthians 13:13." *The Expository Times* 82 (1970–1971): 120.

Moo, Douglas J. "1 Timothy 2:11–15: Meaning and Significance." *Trinity Journal* 1 (1980): 62–83.

O'Connor, J. Murphy. "Interpolations in 1 Corinthians." *Catholic Biblical Quarterly* 48 (1986): 90–92.

Odell-Scott, D. W. "Let the Women Speak in Church, An Egalitarian Interpretation of 1 Cor. 14:33b–36." *Biblical Theology Bulletin* 13 (1983): 90–93.

Overholt, Thomas W. "Prophecy: The Problem of Cross Cultural Comparison." *Semeia* 21 (1981): 55–78.

Packer, J. I. "Theological Reflections on the Charismatic Movement (Part I)." *Churchman* 94 (1980): 7–25.

Petersen, Norman R. "When is the End Not the End? Literary Reflections on the Ending of Mark's Narrative." *Interpretation* 34 (April 1980): 151–166.

Richardson, William. "Liturgical Order and Glossalalia in 1 Corinthians 14:26c–33a." *New Testament Studies* 32 (January 1986): 144–53.

Robertson, O. Palmer. "Tongues: Sign of Covenantal Curse and Blessing." *Westminster Theological Journal* 38 (Fall 1975): 43–53.

Schweizer, E. "The Service of Worship: An Exposition of 1 Corinthians 14." *Interpretation* 13 (1959): 402.

Sigountos, James G. and Myron Shank. "Public Roles for Women in the Pauline Church: A Reappraisal of the Evidence." *Journal of the Evangelical Theological Society* 26 (September 1983): 283–95.

Talbert, Charles H. "Paul's Understanding of the Holy Spirit: The Evidence of 1 Corinthians 12–14." *Perspectives in Religious Studies* 11 (Winter 84): 95–108.

Thee, Francis C. R. "Wherefore Tongues . . ." *Paraclete* 3 (Winter 1969): 14–20.

Thistleton, A. C. "The Interpretation of Tongues: A New Suggestion in the Light of Greek Usage in Philo and Josephus." *Journal of Theological Studies* 30 (April 1979): 15–36.

Thomas, John Christopher. "A Reconsideration of the Ending of Mark." *Journal of the Evangelical Theological Society* 26 (December 1983): 407–419.

Turner, Max M. B. "The Significance of Receiving the Spirit in Luke-Acts: A Summary of Modern Scholarship." *Trinity Journal* 2:2 (Fall 1981): 131–158.

———. "Spiritual Gifts Then and Now." *Vox Evangelica* 15 (1985): 7–64.

Wedderburn, A. J. M. "Romans 8:26: Towards a Theology of Glossalalia?" *Scottish Journal of Theology* 28:4 (1975): 369–377.

Williams, C. G. "Glossolalia as a Religious Phenomenon: Tongues at Corinth and Pentecost." *Religion* 5:1 (Spring 1975): 16–32.

Miscellaneous

Barrett, David B. and Frank Kaleb Johnson. "The World in Figures" in Lausanne II Congress Notebook 13:16. July 1989.

Howard, Rick, pastor in Redwood City, Calif. Assemblies of God Missionary Fellowship meetings, 1986, Philippines.

MacDonald, William. Interview by author, 30 October 1987, Baguio City, Philippines.

———. Lecture notes on soteriology.

Winter, Ralph. Class on perspectives in world missions, January 1985. William Carey University. Pasadena, Calif.

Scripture Index

OLD TESTAMENT

New Testament

Subject Index

321